UNIVERSITY OF CAMBRIDGE
DEPARTMENT OF APPLIED ECONOMICS

MONOGRAPHS

15

PLANNING, PROGRAMMING AND INPUT-OUTPUT MODELS: SELECTED PAPERS ON INDIAN PLANNING

UNIVERSITY OF CAMBRIDGE
DEPARTMENT OF APPLIED ECONOMICS
MONOGRAPHS

This series consists of investigations conducted by members of the Department's staff and others working in direct collaboration with the Department. The Department of Applied Economics assumes no responsibility for the views expressed in the Monographs published under its auspices.

PLANNING, PROGRAMMING AND INPUT-OUTPUT MODELS: SELECTED PAPERS ON INDIAN PLANNING

BY

A. GHOSH

Professor of Applied Economics,
Jadavpur University, Calcutta

CAMBRIDGE
AT THE UNIVERSITY PRESS
1968

Published by the Syndics of the Cambridge University Press
Bentley House, 200 Euston Road, London, N.W.1
American Branch: 32 East 57th Street, New York, N.Y.10022

© Cambridge University Press 1968

Library of Congress Catalogue Card Number: 68–29327
Standard Book Number: 521 07059 7

Printed in Great Britain
at the University Printing House, Cambridge
(Brooke Crutchley, University Printer)

CONTENTS

PREFACE

The Indian Five-Year Plans were initiated in 1951. But it is during the period of the second Five-Year Plan (1956–60) that Indian economists became more deeply involved. Problems of allocation, construction of econometric models suitable to Indian conditions and similar problems were studied by both Indian and foreign economists.

At that time I was on the staff of the Department of Applied Economics at Cambridge working on input-output and allied models for the United Kingdom economy. As input-output and programming models are very relevant to planning models I naturally took great interest in those of importance in India planning. I went back to India in 1959 and as a teacher of planning techniques became concerned with various issues relating to the theoretical and empirical aspects of planning and programming models with special reference to Indian conditions.

The present collection of papers can be divided into three broad categories. Papers 1 and 2 are concerned with a survey of the techniques used in Indian planning, mainly from an econometric angle, and various models of partial and comprehensive planning, worked out in exploratory research. Papers 3 to 8 are mainly attempts I have made at model building to tackle relevant planning problems in the Indian economy. Papers 9 to 14 are empirical applications of some standard models and some models developed by the author in trying to find numerical solutions to various problems.

The review article in the first group contains some results which are discussed separately in papers in the other groups. This could not be avoided as I feel that the completeness of the review paper would suffer if results repeated in detail in later papers are omitted from the review article. The review article as it stands now is comprehensive and gives adequate information to anyone who wants to familiarize himself with the type of work being carried out in India without going into great detail.

The last paper in the third group is a critique of the Indian fourth Plan. This has been included as it contains a numerical demonstration of the model on inflation in the second group of papers and the use of a straightforward econometric model to expose the fallacy of some assumptions around which the Plan is built.

At least two of the papers presented here were published while I was at Cambridge. Some of the other papers were started at Cambridge but finished and published after I had left. Work in connection with two of the papers was done while I was a visiting Fellow at Harvard University and Oslo University. The rest of the papers were mainly prepared while working at Jadavpur University.

In the preparation of many of these papers I have gained much from various discussions I have had with Professor Richard Stone and Mr W. B. Reddaway of the Department of Applied Economics, Professor Lief Johansen at Oslo University, Professor Jan Tinbergen of the University at Rotterdam, and Professor W. W. Leontief of Harvard.

Some of the empirical papers are condensed versions of books dealing with the subject in greater detail. I wish to thank the various publishers for their permission to use condensed accounts of these published books. Most of the other papers were originally published in various journals, to whose editors the author is grateful for permission to reprint them.

Jadavpur University   A. G.
Calcutta

ACKNOWLEDGEMENTS

The papers in this book first appeared in the following books and journals and the author thanks the publishers for permission to reprint them in their present form:

1 *Economics of Planning*, vol. 4. no. 1, 1964, Oslo, Norway.
2 *Economics of Planning*, vol. 6, no. 2, 1966, Oslo, Norway.
3 *Economica*, Feb. 1958, London, w.c. 2.
4 *Metroeconomica*, vol. 12, April 1960, Roma.
5 *Arthaniti*, vol. 3, no. 1, Nov. 1959, Calcutta, India.
6 *Arthaniti*, vol. 3, no. 2, May 1960, Calcutta, India.
7 *Arthaniti*, vol. 8, no. 1, Jan. 1965, Calcutta, India.
8 *The Economic Weekly*, Annual no., Feb. 1964, Bombay, India.
9 *Indian Economic Journal*, vol. 14, no. 2, 1967, Bombay, India.
10 *Efficiency in location and inter-regional flows*, 1965, North-Holland Publishing Company, Amsterdam.
11 *Arthavijana*, vol. 9, no. 2, Jan. 1967, Poona-4, India.
12 *Union budget and prices—A projection*, Asia Publishing House, Bombay, India.
13 *Calcutta—The Primate City*, Census Monograph No. 2, Government of India.
14 *Yojana*, vol. 10, no. 24, 11 Dec. 1966, New Delhi-1, India.

CHAPTER I

THE EVOLUTION OF
PLANNING TECHNIQUES AND
ORGANIZATION IN INDIA

I.I

The share of the public sector in the total economic activity of India is still by no means impressive. In fact, it is much less than similar shares in many of the co-called free enterprise countries of the West, not to speak of the Socialist countries. The following table, giving the share of Government in the total national output, demonstrates the relative weight of the public sector in the United Kingdom and India during 1956–61.

*Share of Government in domestic output in per cent.**

Year	India	U.K.
1956	9·6	19·0
1957	10·3	18·0
1958	9·9	18·0
1959	10·0	19·0
1960	10·4	19·0
1961	11·1	19·0

* In India output refers to net output. In U.K. output refers to GNP.

As may be seen the share of Government expenditure in the total economic activity in India is certainly less impressive than in the U.K.

But if we turn to the relative share of Government and the private sector in current investment the picture is different as is shown below:

Share of Government in total domestic investment in per cent.†

Year	India	U.K.
1955	43·0	26·0
1956	44·0	25·0
1957	49·0	24·0

† In India the share refers to domestic net investment. In the United Kingdom the share refers to gross fixed capital formation at home.

In spite of the comparatively insignificant role of the public sector, in India at present, in a sense the economy is more planned than the economies of Western countries though certainly less than those of Socialist countries.

This is because the public sector is in virtual monopoly of the strategic sectors of the economy that are being newly developed. It is also the more important partner in current investments and has a much larger influence on the future growth of precisely those sectors which involve higher and more advanced technologies. In this sense the public sector is providing leadership and direction while, the private sector, with a much larger share, as far as size is concerned, is following in line.

The planning policy of the Indian Government has two major aspects. The first is to stimulate and accelerate the growth of the industrialization of the country, especially in providing resources for the more expensive types of complex industries and overhead developments.

The second is the welfare aspect of the plan—pushing development along more egalitarian lines. This second aspect has always been a bit fuzzy and problematic and it is difficult to assess its success. But there is no doubt that over the last twelve years of the plan the public sector has to some extent led the country towards a broadly based industrialization process in spite of various failures and shortcomings. It is also widely felt that such a process of industrialization could not have been achieved, in the present state of Indian entrepreneurship, without firm action from the public sector. The purpose of the present paper is to discuss some aspects of the planning process in India concerned with industrialization.

1.2

Planning in India is very different from the planning procedures adopted in the socialist countries, but it is more rigid and direct than planning procedures in the West.

The planning process is initiated by the Planning Commission, which was set up as an advisory body to integrate two trends and give them a sense of coherence and reality. One of these trends was the theoretical process of visualizing the development of the Indian economy, its rate of growth and line of development in the future. This may be called the construction and elaboration of the model of growth, or, the plan-frame. The other trend consists of the process of systematizing and rationalizing the detailed schemes devised by local executive organs which in effect give what they think are the detailed lines of future development as visualized by them. These two aspects are often quite contradictory and have independent lobbies of their own within the Commission. The synchronization and proper integration of the two trends is part of the evolution of the planning process within the Planning Commission over the last twelve years. A historical survey of the process of growth of the three plans shows the gradual integration of the two trends of activity and will be discussed after I have given a purely taxonomic picture of the organs of planning and its execution.

The functions of the Indian Planning Commission, as stated in the Government of India resolution of March 1950, are:

(1) To make an assessment of the material capital and human resources of the country, including technical personnel, and investigate the possibilities of augmenting such of these resources as are found to be deficient in relation to the nation's requirements.

(2) To formulate a plan for the most effective and balanced utilization of the country's resources.

(3) To determine priorities, define the stages in which the plan should be carried out and propose the allocation of resources which in view of the current social and political situation, should be established for the successful execution of the plan.

(4) To determine the nature of the machinery which will be necessary for securing the successful implementation of each stage of the plan in all its aspects.

(5) To appraise from time to time the progress achieved in the execution of each stage of the plan and recommend the adjustments of policy and measures that such appraisal may show to be necessary.

(6) To make such interim or ancillary recommendations as appear to it to be appropriate either, for facilitating the discharge of the duties assigned to it; or, on a consideration of the prevailing economic conditions, current policies, measures and development programmes; or, on an examination of such specific problems as may be referred to it for advice by central or state governments.

No executive functions were allotted to the Commission. The responsibility for implementation rested with the central ministries and the state governments.

The function of the Planning Commission in the USSR may be compared with the above:

(a) To draft and submit to the Council of Ministers of the USSR for approval, national-economic long-range, annual, quarterly and monthly plans.

(b) To submit to the Council of Ministers of the USSR conclusions on the long-range, annual, quarterly and monthly plans submitted by the ministries and departments of the USSR and of the Union Republics.

(c) To verify the execution of the national-economic plans of the USSR that have been approved by the Council of Ministers of the USSR.

(d) To work out, on instructions of the Council of Ministers of the USSR, or on its own initiative various problems of socialist economy.

(e) To direct socialist accounting in the USSR.

It can be seen that as far as conception of the planning process is concerned, there are large areas of similarity.

The big difference, of course, lies in the fact that in the USSR the Planning Commission plans for the whole of the economic activity in the state of the USSR and in the case of India the plan is only a kind of forecasting, as far as the private sector is concerned. But the basic approach regarding the functioning of the Planning Commission and the Gosplan is very similar.

The role of the Planning Commission is partly to include various schemes in its plan and partly to fix priorities among other schemes. For all schemes, whether in existence or not, financial allocations over the five year period, including broad allocations of foreign exchange, are made by the Planning Commission, in consultation with the other organizations concerned. In making these allocations, the Planning Commission conducts a series of discussions with the representatives of state governments and central ministries and with members of the public concerned with economic development, e.g. businessmen, economists, etc. But there is no governmental sanction behind these targets. The plans only indicate what is broadly agreed upon between government representatives, economists and industrialists as feasible targets for achievement which are essential for the balanced economic development of the country.

The institutional structure of the Planning Commission has been taking shape during the last seven years. As well as the chairman, who is the Prime Minister, the Commission consists, at present, of several members of the Cabinet and also non-official economists. The Commission is assisted by officers drawn from the Services, and Research Officers grouped in a number of divisions; for instance, the Economic and Finance Division, the Irrigation and Power Division, the Land Reforms Division, the Food and Agriculture Division, the Industry and Minerals Division, the Progress and Programme Administration Divisions, the Perspective Planning Divisions, etc. The actual plans and estimates come from the Services. Members of the Commission and the Research Division examine the various studies from the point of view of the economy as a whole, as well as from the practical point of view. The schemes of the central and of the state governments are coordinated in the Planning Commission. The Planning Commission is thus a coordinating and priority fixing body working in discussion with representatives of the central ministries and state governments. Before being finalized, these plans are placed before the National Development Council for approval. This Council consists of the Prime Minister, members of the central cabinet, the members of the Planning Commission and the chief ministers of the states. The planning process is thus through persuasion and agreement. Unless the various groups have a substantially similar outlook agreed decisions are impossible.

1.3

The planning process has been in a state of evolution and the process of evolution gives the clue to the nature of the planning process itself. I shall, therefore, discuss in the following pages the nature of the coordination of the two lines of approach outlined before, e.g. the construction of the theoretical model and its synchronization with schemes drawn up by various executive organizations in the three Five-Year Plans.

The first Five-Year Plan

As far as is known the first Five-Year Plan started merely as a process of summarizing, rationalizing and coordinating separate schemes of development and presenting them together, a compilation of the piecemeal projects of the departments, lacking in any theoretical underpinning or overall visualization of the future.

Subsequently, however, a Harrod–Domar model of growth was fitted to the compiled data, more as a mathematical appendix to the plan itself. The Harrod–Domar model was used merely as a curve-fitting technique for projections into the future. Using the Domar model of growth the Commission very roughly estimated a savings ratio of 5 to 6 per cent during the plan period with an incremental capital output ratio of about 3 : 1 giving rise to a rate of growth of 2 to $2\frac{1}{4}$ per cent per annum in the first five year period. There was very little work on the theoretical plan frame itself.

Many of the schemes included in the first Five-Year Plan had already been drawn up during the Second World War and afterwards for post-war reconstruction. Quite a number of these, which were previously only in blueprint, found a place in the first Five-Year Plan. The Plan itself was officially signed on 7 December 1952, although it began from April 1951. Many of the schemes included in the plan were already in execution when the first Five-Year Plan was finalized.

The second Five-Year Plan

This was very much in advance of the first Plan. In a way, real planning in the sense of a formal projection on the basis of certain sets of assumptions about the economy and its working, was started with the second Five-Year Plan.

In this, the theoretical underpinning was supplied by the now well known Mahalanobis model.

The Mahalanobis model was set up on lines analogous to Soviet economic thinking during its earlier plans. In fact, the model of growth demonstrated by Feldman[1] in 1928 is an exact replica of the first model used by Mahalanobis. Analytically, it is a two-sector variant of the Harrod–Domar model, the behaviour coefficient of the Domar model being replaced by institutional allocation coefficients in two sectors, one for investment goods and one for consumption goods.

The two-sector Mahalanobis model is defined below:

If λ_k and λ_c are the relative shares of total allocation to the two industries' investment, α_0, the ratio of national investment to income initially, and β_k and β_c, the output-capital ratios, then national product is given by

<hr>

[1] 'The process of growth of national income', *Sankhya*, 1952. Domar has pointed out that the two-sector model on almost similar lines was first proposed by the Soviet economist Feldman as early as 1928. Domar: *Essays in the theory of economic growth*. New York: Oxford University Press.

$$y(t) = y_0 \left\{ 1 + \alpha_0 \frac{\beta_k \lambda_k + \beta_c \lambda_c}{\beta_k \lambda_k} [(1 + \beta_k \lambda_k)^t - 1] \right\},$$

where $I(t)$ the investment takes the form

$$I(t) = I_0 (1 + \beta_k \lambda_k)^t$$

and $c(t)$ the consumption in t takes the form

$$c(t) = y_0 \left[1 - \alpha_0 \left(1 + \frac{\beta_c \lambda_c}{\beta_k \lambda_k} \right) \right] + \alpha_0 y_0 \frac{\beta_c \lambda_c}{\beta_k \beta_k} (1 + \beta_k \lambda_k)^t.$$

It is interesting to note that in tracing the time path in both cases, λ_k the investment allocation is sufficient. Further disaggregation, therefore, of $c(t)$ into $c_1(t)$ and $c_2(t)$ can be easily done so long as the basic allocation is not altered.

Mahalanobis explains the use of the model in the plan as follows:

'(1) In the two-sector model the pattern of growth of the economy depends on the initial rate of investment (which is given), the values of β_k and β_c, the income coefficients respectively in the industries producing capital goods (k sector) and in the industries producing consumer goods (c sector) which are determined by technological factors and conditions of production and are not at the choice of the planner, and on λ_k, the fraction of the total investment allocated to industries producing capital goods (k sector) with the remaining share of investment $\lambda_c = (1 - \lambda_k)$ going to industries producing consumer goods.

(2) The value $\lambda_k = \frac{1}{3}$ was adopted on the basis of the pattern of growth emerging from certain values of λ_k and λ_c which were considered to be reasonable estimates of these parameters under Indian conditions.'[1]

For a more detailed allocation at one point of time, Mahalanobis further prepared a four-sector model as a special case:

If Y_i and n_i are the sectoral increases in income and employment respectively and λ_i are investment allocation ratios ($i = 1, 2, 3, 4$), we have

$$I_i(t) = \frac{1}{\beta_i} Y_i(t),$$

$$I_i(t) = \frac{1}{\Theta_i} n_i(t).$$

Then it follows that, $I_i(t) = \lambda_i I(t) = \frac{1}{\beta_i} Y_i(t),$

$$I_i(t) = \lambda_i I(t) = \frac{1}{\Theta_i} n_i(t)$$

also, $\Sigma \lambda_i = 1.$

Introducing targets $\Sigma n_i = n$ and $\Sigma Y_i = Y$ and assigning a specific value to one of the λ_i, the system is solved for Y_i, n_i and the remaining λ_i.

Since Y_i is the increase in sectoral income we have, total increase in income

$$\Sigma Y_i = Y = I \Sigma \beta_i \lambda_i = I\beta,$$

[1] P. 38, Appendix to chapter 4: Technical note on the pattern of growth of the economy. 'The approach of operational research to planning in India' by P. C. Mahalanobis. *Sankhya*, vol. 16 (1955-6).

where β is the overall coefficient relating to the increase of income and investment and I is total investment, i.e. $\Sigma_i I_i$.

Treating the increases as instantaneous we have

$$\frac{dy}{dt} = I\beta,$$

β here plays the part of a weighted investment productivity coefficient. If during the plan period we also have I as a constant ratio α of y, i.e.

$$I = \alpha y,$$

this at once gives us Domar's form of the growth model,

$$I = I_0 e^{\alpha\beta t}.$$

Any sectoral increase

$$Y_i = \lambda_i I \beta_i = \lambda_i \beta_i I_0 e^{\alpha\beta t}$$

and

$$\frac{Y_i}{Y_k} = \frac{\lambda_i \beta_i}{\lambda_k \beta_k}.$$

In the Plan-frame[1] the volume of new employment estimated was about eleven million. The estimate was based on the following values of the income-coefficients of investment (β's) and the capital required per engaged person (Θ's) for the different sectors for which they were calculated separately and added up.[1]

Sector of Economy		Sectoral income coefficient of investment	Sectoral value of capital per engaged person
Symbol (1)	Description (2)	(3)	(4)
K	Large-scale industries producing investment goods	0·20	Rs. 20,000
C. 1	Large-scale industries producing consumers goods	0·35	Rs. 8,750
C. 2	Agriculture and small and household industries	1·25	Rs. 2,500
C. 3	Services (health, education etc.)	0·45	Rs. 3,750

Detailed planning from this theoretical background was done on the basis of input-output tables and various sectoral data from which eventually a set of physical targets was worked out.

It may be seen that to a large extent the planning procedure of the second Plan was very much an advance. But targets were often fixed for the whole nation and a substantial part of them were to be produced in the private sector or in cooperation with it. Official instruments of implementation were very indirect and therefore, there was no definite guarantee that the private sector would operate as required. In this sense, there was a dichotomy or dual system in the planning procedure though a sort of general visualization was made of the development of the economy as a whole.

[1] *Ibid.*

The third Five-Year Plan

In the third Plan broadly the trend set up by Mahalanobis was presumably followed though no specific published source is mentioned anywhere. In a sense while there was a definite trend towards more coherent planning from the first to the second Plan there is no evidence of this progress being maintained from the second to the third Plan. It is generally known that the statistical background required to prepare a blueprint was very weak during the second Plan period. This has definitely been strengthened by more elaborate studies, but the kind of imaginative effort of visualizing the economy as a whole and its future which was demonstrated during the second Plan has definitely given way to a more pragmatic and piecemeal effort at solving problems independently of each other. In this sense, the preparation of the third Plan holds out nothing exciting to a student of planning. It is quite true that the attempt at developing workable models for planning, which was initiated during the second Plan, if patiently pursued during the third Plan, would have given greater insight into both the theory and the practice of developmental planning in under-developed countries.

1.4

We come now to a statistical assessment of the net result of planned activity by the Government. What is the position of the Government of India as the leader of industrialization? The following tables give the Government and private share of activities in per cent of the GNP.

It will be seen that over all the position of the Government is still not impressive though its rate of growth in the matter of new capital formation and especially in industrial concerns is more impressive. This is shown below.

In the field of new investment the Government is already the leading investor. This is especially so in the sectors involving more complicated technology. In total capital formation the Government is clearly emerging as an important factor.

The nature of government activity has considerably changed during this period as may be seen from the breakdown of Government expenditure into administrative and commercial enterprises.

Previously, the government activity included very little industrial or commencial entrepreneurship. But this type of entrepreneurial activity has been steadily growing as a result of changes in the basic approach to government functions.

All this goes to show that the Government has been playing an increasing role in the development of the Indian economy, especially relating to its industrialization.

The nature of the Indian economy and the volume of activity in the private sector makes it obvious that the Government has operated in a narrow field here insofar as direct involvements are concerned. Indirectly,

Government share in the generation of net domestic product.

Unit-Rs. 100 crores at current prices. (1 cr = 10 million)

Year	Net output of Government enterprises	Net output of Government administration	Net output of private sector
1948–49	2·4 (2·8)	4·0 (4·6)	80·3 (92·6)
1949–50	2·7 (3·0)	4·1 (4·5)	83·5 (92·5)
1950–51	2·9 (3·0)	4·3 (4·5)	88·3 (92·5)
1951–52	3·2 (3·2)	4·5 (4·5)	92·2 (92·3)
1952–53	3·1 (3·1)	4·6 (4·7)	90·6 (92·2)
1953–54	3·2 (3·0)	4·9 (4·7)	96·7 (92·3)
1954–55	3·6 (3·8)	5·2 (5·4)	87·3 (90·8)
1955–56	4·2 (4·2)	5·7 (5·7)	89·9 (90·1)
1956–57	4·8 (4·2)	6·1 (5·4)	102·1 (90·4)
1957–58	5·1 (4·5)	6·6 (5·8)	102·3 (89·7)
1958–59	5·2 (4·1)	7·3 (5·8)	113·7 (90·1)
1959–60	5·1 (3·9)	7·9 (6·1)	116·8 (90·0)
1960–61	5·7 (4·0)	9·1 (6·4)	127·3 (89·6)
1961–62	6·1 (4·2)	10·2 (6·9)	130·6 (88·9)

Figures in parentheses indicate percentage distribution.

An estimate of domestic net investment and saving in India (1952–3 prices).

Unit = million rupees.

Year	Government	Corporations	Individuals	Total Domestic
1948–49	1702	1466	2863	6031
1949–50	2073	1525	3059	6657
1950–51	2035	758	3048	5841
1951–52	2112	1543	3151	6806
1952–53	2460	820	3357	6637
1953–54	2735	475	3631	6842
1954–55	3813	1402	4360	9575
1955–56	5360	1850	5276	12486
1956–57	6158	2245	5438	13841
1957–58	7893	2418	5958	16269
1958–59	8600*	N.A.	N.A.	N.A.
1959–60	7000*	N.A.	N.A.	N.A.
1960–61	7900*	N.A.	N.A.	N.A.
1961–62	10500*	N.A.	N.A.	N.A.

* Gross investment on government account.

there are various ways in which the Government is channelling the growth of the economy in certain directions, e.g. its licensing policy, tariff policy, subsidy policy, etc. But these are all indirect and non-coercive and their overall effect, though considerable, cannot easily be measured.

Granting that the present trend continues into the future, the Government will emerge as the single most important investor in the country, but not the biggest investor in any sense. The Government, then will have

Capital outlay (net of maintainance), in commercial enterprises and administrative departments respectively, of the Government of India.

Unit = Rs. 100 crores at current prices.

Year	Capital outlay in commercial enterprises	Capital outlay in administrative departments
1948–49	0·92	0·70
1949–50	1·15	0·87
1950–51	1·33	0·71
1951–52	1·47	0·73
1952–53	1·41	0·76
1953–54	1·63	0·96
1954–55	2·18	1·16
1955–56	2·93	1·77
1956–57	4·02	1·77
1957–58	5·18	1·77
1958–59	4·98	1·87
1959–60	3·24	2·17
1960–61	3·38	2·84
1961–62	5·30	3·34

Source: Estimate of National C.S.O. January 1963.

an immense influence on the economy of the country but not an adequate control over it.

What are the prospects for planning in India in the future? Is it going to increase, or stabilize somewhere or have a slow fade out? This is a question many have been confronted with. It is true that we are still at a cross-roads in the sense that basic shifts of industrial policy are not completely ruled out. In an economy where the public and private sectors are both existing and growing, there is a continuous tension, with lobbies for both sectors, national and international, trying to steer policy in their own direction.

We cannot say that a stable balance has yet been worked out. But a basic shift in policy is becoming more and more difficult. Every system generates its own political and economic support by expanding groups and sectors interested in the growth of the system. With its growth the public sector is creating a large body of people who are vitally interested in the growth of the public sector. The public sector is coming more and more into control of strategic points of the economy. The public at large may have various complaints but are definitely in favour of more public ownership, from a sense of social justice, and public control. The private sector in India has never impressed the general public with its vigour or with its long range vision. It has generally been conservative and out to get short-range returns.

It seems, therefore, that the present trend of development and the policies associated with it is likely to become increasingly our way of life and will continue to be so.

CHAPTER 2

MATHEMATICAL MODELS IN RESEARCH RELATED TO PLANNING IN INDIA (A REVIEW)

In an earlier paper[1] an attempt was made to review the planning effort in India and the integration of theoretical planning models with actual planning problems.

In the present paper, a detailed review has been made of economic models constructed in India stimulated by problems of planning which emerged during this period. The models selected for discussion have either been empirically fitted, or are in the process of being fitted, to Indian data. In this sense the selection is oriented to actual empirical work. It is to be understood, however, that these models are still in their initial stages, and their impact on direct planning itself remains negligible. They are in a stage which may be described as research and exploration for shaping the tools of prediction and planning but their use as instruments of planning is not yet on the agenda. These models, however, are influencing the approach of our planners and in this sense they are of importance to our planning process.

In most of these models, programming and input-output techniques are combined. This combination of two essentially allied techniques will, therefore, receive special attention. These models have been used both at regional and national levels and the problems treated are of interest to economists concerned with various questions of growth and regional balance. A portion of this study will consequently be devoted to problems relating to regional allocation, using input-output models, with or without programming.

The paper is divided into several sections:

In § 2.1, we review, briefly, work relating to the construction of input-output tables in India at different times and present a group of consistency models, some of them using input-output techniques, and others influenced by such techniques.

In § 2.2, we report on work combining input-output with programming models at a national level.

In § 2.3, we discuss planning models involving problems of inter-temporal efficiency.

In § 2.4, we present some demonstrations of inter-regional allocation models combining input-output and programming techniques.

[1] A. Ghosh, *Economics of Planning*, vol. IV, no. 1, 1964. Chapter 1 of this book.

In § 2.5, we briefly discuss some models which are being developed to consider dynamic complications and problems requiring integer solutions.

2.1

In India, as in most other developing regions, an input-output approach was found to be ideally suited to a comprehensive planning effort, since it gave a reasonably simple but overall approach with which the first blueprints could be drawn up and interrelations of the effect of growth between different sectors worked out. Therefore, input-output models were used from the beginning.

The first input-output table was constructed for India in the Indian Statistical Institute under the direction of Goodwin and Choudhury.[1] The table was of twelve sectors and, being the first of its kind, it was full of rather unreliable estimates made on an *ad hoc* basis. It is not known to what extent this table was directly used in making estimates for the second Five-Year Plan. Presumably it was used as an additional check on estimates of intermediate requirements and total outputs.

A number of more detailed and reliable tables have been prepared since then under the direction of the Inter-Industry Unit of the Indian Statistical Institute[2], Perspective Planning Division[3] and elsewhere. These tables are of varying sizes and, due to the steady building up of the statistical base, have greater accuracy.

A new development in the construction of input-output tables was the work carried out by Dhar and others in Jadavpur University and elsewhere under the guidance of the author. Dhar prepared an inter-regional input-output table for India in 1954.[4] This work was again a pioneer attempt at building a table combining inter-regional flows and inter-sectoral flows. Dhar's table opened possibilities of building multi-regional planning models. The use of this table in inter-regional models will be discussed in a later section.

Dhar went on to the difficult task of trying to build up tables showing the regional input-output flows and external links of the West Bengal state[5] and later of the Calcutta Metropolitan Area.[5] The attempt was very ambitious, considering the lack of data, and the results were not of a type to be practically useful in the first instance. Later on, however, the table was further improved by *ad hoc* surveys of the flow between the

---

[1] T. P. Choudhury & R. M. Goodwin, *Transaction matrices for the Indian Union, 1950–1* (Indian Statistical Institute, Planning Division, Inter-Industry Unit, Calcutta).

[2] U. Dutta, A preliminary study of inter-industry relations in India in papers in *National Income and Allied Topics*, vol. 1. Asia Publishing House.

A. K. Chakraborty & S. S. Sengupta, *Inter-industry relations of the Indian economy, 1953–4, at market prices*. (Indian Statistical Institute, Planning Division, Inter-Industry Unit, Calcutta, Working Paper Series).

[3] Perspective Planning Division, 1964.

[4] R. Dhar, *Inter-regional input-output analysis of the Indian economy (1953–4)*, (Unpublished thesis).

[5] R. Dhar, *An input-output table for W. Bengal and the Calcutta Metropolitan District: first and second interim reports* (Calcutta Research Studies, Occasional Reports, I.P.A. New York).

Calcutta Metropolitan Area and other areas. A planning model based on such a table is discussed later in this section.

Compared with the effort spent in the construction of tables, the amount of published material involving the use of input-output models is not impressive. It is assumed that these models are used in the Planning Commission to project sectoral output levels, but there are, unfortunately, very few published reports concerning them. An important paper on this subject was presented by Manne & Rudra[1] projecting consistent sectoral outputs for 1970–1 from the 1960–1 table using the open model of input-output.

The authors describe their paper as a consistency model for the fourth Five-Year Plan and base their work on the transaction matrix of 1960–1 produced by the Planning Commission.[2] They have considered a consistency model, rather than an optimizing model, under the conviction that the relative scarcities are well known and most of the alternative choices could be eliminated by a careful scrutiny of the realistic bounds of import substitution and export possibilities. According to them, although formally more satisfying, an optimizing model may not really yield substantive conclusions very different from a simple consistency model, provided the targets are fixed on the basis of known preferences and scarcities, since the range of choice is greatly limited.

In their model, the authors use a stock-flow conversion factor to relate the investment in any year to the total capital formation in the period, thus enabling the investment activity to be built endogenously into the model in terms of the target capital formation. If r is the rate of annual investment, then e^{rt} is the index of gross annual investment t years from the base date, and $\int_0^t e^{rt}\,dt$ becomes the index of capital formation; conversion factor between stocks and flows is defined as

$$\frac{e^{rt}}{\int_0^t e^{rt}\,dt}.$$

With a lag of θ years, the start must be θ years before the base period and have to be completed θ years before the target date so that we get, for the conversion factor with a gestation of θ, the expression,

$$\frac{e^{rt}}{\int_{-\theta}^{t-\theta} e^{rt}\,dt}.$$

The projection of coefficients for 1970–1 depended largely on the existing transaction table for 1960–1, prepared by the Perspective Planning Division, and adjustments were made on the basis of anticipated changes. Specially affected by changes were sectors like chemical

[1] A. Manne & A. K. Rudra, A Consistency Model of India's Fourth Plan, *Sankhya*, vol. 27, parts I and II, 1965.

[2] Perspective Planning Division, 1964.

fertilizers, petroleum, etc. Import coefficients were adjusted on the basis of the most likely conjectures for 1970–1 and anticipated structural changes in the economy.

In projecting final demand for the open model, it was assumed that 'Government has sufficient fiscal powers so that it is unconstrained by the fixed back link that operates in a market economy.... If the goods can be produced, the domestic finances can be found'.[1] While this was the main guiding principle, the broad policy statements of the government regarding the target of consumption, capital formation, etc. were also kept in mind.

Several sets of 'optimistic' and 'pessimistic' projections were obtained with varying alternatives, showing a growth rate of between 6·6 to 4·9 per cent in domestic expenditure, and 9·8 to 7·8 per cent in capital formation.

Though a simple and straightforward application of the input-output model, it is a competent and useful piece of work based on a wealth of empirical data from the best available sources.

As a continuation of the Manne & Rudra study, Manne & Bergman[2] have constructed what they call an almost consistent intertemporal model for the fourth and fifth Indian Plan. Their approach to the calculation of terminal year output levels does not differ substantially from that of Manne & Rudra. But they proceed from this to calculate annual output rates log-linearly from the terminal year output and initial year outputs. Since such annual rates will not necessarily be consistent in the framework of the model, they use these rates to make the necessary changes in the outputs and final demands. Iterating in this way, they have arrived at a set of annual figures for the thirty sectors which are self-consistent within the framework of the input-output model and present also a set of growth rates which are determined as a long-linear trend during the five years of the plan. In the model the foreign trade balance position each year is an important objective for study under different growth targets. The model works on the assumption that the demand-supply gap for any commodity could be met either by imports, by increasing domestic service, or by consumption shortfalls. As this work is very similar to Rudra & Manne in basic approach it is not taken up in detail here.

Dhar has used his own input-output table for West Bengal to make a projection of the final demands of West Bengal.[3] His objective in this exercise is a feasibility study of certain proposed targets of outputs approved by the authorities.

Dhar's main purpose was to calculate the level of final demand for officially given output targets, and to analyse the feasibility of this final demand in terms of available local and national resources. It was found

---

[1] Perspective Planning Division, 1964.

[2] Manne & Bergman, An almost consistent inter-temporal model for India's fourth and fifth Plans. *Economic Weekly*, vol. XVII, no. 47.

[3] R. Dhar, Input-output and regional plan formulation: a case study of the economy of west Bengal during the fourth Five Year Plan (1965–6 to 1970–1).

from his projection that an increased surplus for export to other regions will be possible in food processing, jute, iron and steel and engineering. He draws up a net balance of inter-regional trade, and estimates the surplus and deficit in the different commodities, on the basis of the given output level.

Ghosh[1] used a two-sector flow table of the Calcutta Metropolitan Area in a projection model for the growth of the area up to 1981. At a two-sector level this does not make an impressive show for inter-sectoral analysis, but the main objective was a projection of population and employment as a whole, and the inter-industrial part was therefore secondary to the study.

The objective of the complete model constructed by Ghosh was to predict the population, employment, output, and net immigration to the Calcutta Metropolitan Area through a system of equations with estimated parameters.

The model has three structural parts. The first part $(1 \cdot 1 - 1 \cdot 3)$ consists of the demographic variables, and their inter-relation with each other, and with economic variables. The interesting equation in this system is the one relating the immigrant population to the 'pull' factor defined by employment opportunities in the city and the 'push' factor denoted by the scarcity of land in the surrounding rural areas. The immigrant flow here is determined by the man-land ratio of the region from which migrants come, and the index of employment of the metropolis itself, as follows:

$$_mP(t) = a + bE_t + c_{ag}I(t),$$

where $_mP(t)$ is the immigrant population, $E(t)$ is employment in the metropolis, and $_{ag}I(t)$ is the agricultural land-to-labour ratio in the neighbouring rural hinterland. The obvious assumption was that the rural immigrants to the city are mainly from the class of agricultural labourers and tenants suffering from an increasing shortage of arable land. They come into the city lured by prospects of employment.

The second part $(2 \cdot 1 - 2 \cdot 3)$ gives the input-output equations in two sectors, 'primary plus secondary' and tertiary.

Finally, there are equations $(3 \cdot 1 - 3 \cdot 3)$ giving the interrelations between final demand, population, and other variables.

Using productivity and export–import balance as exogenously given, a projection of the population to 1961, 1971 and 1981 was obtained. Agreement with the 1961 data, which was available only after the model was fitted, was found to be reasonably satisfactory.

A rather straightforward projection by input-output model was also carried out on a four sector model by Padma Desai[2] as a research exercise.

[1] A. Ghosh, A growth model of the Calcutta Metropolitan Area. Census (1961) Monograph, No. 2, Government of India. See Chapter 13 of this book.
[2] Padma Desai, A short-term planning model for the Indian economy, *Review of Economics and Statistics*, 1961.

2.2

During the second Five-Year Plan, great stress was laid on central plans to stimulate growth in various sectors. Input-output was the first available technical tool that was taken up. The planners also took up a study of the feasibility of programming techniques, at least in an exploratory manner, in order to judge the desirability of different methods of growth. Given the data base required to work out an input-output model, its extension to linear programming models really involved only some suitable preference functions and certain additional constraints. Studies of various programming models of the economy were therefore initiated under the inspiration of Mahalanobis.[1] Two interesting studies carried out are by Sandee[2] and Frisch[3] who worked in India during 1954–5.

Sandee considers a combination of input-output techniques with linear programming. He considers the usual form of an open input-output model, but instead of assigning the exogenous vectors arbitrarily, he tries to obtain them by maximizing the consumption in the target period. Let C stand for the increase in total consumption where C' is the initial value. Then, C/C' is the relative rise in consumption. Let p be the relative rise in population, then $C/C' - p$ is the per capita increase in consumption.

Given η_j as the expenditure elasticity of the jth commodity, *per capita* increase in jth commodity is $\eta_j(C/C' - p)$, and the total increase represented by c_j/c_j' for the jth commodity is

$$\frac{c_j}{c_j'} = \eta_j \left(\frac{C}{C'} - p \right) + p$$

so that

$$c_j = \eta_j c_j' \frac{C}{C'} - \eta_j p c_j' + p c_j'.$$

Defining incremental consumption as above, in terms of initial consumption, population increase and ultimate consumption, the preference function maximizes the level of material consumption in 1970, subject to a set of constraints in the form of input-output equations.

Sandee relates investment to output by introducing a stockflow conversion factor and a capital-output ratio. If T is the number of years and Δ the increment of investment each year, then the accumulation of capital is given according to his method by $T I_o + \frac{1}{2}[(T-1) T\Delta]$, where I_o is the initial investment and this is equal to rx. Inventory is related to output in a similar way.

Additional constraints are brought as realistic limits to production, e.g. the equalization of imports with exports, reflecting balance of payments difficulties; fixing a size of total investments; fixing an upper limit for exports, for steel imports, transportation, and similar scarcities.

[1] P. Mahalanobis. See Preface.

[2] J. Sandee, A demonstration planning model for India, Indian Statistical Institute, *Studies Relating to Planning for National Development*, No. 4, Calcutta, 1960.

[3] R. Frisch, Planning for India: Selected explorations in methodology, studies relating to planning for National Development, Indian Statistical Institute, Calcutta, 1960.

Sandee's model has value as a pioneer effort describing a simple decision model relevant to planning in India, and it played a useful part in developing the methodology for application in an Indian context.

The model used by Frisch is similar to Sandee's as far as the structure is concerned. He uses a variant of an input-output model with linear programming. His model, however, is rather more elaborate as he uses several variables for the objective function, one of which also introduces consideration of long-range requirements and adjusts short-range requirements to long-range problems of balanced growth.

To solve the long range growth problem, Frisch uses a deterministic set up. The basic equations in his model are a balance relation, setting up equivalence between output and its allocation to different uses during a specific period.

He now adds to the system a set of input coefficients and a set of investment coefficients which transform the balance equation into the form

$$X_i = \sum_j a_{ij} X_j + C_i + \sum_j b_{ij} I_j^d$$

where $a_{ij} x_j$ is the requirement of the ith output for current production in the jth sector, b_{ij} denotes sectoral capital coefficients from ith to jth sector I_j^d being the sectoral investments, and C_i denotes final consumption of commodities of the ith sector. Further structural equations used by Frisch are a depreciation equation of the form,

$$D_i = d_i X_i$$

a labour equation of the form,

$$N_i = n_i X_i$$

and a capacity to production relation given by

$$K_i = b_i X_i,$$

where capacity K_i fully used stands in a given proportion to production in ith sector.

Finally, the growth of capacity K_i at t is given by

$$K_i^t = K_i^{t-1} + I_i^{t-si-1} - D_i^{t-1},$$

where s_i is the maturity lag in ith sector. Making the necessary substitutions he gets the equation for investments at time t

$$I_i^d(t) = \frac{b_i}{n_i} N_i^{t+s_i+1} - \frac{b_i - d_i}{n_i} N_i^{t+s_i}. \tag{1}$$

It is thus demonstrated that using the above structural equations, investment is uniquely determined by labour supply, and therefore by population growth. It follows that if the growth level of employment is assigned for a given population, then the investment requirement is determined uniquely. The cross-delivery coefficients are now used for determining consumption resulting from a given population growth as a residual item from the balance equation.

Coming to the short-term problem of growth, he maximizes a preference function of the form

$$f = au + bv + cw, \tag{2}$$

where u denotes the number of new jobs created annually, $v =$ the annual rate of investment, and $w =$ the net annual increase in India's foreign assets. The weights a, b, c are fixed by an arbitrary political authority.

The above function does not automatically ensure that short-term growth takes place in a manner which will satisfy the requirements of long-term balance. Therefore, he brings the consideration of long term balanced growth into the preference function in the following way. He considers the capacity K_i that should be generated on consideration of the long run balance given in (1) and the capacity actually acquired in the beginning of any short-term planning period for any sector. Thus $\bar{K}_i - K_i^0$ expresses the discrepancy, at the beginning of a short-term plan, between desired and actual growth. He now forms the weight,

$$w = (\bar{K}_i - K_i^0)$$

denoting the deviation of a sector from its ideal balanced path, and considers the investment, net of depreciation, in each sector weighted by w_i, so that he maximizes

$$\frac{\sum\limits_i (\bar{K}_i - K_i^0)\, (I_i - D_i)}{\sum\limits_i (\bar{K}_i - K_i^0)}.$$

This ensures that sectors which are under capacity, in terms of the warranted growth path, will get preference in investment, and sectors with excess capacity will be discriminated against.

Using the relations between labour, output, and investment, by straightforward substitution he reduces u to a function of the output, w is assumed proportional to exports, and the coefficient of proportionality used is based on the export surplus in 1950–1. Subject now to the usual balance equations, he maximizes the preference function noted above.

Apart from using a more elaborate structure than Sandee, Frisch adds the notion of balanced long-term growth and adjustments of short-term plans, according to performance in preceding years, so that eventually, through such adjustments, the long-term balance may be maintained. In this way Fisch develops an empirical model where principles of long term perspective planning are made consistent with short term three to five year plans.

The Sandee and Frisch models are examples of the organic link between linear programming models and input-output models both being generalizations of the classic input-output model along lines where some degree of freedom is encouraged and problems are solved by introducing a system of choice.

The two models described above emerge directly from planning efforts and for this reason there is a strong tendency in both to tackle problems which have an empirical base and to obtain answers which are in the region of feasibility.

As a check on the consistency of the third Five-Year Plan some exercises were carried out by the Perspective Planning Division. Plant & Little[1] used a decision model in order to check the consistency of some broad magnitudes relating to it.

The model consists of fifteen variables of which population, government current expenditure, operating surplus from public enterprise and taxes which are independent of income are considered as given data. Technological equations relate the increase in total income to investment and agricultural income to agricultural investment; a set of definitional identities is used to bring consistency among several magnitudes such as total taxes, taxes from income and other taxes, total investment with savings, foreign aid which goes into capital formation, and so on. A behaviour equation expresses the demand for agricultural goods in terms of population, *per capita* income, and income elasticity, as below,

$$D_A(t) = P_t \left(\frac{Y}{P} \right)_t^{\eta},$$

where D_A indicates demand for agricultural output, P is the population, Y is income, η is the income elasticity of demand for agricultural production, all referring to the time period t. Certain institutional equations are used to relate taxes from current consumption, current agricultural income, and non-agricultural income. This is given as

$$T^d = C^{r_1} Y_{na}^{r_2} Y_a^{r_3},$$

where T denotes the total tax revenue, C refers to consumption, Y_a and Y_{na} to agricultural and non-agricultural production, which gives on differentiation

$$\frac{\Delta T}{T} = r_1 \frac{\Delta C}{C} + r_2 \frac{\Delta Y_{na}}{Y_{na}} + r_3 \frac{\Delta Y_a}{Y_a} = \frac{\Delta T'}{T'}$$

since $T = T' + T''$, where T' and T'' refer to tax revenue components dependent on income and independent of income, and T'' is fixed. This solution expresses taxes as a weighted sum of the rate of increase in consumption, in agricultural income, and in non-agricultural income. Given the parameters and the assigned variables $P(t)$, $E_c(t)$, $R(t)$ and $T''(t)$, the other variables e.g. savings, net foreign aid, consumption, investment, etc. are determined through the system.

The difficulty with the eventual interpretation of such models is that even slight changes in the given values of the parameters and assigned variables means a considerable change in the other endogenous variables, and the use of such models is expedient only if an adequate practical knowledge of the economy and its behaviour is available, so that suitable parameter values may be selected from a wide range of likely values.

[1] Pant & Little, Dimensional hypotheses concerning the third Five Year plan (unpublished), New Delhi, February 1959; Public finance and the third Plan, M.I.T., New Delhi, May 1959.

Another deterministic model was constructed by Ghosh[1] to predict the Union Government expenditure during the third Five-Year Plan by a system of simultaneous equations.

The model is an elaborate system with twenty-one variables defining various items of Union Government expenditure, income, and other relevant variables.

Apart from several straightforward definitional identities the model uses several equations of significance. Thus, the earned income of the government (y) is expressed as a function of its expenditure E as below:

$$Y = a_E^Y E + a_t^Y t + \lambda^Y,$$

where a_E^Y, a_t^Y and λ^Y are constants. It is thus assumed that government income depends on its own decisions to spend, subject only to a time trend.

Another equation relates price to government income, expenditure, and a time trend as follows

$$P = a_E^P E + a_y^P y + a_t^P t + \lambda^P.$$

This equation makes the price rise dependent upon government income and expenditure as major determinants in conjunction with a time trend.

Several equations are also introduced based on the assumption that expenditure under various heads and incomes from various sources are given fractions of total expenditure and income.

2.3

We shall now describe experiments which are more of an exploratory methodological type and handle optimizing problems involving time in various ways. An ambitious example of this type of model is one by Chakravarti & Lefeber.[2]

The model for Indian planning constructed by Chakravarti & Lefeber carries the earlier models some steps further in complexity and elaboration of detail. It is multi-sectoral and uses input-output coefficients to relate the sectors. It is an optimizing model but it also introduces notions of inter-temporal efficiency in a finite planning horizon. It considers capital goods of two types for each sector consisting of 'construction' and 'equipment' and uses a fixed lag of three years as a gestation period. It further assumes that the investment in a capital installation completed in three years is consistently spread over the three-year period in a uniquely defined way. For the objective function, it uses a discounted value of consumption over the planning horizon as a maximizing function. We discuss in detail some of its additional features as compared to

---

[1] A. Ghosh, *Union budgets and prices*, Asia Publishing House.
[2] Chakravarti & Lefeber: An optimizing planning model, *The Economic Weekly*, vol. xvii, no. 5, 6 and 7, February 1965.

the models of Sandee, Frish, Manne & Rudra, etc. The objective function is defined as

$$U = \sum_{t=1}^{T} W(t)\, C(t),$$

where $W(t)$ s are the relative weights, so that a ratio between a pair of $W(t)$ s represents a 'social discount factor', and $C(t)$ the consumption in t. It is assumed that the discount rate is constant over the plan horizon.

The sectoral composition of final consumption is always fixed, so that sectoral consumption enters in fixed proportion to total consumption.

For capital, the production function is considered as

$$bX(t) - K(t) \leqslant 0,$$

where $X(t)$ and $K(t)$ refer to output and capital in period t, where b is a diagonal matrix of capital-output ratios.

The depreciation is exogenously accounted for by $\overline{R}(t)$, a replacement requirement for each planning period.

If $Z(t)$ is the gross addition to productive capital in t, then it is assumed that it has come as a result of investments in $t-1$, $t-2$, and $t-3$, in an assigned ratio. Thus, if $Z(t)$—a steel mill, for example— is brought into action in t, it is assumed that a fixed part of this was invested in $t-1$, another fixed part in $t-2$ and a third part in $t-3$. Thus $I(t-k)$, the investment in $t-k$ is an assigned fraction of $Z(t)$ the capital formation in period t,

$$_q{}^k Z(t) = I^t(t-k), \quad \sum_k q^k = 1 \quad (k = 1, 2, 3).$$

Further, these investment components are assumed to have fixed sectoral production coefficients b_{ij} analogous to Frisch's capital coefficient matrix.

Government, foreign aid, exports are determined exogenously, and import is subject to a constraint that it cannot exceed the sum of foreign aid plus exports in constant domestic currency. Non-competitive imports have a *floor* in terms of sectoral domestic outputs, while competitive imports, which are admissible only after non-competitive imports are satisfied, have been allocated by fixed proportion among the sectors.

The initial conditions refer to the state of the economy before the planning period.

The terminal conditions are prescribed according to specific rates of growth for the exogenous elements which, combined with the other constraints in terms of production coefficients, investment coefficients, etc., prescribe the output levels that must be met from the end of the planning period onwards. This is given by,

$$\begin{aligned}
X(T+\theta) = {}&AX(T+\theta) + (1+r)^\theta F(T) + (b^1 + d^1 + s) \\
&\times [X(t+\theta+1) - X(T+\theta)] + (b^2 + d^2) \\
&\times [X(t+\theta+2) - X(T+\theta+1)] + (b^3 + d^3) \\
&\times [X(t+\theta+3) - X(T+\theta+2)] + (1+g)^\theta G(T) \\
&+ (1+c)^\theta E(T) - (1+f)^\theta M(T).
\end{aligned}$$

If T is the terminal year of the plan and if θ is the period after the terminal year that we are considering, the output at time $T+\theta$ must satisfy the scheduled growth of the exogenous elements $F(T), G(T), E(T)$, and $M(T)$, which have assigned growth rates r, g, c and f. Terms like $[X(T+\theta+1) - X(T+\theta)]$ give the output in $T+\theta$ which must go as capital formation for the years $T+\theta+1$, $T+\theta+2$ and $T+\theta+3$ to sustain the required growth after $T+\theta$; b and d are the coefficients transforming this output into the necessary capital that must be provided for, in order to produce in $X(T+\theta)$, while s gives the corresponding inventory requirement. This equation presents the condition that has to be met in the terminal year, depending on the post-terminal horizon θ. A set of particular solutions to the above, corresponding to the assigned growth rate, has been presented as a constraint to be met so that the programme may satisfy the assigned growth rate with a specific solution based on present day information.

Using available official and semi-official data relating to the Indian third Five-Year Plan, this model was applied to discover the optimal consumption levels in the model, and was compared with the third Plan targets.

Being quite an ambitious model, its solutions are of course open to many questions, some of which have been put to the authors in a rejoinder by Srinivasan.[1] As Srinivasan observes, the extremely short period for which consumption is taken in the objective function makes the model most insensitive to the discount rate. If the time horizon was made longer, even with small discount rates, it might become profitable to accumulate in the earlier years.

As the authors admit, this is only a tentative exercise which should open the way to more practical work on a larger scale over varying assumptions, so that knowledge of the behaviour of these models under changes in the parameters b may be gained. Such work is necessary before practical use can be made of such models in planning work, even on an elementary level, apart from the fact that, for working such models, a greater wealth of accurate statistics has to be made available. But such models do provide the future possibility of utilizing quite complicated models empirically.

Mathur[2] considers a developmental problem of a new type. He is concerned with the shortest path in time that an economy should take in transforming its base from an old to a new technology.

He divides total production into two groups under 'old technology' and 'new technology'.

Then he considers the intermediate requirements for output by these two technologies and the consumption requirement of the workers of the two technologies in the style of the Leontief closed model, denoting by

[1] T. N. Srinivasan, Critique of the optimising planning model, *The Economic Weekly*, vol. XVII, no. 5, 6 and 7, February, 1965.

[2] P. N. Mathur, An efficient path for the technological transformation of an economy in *Structural Interdependence and Economic Development*, edited by T. Barna.

a_{ij} and a'_{ij} the input coefficients of the two technologies, C_{ij} and C'_{ij} the consumption coefficients for the two technologies, b_{ij} the capital coefficient in the new technology. He assumes that capital creation takes place only in the new technology. The requirements of the economy p years from the initial period are now expressed as:

$$\sum_{j=1}^{n} (a_{ij}+C_{ij})\, {}_oX_j + \sum_{j=1}^{n} (a'_{ij}+C'_{ij}) \sum_{k=1}^{p-1} \Delta_k X_j$$

$$+ \sum_{j=1}^{n} b_{ij} \Delta_p X_j + Y_i^p - \sum_{j=1}^{n} (a_{ij}+C_{ij})\, u_j^p,$$

where ${}_oX_j$ is the initial capacity in the jth sector, $\Delta_k X_j$ is the increase in X_i in the kth period, Y_i^p is final demand in the pth period, u_i^p is unused capacity in the old technology.

The above expression can be elaborated as follows:

The total requirement in the pth period consists of the intermediate requirements and consumption requirements for producing the initial output by the old technology, plus some requirements for all output increments from the initial to $(p-1)$th period using the new technology, plus capital formation needs for the pth period, plus consumption of the pth period less the intermediate requirements not absorbed, due to slack in the productive capacity in the old technology.

The supply side now consists of the used capacity of the old and new technologies, plus imports, less unused capacity, given as,

$$X_i^o + \sum_{k=1}^{p-1} \Delta_k X_i + I_i^p - u_i^p.$$

Obviously, to maintain production, supply must be $\geqslant$ requirement.

This system represents inequalities for each commodity and for each of the m periods which are within the horizon. Apart from these mn inequalities, there are m inequalities denoting import constraints, and other m inequalities denoting labour constraints. These are:

$$\sum_{i=1}^{n} I_i^p \leqslant E^p, \quad \sum_{i=1}^{n} \left\{ l_{i\,o}X_i + l'_i \sum_{k=1}^{p-1} \Delta_k X_i - l_i u_i^p \right\} \leqslant L^p \qquad (p = 1, 2, ..., m),$$

where E^P and L^P are fixed values dependent on other considerations and assigned to the system, and l_i and l'_i represent the labour requirement of the ith industry per unit of its output in the old and new technologies respectively. As unutilized capacity is assumed to be only that of the old technology, it cannot be greater than the initial capacity of the economy.

Like Frisch, Mathur also finds that at the end of the plan period, growth will be balanced and proportional to the rate of increase of labour.

Mathur's original objective was to develop such a growth path that the transition time from the old to the new technology would be minimized. This, however, was found to be rather intractable. Mathur therefore used a preference function for a terminal year, maximizing in turn:

(a) the total value added by the use of new technology;

(b) total growth of profit of all firms using the new technology;

(c) products of all firms using the new technology.

With these objective functions, different sets of solutions were obtained. The paper is primarily of academic interest, but it also has points regarding practical problems of growth. The original problem posed by Mathur was not solved in his paper. A smaller version of this problem was taken up and solved from a purely theoretical angle by Srinivasan.[1] As Srinivasan has not obtained any empirical demonstration of this exercise, the solution of the problem by Srinivasan is not taken up in this paper.

2.4

In the following section, we consider planning models in which an attempt has been made to solve regional allocation problems.

In a study by Ghosh on the cement industry in India[2] a model to solve transportation problems between regions, and the problems concerned with the installation of new units in different regions of India was applied.

The object was to assess to what extent the present system of inter-regional trade is optimal from a national standpoint, using the conventional transportation model.

The table below gives some of the results of the programming for 1950, 1954 and 1957.

Years	Actual	Optimal	Savings	Saving as % of actual
1950	1·41	1·32	0·09	6
1954	2·16	1·80	0·27	12
1957	1·83	1·78	0·07	4

It is realized that such a national optimum may go against genuine regional interests and produce undesirable consequences. The problem was therefore solved in alternative ways by assuming certain restrictions on regional targets and inter-regional movements.

The general conclusion seemed to be that in the cement industry the allocation had been gradually becoming more efficient since 1954, while it presumably operated earlier at moderate levels of efficiency.

The problem of finding an optimal location pattern for future expansion was also considered. The main assumption here was that regional average costs were unaltered by the addition of new units.

Using present techniques, the problem was formulated as below:

Let x_{ij} indicate the regional deliveries, r_j the requirement of the jth region, k_i the existing capacities in the ith region, and n_i the additional capacity installed in the ith region. Given regional requirements

$$\sum_i x_{ij} \geq r_j$$

[1] T. N. Srinivasan, *On a two-sector model of growth*, Cowles Foundation Discussion Paper, 1962.   [2] See Chapter 10.

and given regional delivery capacities

$$\sum_j x_{ij} \le k_i + n_i$$

such that total requirements exceed total capacities of the old installations denoted by k_i. If c_{ij} is the associated total cost, find the deliveries x_{ij} such that the expression,

$$\sum_i \sum_j c_{ij} x_{ij} \quad \text{is minimal.}$$

For a more efficient approach the capacity equation was taken in the form

$$\sum_j x_{ij} - n_i \le k_i.$$

Since n_i does not enter into the objective function, arbitrary values of n_i may be taken, subject only to the fact that we do not require excess capacity to be more than the amount

$$\sum_j r_j - \sum_i k_i.$$

We can, therefore, initially set forth,

$$n_i = \sum_j r_j - \sum_i k_i.$$

Since we have to minimize the objective function involving the x_{ij}'s, the requirement equation will ultimately determine the effective levels of the excess capacity that will be utilized regionally.

Assuming the requirement targets of the future for the region as given, and on the assumption that these requirements will exceed existing capacity, this excess over existing capacity may be called Δ, so that Δ is the excess of planned requirements over existing capacity, and, by previous assumption, production of this excess will not change any regional costs per unit. Assume that there are unused resources of the size Δ in every regional unit. This makes the capacity equations

$$\sum_j x_{ij} \le k_i + \Delta \quad \text{when} \quad \Delta = \sum_j r_j - \sum_i k_i.$$

On the assumption that unused capacity of magnitude Δ exists in every region all that is now needed is to determine an optimum programme, on the basis of the increased requirements as planned, and see which of the assumed excess capacities are really used in the new optimal flow and which are left unused. It is argued that if newly installed capacity is left unused somewhere, there was no point in increasing capacity, since the increased capacity in that region will not be needed in the optimal solution. If this excess is utilized in more than one region, it indicates that those regions benefit from an expansion of capacity in the optimal solution. That is, their expansion will be consistent with a reduction of total costs.

A demonstration was carried out with the requirements of 1957, while the capacity was made equal to that of 1954, plus the difference in capacity and requirement added over all.

Some interesting features of the relative cost components of the cement industry became obvious. If there was no change in the cost of production, then the lowest cost solution would be for each unit, with the exception of Uttar Pradesh, to produce its own requirements. That is, if the relative cost structure is unaltered, proximity to consumers under the present cost structure is rather more important than proximity to raw material in considering expansion. This is probably due to the fact that power and several other important cost components are cheaper near the centres of consumption. This makes the cost of production differential smaller than the transport cost differential.

A more ambitious work on a similar problem in many sectors and in many regions, still in its working stage, is described below.

In this investigation, a study has been made into the optimal regional exchange pattern for a number of commodities e.g. iron and steel, coal, engineering, etc., which are being produced and exchanged.

The balance relation for the output of the ith sector in region p may be written as

$$\sum_j \sum_q {}_{pq}x_{ij} + \sum_q {}_{pq}f_i = {}_pX_i.$$

This indicates that all inter-industrial deliveries and final demand deliveries to all other regions from any one region must equal that region's production.

The second balance equation relates to regional inputs and may be stated thus for inputs of a single sector and region:

$$\sum_p \sum_j {}_{pq}x_{ij} + \sum_p {}_{pq}f_i = {}_qR_i.$$

Technical coefficients of the Leontief type are introduced as below, and it is assumed that they are similar from region to region.

$$\sum_p {}_{pq}x_{ij} = a_{ij}. {}_qX_j.$$

The earlier balance requirement is now written as

$$\sum_j a_{ij}. {}_qX_j + \sum_p {}_{pq}f_i = {}_qR_i.$$

With these constraints, if ${}_{pq}C_{ij}$ is the cost of delivery from i to j in the regional group p to q, the objective is to minimize

$$\sum_p \sum_q \sum_i \sum_j {}_{pq}C_{ij}. {}_{pq}x_{ij}.$$

Assume that total final demand supplied by a region is assigned. Let us further assume that the total final requirements of a region are also assigned. This is to imply, that on an *a priori* basis, we have fixed the absorptions and deliveries of the final output from every sector for every region; then the model can be simplified as below.

Since regional final demands are assigned, this means that regional deliveries are determined by using these final demands with the input coefficients in the balance relation. The objective function is:

$$\sum_p \sum_q \sum_i \sum_j {}_{pq}C_{ij}. {}_{pq}x_{ij} = \text{minimum}$$

subject to
$$_qX_j = \sum_j A_{ij}(_pR_i - \sum_p {}_{pq}f_i),$$

where A_{ij} are the inverse elements of the matrix formed by the a_{ij}'s.

As final demands, etc. shift, the requirements will also shift and so will the optimum programme. The allocation may thus be linked up to the changing character of the regional final demand targets and total requirement targets.

The nature of the available data made it necessary to modify this rather straightforward framework.

Thus, in the balance relation, since the system is open in an inter-regional sense, we must consider the flows to and from the regions, as well as the local consumption, before we can obtain an identity where the production of the region may be balanced against all forms of delivery. Also, since the flows from any region to other regions cannot be easily allocated to different sectors without assuming some form of arbitrary levels of allocation, no possibility of transforming the flows into functions of output, by using the production function, exists. Hence, the only other balance relation that could be used is the type which relates regional inputs irrespective of origin to outputs.

In the present case, regional input-output tables are available. Therefore, any regional balance equation may be written for the ith sector, as

$$\sum_j {}_qx_{ij} - \sum_p \sum_j {}_{pq}x_{ij} - \sum_p {}_{pq}f_i + {}_qf_i + \sum_p {}_{qp}X_i = {}_qX_i$$

which means that inter-industrial absorption from all regions, plus final deliveries from all regions, plus export must equal home production plus import from all other regions.

Since any $_qx_{ij}$ absorbs $_qa_{ij}\,_qx_j$ units of the ith commodity, irrespective of the origin of the materials, we can replace the elements $_qx_{ij}$, which denote the total absorption in the jth sector of the region q of ith commodity, by $_qa_{ij}\,_qX_j$, the output of jth sector in q.

Then the balance relation can be rewritten, as

$$\sum_j {}_qa_{ij}.\,_qx_j + \sum_p {}_{qp}x_i - \sum_p \sum_j {}_{pq}x_{ij} - \sum_p {}_{pq}f_i + {}_qf_i = {}_qX_i,$$

where, as before, the symbols pq and qp indicate the direction of the flow from p to q and from q to p respectively.

The transportation limits are now considered in the following way. Let a 'Leontief' unit of material (in the accepted sense) of any type i be associated with a weight W_i, so that $W_i X_i$ denotes that weight of X_i units in the Leontief sense. Then the model requires that balance be kept between the transport availability from region p to region q, and the total material transported, as in the following equations:

$$\sum_p \sum_j W_{j\,.\,pq}x_j \leqslant T_{pq}.$$

We now come to the minimizing function. Since we have considered gross production, to avoid duplication in production costs, the minimization may be effected considering labour costs together with transportation costs. We thus minimize the following function:

$$\sum_p \sum_q \sum_i {}_{pq}x_i({}_{pq}\pi_i + {}_p\pi_i),$$

where ${}_p\pi_i$ denotes the labour cost of producing ith commodity, and ${}_{pq}\pi_i$ the transportation costs of the same from p to q.

The empirical implementation of the model is based on data relating to the Indian Union in 1954. A regional input-output table which has been prepared by Sri. R. Dhar[1] has been used as the basic table from which the present aggregation has been completed.

In the first experiment, the assumption was made that capacity limit on production does not exist in any sector or region. This implied that an optimal solution will have only to conform to the restrictions on the balance relations.

It was seen that the deviation between optimal and actual was not large with respect to production. But the actual inter-regional flows were quite different from the optimal. The latter, however, should not be immediately interpreted as a sign of the inefficiency of the trade pattern for reasons of capacity limits.

It was noted that some regions are producing more than the actual in the optimal. In the existing cost and transport situation such cases show the comparative advantages of producing more in the regions. In a later experiment, however, this assumption of unlimited capacity has been withdrawn and some capacity limits have been imposed to study a more realistic situation.

It was seen that the introduction of a number of constraints does improve the nature of the agreement between the actual and the optimal flow.

2.5

In the course of completing the above empirical work a variety of problems requiring solution were brought to light. Some of these problems and the methods of approaching them in empirical exercises have been reported by Ghosh[2] and are summarized here.

Complications of a dynamic nature, relating output to input and supply to requirements with different time labels, naturally arise in a model. The following problem should be considered.

During a five-year period a planning body anticipates a certain increase in demand for a commodity and decides to expand existing units, or to establish new units. The objective of the body is to increase capacity in such a way that the demands of the region are met.

Further, the objective is to choose the location of the units in such a way that the terminal cost of production of the given commodity is

[1] R. Dhar, An input-output table for W. Bengal and the Calcutta Metropolitan District: first and second interim reports (Calcutta Research Studies, Occasional Reports, I.P.A., New York).   [2] See Chapter 10.

minimal. (In the first formulation we assume some drastic over-simpli-fications. The production costs are as given in the initial period for the regions. So are the transportation costs. Installation costs are not con-sidered at all. It is initially assumed that there is no excess capacity.) A further objective is, that given the location objective as above, the phasing of the installations should be such as to minimize the total cost of both production and distribution over the five-year period.

Let x_{ij} be the unit of shipment from any region i to a region j in time t. Let c_{ij} be the production cum transportation cost which is treated as a constant.

The initial capacities are denoted by $_0C_i$ for the ith region, and the requirement of the jth region in *period t* by $_tR_j$.

Then the rule that the terminal demands must be met and regions selected optimally may be stated thus:

If $_TC_i$ are the terminal capacities:

$$\sum_j {_TR_j} = \sum_i {_TC_i}.$$

Let $_tC_i$ denote new capacities created in the 't'-th period in region i. Then $_TC_i = {_0C_i} + {_1C_i} + {_2C_i} + \ldots + {_KC_i}$, where $t = 1, 2, \ldots, K$.

Let $_Tx_{ij}$ be the terminal shipments from i to j. Then

$$\sum_j {_Tx_{ij}} \leqslant {_TC_i}, \quad \sum_i {_Tx_{ij}} \geqslant {_TR}$$

subject to the above minimize,

$$\sum_i \sum_j C_{ij} \cdot {_Tx_{ij}}.$$

Since $_tC_i$ are not known except that

$$\sum_t {_tC_i} = {_TC_i} \quad \text{and} \quad \sum_i {_TC_i} = \sum_i {_TR_i}$$

we have to devise such a method that we can find $_tC_i$ separately for each phase.

In an earlier section, the method for determining the location of new units is described. The next problem is to phase it over time, so as to minimize the total cost over the Five-Year Period as a whole.

Let $_tC_i$ denote the new capacities to be created in the ith region in time t. Then minimize

$$\sum_t \sum_i \sum_j C_{ij} \cdot {_tx_{ij}}$$

subject to,

$$(a) \quad \sum_j {_tx_{ij}} \leq {_0C_i} + \sum_{t=1}^{T} {_tC_i}; \quad (b) \quad \sum_i {_tx_{ij}} \geq {_tR_j}.$$

This will ensure that, during the plan period, the phasing will be done so as to reduce expenditure as much as possible up to the terminal period.

The problem of location over regions and phasing the same is then split into two problems. One is the problem of terminal location which ensures that an optimal location is decided for the future. Future, however, is envisaged as the period after the plan period. There is thus no assurance that whatever is undertaken during the following plan period will not disturb the optimality of future terminal locations. It is quite possible that if the plan period was extended more and more into the future, the optimality of the terminal plan would have been more complete.

We now consider a more complex case where more than one commodity enters into our problem and the equations relate to some intertemporal conditions of dependence as well.

Let us consider an economy with three sectors: coal, engineering, and iron and steel. The problem may be elaborated as follows.

Coal requires machines from engineering for capacity production; the coal supply to other units has a lag of one year from the time of production; engineering requires iron and steel, and there is a lag of one year before iron and steel passes into engineering goods. Engineering produces its own machine, a machine for coal, a machine for iron and steel. The gestation period for all types of machines is one year. Some machines-to-output ratios are given, and also some current input-to-output ratios. Iron and steel supplies raw inputs to engineering. Coal supplies raw inputs to engineering and iron and steel. Thus we have the following inter-dependence.

Coal supplies coal to (1) iron and steel; (2) engineering.

Iron and steel supplies iron goods to engineering.

Engineering supplies machines to (1) engineering; (2) iron and steel; (3) coal.

The balance equation may be described as follows:

$$X_C(t-1) = X_{CI}(t) + X_{CE}(t),$$
$$X_I - (t1) = X_{IE}(t),$$
$$X_E(t-1) = x_{EC}(t) + x_{EI}(t) + x_{EE}(t),$$

where the x_{CI} denotes coal delivered to iron and steel, and x_C denotes the output of coal, and so on.

The input-output relations are

$$x_{CI}(t) = a_{CI} X_I(t),$$
$$x_{CE}(t) = a_{CE} X_E(t),$$
$$x_{IE}(t) = a_{IE} X_E(t).$$

The capital-output relations are

$$X_E(t) \leqq \sigma_{EE} X_{EE}(t),$$
$$X_C(t) \leqq \sigma_{EC} X_{EC}(t),$$
$$X_I(t) \leqq \sigma_{EI} X_{EI}(t),$$

where σ_{EE}, σ_{CE} and σ_{IE} are the output-capital ratios, and capital is obsolete after one year.

Given the above system of constraints, let us have, as an objective function, the maximizing of engineering output from $t = t_0$ to t_5:

$$\text{maximize} \quad \sum_{t=0}^{5} X_E(t).$$

It is obvious that the problem has entered the dynamic field. There is interdependence of a dynamic type, and a necessary condition for the system is that the dynamic equilibrium conditions are to be met. The choice in this particular case is over the entire planning period; the optimization process will pick up such activity levels at different time periods as will lead to the total engineering output being a maximum over the whole period.

We now consider an extension of the previous transportation models to consider problems involving discreet variables. Suppose a unit that is installed can only be either x_1 or x_2 or x_3, where $x_1 < x_2 < x_3$ but that no intermediate value is possible.

The problem may be stated thus. A certain increase in demand over all regions has to be met. New installations can either be of a size of $x(1)$ unit or $x(2)$ unit or $x(3)$ unit. Thus, a cement factory may be designed for 20,000 tons or 30,000 tons or 40,000 tons but not for 32,500 tons.

Let x_{ij} be the flow as before, so that

$$\sum_i x_{ij} = R_j \quad \text{the increased requirement so that} \quad \sum_j R_j > \sum_i \sum_j x_{ij}.$$

Let λ_i be a given integral number in ith region consisting of old capacity and new capacity so that

$$\sum_i \lambda_i \geqslant \sum_j R_j.$$

Let s_i be the slack variable showing idle capacity installed in a region, and s'_i be a disposal activity for uninstalled capacity. We consider,

$$\Sigma x_{ij} + s_i + s'_i = \lambda$$

as the flow equation giving the balance relation. It is to be noted that we attach additional integral capacities to all regions and λ is used in a role similar to that of Δ in §2.3 to find potential location.

Let a_k be a set of integral numbers giving possible capacities of the plants.

Let $s'_i = \sum_k a_k \delta_k$, where δ_k is either 0 or 1 and $\sum_k \delta_k = 1$, further let $\sum_i x_{ij} = R_j$. Minimize, $\Sigma c_{ij} x_{ij}$ as the integer expression for all extra requirement in all regions.

By our definition s'_i is integral.

$\Sigma x_{ij} + s_i$ is bound to be integral. It will take integral values depending on the value of s'_i and therefore of δ_k. This integer programming formulation is now amenable to the cutting plane approach as developed by Gomory and others.

It is evident that building practically useful planning models and attempting to employ present day techniques of econometric analysis has been stimulated by planning efforts in India. It is to be hoped that with the accumulation of better data and more experience, the art of model building will be closely integrated to our planning efforts. This will be the only way by which present theories can be enriched and put to more practical use.

APPENDIX

Ghosh's condensed Model (for the projection of government expenditure and income)

1. $E^{c \cdot dev} = a_M^{c \cdot dev} M + a_{Ig}^{c \cdot dev} Ig + a_t^{c \cdot dev} t + \lambda^{c \cdot dev}.$
2. $E^{c\Sigma} = a_E^{c\Sigma} E^{c \cdot dev} + a_t^{c\Sigma} t + \lambda^{c\Sigma}.$
3. $E^{r\Sigma} = a_E^{r\Sigma} E^{c\Sigma} + a_t^{r\Sigma} t + \lambda^{r\Sigma}.$
4. $E^d = a_t^d t + \lambda^d.$
5. $E = E^{c\Sigma} + E^{r\Sigma} + E^d.$
6. $Y = a_E^Y E + a_t^Y t + \lambda^Y.$
7. $P = a_E^P E + a_Y^P Y + a_t^P t + \lambda^P.$

Variables explained:

$E^{c \cdot dev}$ = expenditure on capital account of developmental type;

$E^{c\Sigma}$ = total capital disbursement excluding defence;

$E^{r\Sigma}$ = total revenue disbursement excluding defence;

E^d = total defence expenditure on revenue and capital;

Y = earned income of the government, i.e. excluding foreign aid and deficit spending;

M = total imports;

Ig = planned expenditure by the government as proposed in the Five-Year Plans;

t = time;

P = general price level.

a's and λ's (with subscripts and superscripts) are parameters.

The variables may be classified as:

(1) projection variables: E, Y;

(2) associated endogeneous variables: $E^{c\Sigma}$, $E^{r\Sigma}$, E^d, $E^{c \cdot dev}$;

(3) associated exogenous variables: M, Ig, t.

Ghosh's Model (for population growth in the metropolis of Calcutta)

1. $P(t) = {}_nP(t) + {}_mP(t).$
2. ${}_nP(t) = {}_nP(t-1) + b_r\{{}_nP(t-1) + {}_mP(t-1)\} - d_{r}\,{}_nP(t-1).$
3. ${}_mP(t) = a + b\,E_t + c_{ag}I(t).$

4. $\quad E_t = \dfrac{1}{\lambda(t)}\, X(t).$

5. $\quad X(t) = X_1(t) + X_2(t).$

6. $\quad X_1(t) = a_{11}\, X_1(t) + a_{12}\, X_2(t) + F_{1h} + F_{1g} + E_{ext} - I_{ext} + K.$

7. $\quad X_2(t) = a_{21}\, X_1(t) + a_{22}\, X_2(t) + F_{2\Sigma}.$

8. $\quad F_{1h} = b_{11}\, P(t) + b_{12}\, X(t) + b_{10}.$

9. $\quad F_{1g} = b'_{11}\, P(t) + b'_{12}\, X(t) + b'_{10}.$

10. $\quad F_{2\Sigma} = b''_{21}\, P(t) + b''_{22}\, X(t) + b''_{20}.$

Symbols explained:

$\quad P(t) =$ total population at time t;

$\quad {}_nP(t) =$ natural population at time t;

$\quad {}_mP(t) =$ migrant population at time t;

$\quad b_r =$ birth rate in the metropolis;

$\quad d_r =$ death rate in the metropolis;

$\quad {}_{ag}I(t) =$ index of land to man ratio at time t of the regions from which migrants come;

$\quad E_t =$ total employment at time t;

$\quad t =$ average productivity of labour at time t;

$\quad X(t) =$ total output at time t;

$\quad X_1(t) =$ output of sector 1 at time t;

$\quad X_2(t) =$ output of sector 2 at time t;

$\quad a_{ij} =$ input coefficient of Leontief type;

$\quad F_{1h} =$ final demand of household or private account in sector 1;

$\quad F_{1g} =$ final demand of government account in sector 1;

$\quad F_{2\Sigma} =$ final demand of government account and household account in sector 2;

$\quad K = E_{int} - I_{int}$;

$\quad E_{int} =$ flow to other regions in India for sector 1;

$\quad I_{int} =$ imports into the metropolis of sector 1 goods from other regions of India;

$\quad E_{ext} =$ flow to other regions outside India for sector 1;

$\quad I_{ext} =$ import from other regions outside India for sector 1;

$\quad E_{ext},\, I_{ext}$ and K are exogenous variables and $b_r,\, d_r,\, a,\, b,\, c,\, a_{ij},\, b,\, b'$ and b'' are parameters.

Sector 1 means the primary and secondary sector and sector 2 means the tertiary sector.

Pant and Little's Model

1. $I = \Sigma I_t = \Sigma S_t + F.$
2. $\Delta Y = \beta I.$
3. $S_t = S_0 + t a.$
4. $D^A(t) = P_t \left(\dfrac{Y}{P}\right)_t^{\eta}.$
5. $\Delta Y_A = \beta_a I_A.$
6. $T_t = T_t' + T_t''.$
7. $T_t' = C_t^{r_1} Y_{NA}^{(t)r_2} Y_A^{(t)r_3}.$

8. $\Sigma E_t = \Sigma E_{c,t} + s_i I.$
9. $\Delta D = \Sigma E_t - (\Sigma T_t + \Sigma R_t).$
10. $\Delta Y_A + \Delta Y_{NA} = \Delta Y.$
11. $I = I_A + I_{NA}.$
12. $\Delta C_t + \Delta S_t = \Delta Y_t.$
13. $\Delta D_A = \Delta Y_a.$

Variables Explained:

I = total investment;

S_t = savings in period 't';

F = the amount of 'net' foreign aid;

ΔY = the increase of income over the five-year period;

D_A = demand for agricultural output;

ΔY_A = increase in agricultural production;

T_t = total amount of tax revenue in year 't';

T_t' = part of tax revenue dependent on income or some component of income;

ΔY_{NA} = non-agricultural production;

C_t = consumption in period 't';

E_t = total government expenditure over the period;

D = increase in government debt, tax rates remaining unchanged;

I_A = investment in agriculture;

I_{NA} = investment in non-agriculture;

α = the annual increment in savings;

P_t = population in year 't';

$E_{c,t}$ = government current expenditure in period 't';

R_t = operation surplus from public enterprises in period 't';

T_t'' = the part of tax revenue which is roughly autonomous with respect to income;

$P_t, E_{c,t}, R_t$ and T_t'' are exogenous variables.

Parameters explained:

β = the global output-capital ratio;

β_a = the output-capital ratio in agriculture;

s_i = the proportion of investment expenditure undertaken by the government;

r_1, r_2, r_3 = the proportions in which existing tax revenue is earned from current consumption, current agricultural income and non-agricultural incomes;

η = the income elasticity of demand for agricultural production.

Chakravarty and Lefeber's Optimizing Planning Model

Maximize $u = \sum_{1}^{T} w(t)\, c(t)$ subject to:

1. $_c C(t) \leqq F(t); \quad c = |c_i| \quad \Sigma c_i = 1;$

2. $C(t+1) \geqq C(t)\,[(1+n)];$

3. $C(I) \geqq \overline{C(I)};$

4. $AX(t) + F(t) + N(t) + H(t) + G(t) + E(t) - M(t) - X(t) \leqq 0;$
   $A = |a_{ij}|;$

5. $bX(t) - K(t) \leqq 0; \quad b = |b_i|;$

6. $K(t) - K(t-1) - Z(t) + \overline{R}(t-1) \leqq 0;$

7. $q^k Z(t) = I^l(t-k); \quad \sum_{k} q^k = 1; \quad k = 1, 2, 3;$

8. $\sum_{k} p^k_{ij} I^{l+k}_j(t) - N_{ij}(t) = 0; \quad \sum_{j} N_{ij}(t) = N_i(t);$

9. $s[X(t+1) - X(t)] = H(t); \quad = s|S_{ij}|;$

10. $G(t) = \overline{G(t)};$

11. $E(t) = \overline{E(t)};$

12. $\sum_{i} M_i(t) \leqq FA(t) + \sum_{i} E_i(t);$

13. $\Sigma_i M_i(t) = \Sigma_i M^1_i(t) + \Sigma_i M^2_i(t);$

14. $M^1_i(t) = m^1_i X_i(t);$

15. $M^2_i(t) \leqq m^2_i [FA(t) + \sum_{i} E_i(t) - \sum_{i} M^1_i(t)];$

16. $K(I) = \overline{K(I)}; \quad I^3(0) = \overline{I^3(0)}; \quad I^2(-1) = \overline{I^2(-1)}; \quad I^2(0) = \overline{I^2(0)};$

17. $X(T+\theta) = AX(T+\theta) + (1+r)^\theta F(T) + (b^1 + d^1 + s)$
    $\times [X(T+\theta+1) - X(T+\theta)] + (b^2 + d^2)$
    $\times [X(T+\theta+2) - X(T+\theta+1)] + (b^3 + d^3)$
    $\times [X(T+\theta+3) - X(T+\theta+2)] + (1+g)^\theta \overline{G(T)}$
    $+ (1+c)^\theta \overline{E(T)} - (1+f)^\theta M(T),$

where
$$b^k + |b_{ij}^k| \quad (\theta = 1, 2, 3);$$
$$d^k = |d_{ij}^k| \quad (k = 1, 2, 3).$$

18. $\begin{aligned} X(T+\theta) = &[I - A - (b^1 + d^1 + s)\,r - (b^2 - d^2)\,(1+r)\,r \\ &- (b^3 + d^3)\,(1+r)^2 r]^{-1} F(T)\,(1+r)^\theta \\ &+ [I - A - (b^1 + d^1 + s)\,g - (b^2 + d^2)\,(1+g)\,g \\ &- (b^3 + d^3)\,(1+g)^2 g]^{-1} \overline{G(T)}\,(1+g)^\theta \\ &+ [I - A - (b^1 + d^1 + s)\,e - (b^2 + d^2)\,(1+e)\,e \\ &- (b^3 + d^3)\,(1+e)^2 e]^{-1} \overline{E(T)}\,(1+e)^\theta \\ &- [I - A - (b^1 + d^1 + s)\,f - (b^2 + d^2)\,(1+f)\,f \\ &- (b^3 + d^3)\,(1+f)^2 f]^{-1} \overline{M(T)}\,(1+f)^\theta \quad (\theta = 1, 2, 3). \end{aligned}$

19. $b_{ij}^k = p_{ij}^k\, b_j\, q_j^k \quad (k = 1, 2, 3).$

Symbols explained:

$W(t)$ = the relative weight consumption in period t;

$F(t)$ = the column vector of sectoral outputs designated for consumption;

c = a diagonal matrix whose elements denote the proportionate composition of $C(t)$;

$(1+n)$ = growth factor where n is either the population growth rate or some other politically determined parameter;

$C(I)$ = a lower bound on consumption to be attained in the first period;

A = the Leontief matrix of input coefficients;

$X(t)$ = the column vector of the domestic outputs corresponding to all sectors;

$F(t)$, $N(t)$, $H(t)$, $G(t)$ and $E(t)$ are column vectors representing consumption, capital, inventory formation, government consumption and exports respectively. The last two of these are exogenously stipulated;

$M(t)$ = vectors of supplies from imported sources;

$K(t)$ = composite capital which is fixed in each sector but changes from period to period according to depreciation and gross investment;

b = diagonal matrix composed of capital-output ratios;

$\overline{R(t)}$ = vector of depreciation rates;

$Z(t)$ = vector of new capacities available for use in period t;

q^k = the proportion of total capacity increase that must be completed k periods in advance;

$I^l(t-k)$ = the part of $Z(t)$ that is completed in period $(t-k)$;

p_{ij}^k = fixed production coefficient;

I_j^{t+k} = that part of capacity in the jth sector that is to be completed in the $(t+k)$th period;

s = matrix of coefficient for inventory change;

$M^1(t)$ = non-competitive imports;

$M^2(t)$ = competitive imports;

m_j^1 = constant of proportion;

m_i^2 = constant of proportion;

$K(I)$ = active productive capacity at the beginning of the plan;

$I^2(o), I^3(o)$ = incomplete projects from the pre-plan period that will be available for completion during the second and third year of planning;

r, g, e and f are the exogenously stipulated growth rates of C, G, E and M respectively;

T = planning horizon.

CHAPTER 3

INPUT-OUTPUT APPROACH IN AN ALLOCATION SYSTEM

3.1

An input-output transaction matrix may be conceived in terms of an equilibrium position of two sets of interacting forces. The broadest way in which we can define them is to denote one set of forces as technical factors expressed through production functions and the other set as market factors expressed through allocation functions. Though technical factors influence production, it is widely recognized that there are various alternative technical combinations in any economy and under different market situations different combinations are actually taken up. An input-output matrix then represents an equilibrium solution for two sets of equations somewhat analogous to demand and supply functions.

Under a competitive market where resources are not scarce allocation functions will play a minor role in the set up, and special conditions may be formulated under which production coefficients will determine the equilibrium.

But under a monopolistic market scarce resources, allocation functions will determine which, among a large group of alternative processes and combinations, will be taken up by any particular sector. That is production functions are forced to play a minor role.

In this sense we can, associate two sets of coefficients with an input-output matrix. One of these sets has been familiarized by Leontief as production coefficients, or, technical coefficients. It expresses the relationship

$$x_{ij} = \alpha_{ij} X_j,$$

where x_{ij} is the output of the ith sector sold to the jth sector and X_j is the output of the jth sector.

We can similarly assume the existence, under different circumstances, of the relation

$$x_{ij} = A_{ij} X_i,$$

where x_{ij} is as before, the output of the ith industry going to the jth sector and X_i is the output of the ith sector.

As supply or demand conditions predominate either of the relations may approximate to reality or neither of these simplified situations may actually approximate to reality at all.

Leontief has formulated an idealized situation where the set α_{ij} is assumed fixed and the set A_{ij} is allowed to change freely with any change in the final demand. Such conditions may be assumed to hold approximately, so long as there is no scarce factor, and so long as suppliers are able to offer more of any commodity at the existing price.

Leontief's formulation thus takes up a situation for consideration where there is a large unused capacity in most sectors even in the short period such that any change in the final demands does not set up any disturbance in relative prices and certainly does not bring in any question of limited supply. Ignoring other criticisms of this simplified approach for the moment it may be said that even in the short period where nearly all industries have a large surplus of plant and labour at their disposal, the supply curve is bound to be very elastic and the overall situation would be dominated very much by buyers' requirements. This position is illustrated easily by an advanced capitalist economy in depression.

It is possible to build up a similar model with allocation functions in an economy where different sectors are under monopoly control and all except one resource is scarce. We can consider a planned economy under centralized control with scarce material resources and productive capacity with an ample supply of available labour. The central authority has allocation schedules for each sector defining national or social welfare and it has been seeking that allocation which maximizes welfare, subject to possible production combinations. That is, any feasible combination of inputs which gives a higher welfare value may be preferred to one which may be more efficient as a production combination but is lower on the welfare scale. An illustration may be given of a controversy in the Indian second Five-Year Plan which is centred around the objective of reviving cottage industries which are productively less efficient but which give employment rather than keeping people on the dole. The objective of the planning authority is not a search for the optimum technical combination of production but for that feasible combination which makes the best use of resources made available to it on the basis of a welfare function.

It is obvious that in cases of this type the production combinations are forced on the industries, not by technical considerations, but by scarcity and consequent rationing. In any alternative situation, where scarcity has eased or quotas have been changed, the industries will seek combinations which are completely different. Input ratios here, therefore, are conditioned by the assigned quota and any change of the assigned quota will alter such ratios. If such a situation is postulated it is evident that the stability of production coefficients cannot, by any means, be assured for a change in the final demand of the community.

In this paper we shall investigate the use of input-output methods in economies of this type. This means that the discussion is confined to a consideration of economies with a high rate of investment, with an inadequacy of supply of productive plants and materials and with a rationing system in allocation.

The purpose of the present paper is not to search for optimum allocation combinations but to accept that the rationing authorities have, in fact, arrived at some optimum allocation factors on the basis of a national welfare function. An input-output table gives such a set of allocation coefficients defined by the second set of functions. For simplicity we assume further that any allocation has, corresponding to it, at least one feasible combination of products.

In the present paper it is our contention that the general background provided by these economies makes the supply factors of greater pre-dominance and one may consider the second set of coefficients more stable in these economies than the first set defined by Leontief. The basic difference between such economies and that illustrated earlier is that there is an almost unlimited demand for goods stimulated by development plans which is undiminished by higher prices. The only way such a situation can be handled is by rationing, 'that is, if price increases prove ineffectual in reducing the expenditure function suffi-ciently, suppliers [here the Government] may decide that nevertheless they will produce only the output they desire and allocate it among consumers on some arbitrary rationing basis (first come first served, fixed percentage of purchases in previous years, etc.). In this case it is the spenders who are forced into involuntary actions, they must buy less than they desire.'[1]

In economies of rationing, since every sector registers a high demand for the scarce factors, the general tendency of the rationing authorities is not to change the relative shares of each sector in the short run, since such relative shares are determined by a delicate balancing of different sectors' claims and counter-claims. This tendency, considered from the problem of projection, makes the allocation coefficient more stable in the short run than production coefficients.

Though such situations are a commonplace feature in controlled economies only under certain conditions, we may imagine a volunatry allocation system being taken up even by free enterprise in scarcity. This might happen when the producer of the scarce article feels that he should keep his market in his grip rather than sell only to the highest bidder. But of course such a situation over the whole economy in a free enterprise is not quite feasible, and sooner or later authority has to step in and dictate the respective quotas on the basis of national needs rather than leave it as a free for all. This happens during wars. Under such basic change in the background it may be of interest to use the second set of coefficients and develop an allocation model as an extension of the original Leontief system.

With this adaptation the Leontief model and its inverse may be used to provide answers to questions which are very similar, though not identical, to those of the conventional input-output model.

---

[1] Don Patinkin: 'Involuntary unemployment and the Keynesian supply function.' *E.J.*, LIX, 1949, p. 375.

3.2

Our basic model is very similar to the conventional input-output model, that is, we consider the economy as consisting of sectors defined by general economic considerations. We then replace the Leontief production function by a different postulate.

A sector's receipts from every other sector are given linear functions of its own disbursements.

Let E_i be the total external outlay of sector i and e_{ij} the outlay of sector i in sector j. Then we have the identities

$$\sum_j e_{ij} = E_i \quad (i \neq j).$$

Consider functions of the form

$$e_{ij} = A_{ij} E_j.$$

This implies that the ith sector's outlay in the jth sector is a function of the total outlay of the jth sector. That is, not production coefficients α_{ij} but supply coefficients A_{ij} are constant. Any increase of sector j will be allocated in a fixed ratio to all the receipts from other sectors. Then we get a system of homogeneous linear equations

$$\sum_j A_{ij} E_j = E_i \quad (i,j = 1, 2, \ldots, n).$$

This set of equations leads to the closed system considered by Leontief. As, for purposes of projection, we are concerned only with the open case we modify the above system slightly by considering E_n as autonomous such that now we get a system in $n-1$ unknowns

$$\sum_j A_{ij} E_j = E_i - e_{in} \quad (i,j = 1, 2, \ldots, n-1),$$

where e_{in} is the vector of autonomous outlay elements included in every equation. The open case thus reduces to

$$(I - A) E = e,$$

where A is the matrix of coefficient, I a unit matrix and e a column vector of assigned autonomous cost elements in each sector.

The solution vector is given by

$$E = (I - A)^{-1} e.$$

In this readapted system the column vector e is best interpreted as the net national income generated in the sectors. E is the vector of total outlay by the different sectors.

For any given vector of national income to be generated we shall get a unique vector of outlays likely to the sectors. We have arrived through this approach not at an estimate of output (value) but at an estimate of likely costs.

The equation system in the open Leontief model is

$$X_i - \sum_j \alpha_{ij} X_j = x_{in} \begin{cases} (i,j = 1, 2, \ldots, n-1), \\ (i \neq j). \end{cases}$$

Then we have the solutions

$$X_i = \sum_j \alpha_{ij}^* x_{jn},$$

where α_{ij}^* are the elements of the inverse of the coefficient matrix. The income or equivalent employment is obtained by applying the labour input coefficients to the expression for total output in the solution set. Thus employment

$$x_{ni} = \alpha_{ni} X_i = \alpha_{ni} \sum_j \alpha_{ij}^* x_{jn}.$$

In an exactly similar way, the net output, is obtained in the present case as

$$e_{ni} = A_{ni} E_i = A_{ni} \sum_j A_{ij}^* e_{jn},$$

where e_{jn} are the assigned income to be generated and A_{ij}^* are the inverse of the coefficient matrix.

We do not consider the production possibilities in the system and the employment or income generation following from a particular bill of final demand but the income generating or employment possibilities of the system and the resultant net output from the system.

The simplest way of interpreting the use of these cost estimates is to assume that normally every sector will have to balance its outlay and its receipts. We then equate the costs to the value of the output that the sector must produce in order to generate a national income assigned to it. This approach may be used in the same way as an input-output approach is used to locate bottle necks, and for testing the consistency of different bill of goods with different employment programmes.

Let the open allocation model in the base period be

$$E_i - \sum_j A_{ij} E_j - e_{in} = 0 \quad \begin{cases} (i,j = 1, 2, \ldots, n-1), \\ (i \neq j), \end{cases}$$

then we may write the solution set as

$$E_i = \sum_j A_{ij}^* e_{jn}.$$

Let the planning authorities decide that the income in the planned period in the ith sector will be related to the income in the ith sector in the base period by the ratio

$$\frac{e_{in}^*}{e_{in}} = \lambda_i,$$

where e_{in}^* refers to the planned period and e_{in} to the base period. Then the costs in the planned period

$$E_i^* = \sum_j A_{ij}^* e_{jn}^*$$

$$= \sum_j \lambda_j A_{ij}^* e_{jn}.$$

Let the outputs of sector i be denoted by Q_i and Q_i^* in the two periods such that $Q_i^* = K_i Q_i$ and let P_i and P_i^* be the respective prices under equilibrium.

Then
$$E_i = P_i Q_i, \quad E_i^* = P_i^* Q_i^* = P_i^* K_i Q_i,$$

$$\frac{P_i}{P_i^*} = \frac{K_i E_i}{E_i^*} = \frac{\sum\limits_{j} K_i A_{ij}^* e_{jn}}{\sum\limits_{j} \lambda_j A_{ij}^* e_{jn}}.$$

The planning authority has the values of λ_j as data in the form of income ratios between the two periods in different sectors. We may assume that it has certain tentative estimates of the quantity ratios K_i of the two periods. Then the new price ratio P_i/P_i^* is determinate. That is, assuming that the allocation and the suggested income generating plans will lead to specific changes in output the equilibrium price of the planned period is obtained as a solution. Alternatively, assuming certain price ratios between the current and previous period, we can estimate what the equilibrium quantities in different sectors should be. We can thus use this model for the purpose of measuring the inflationary effect on prices which may have to be faced, due to a particular income generating policy.

Assuming that the ratio of prices (quantities) in the planning period should remain as in the base period we get the quantities (prices) that must be obtained in order that the required employment programme is maintained and no sector runs at a loss. Obviously, any sector that reveals a quantity bottle-neck here will be forced to raise prices in order to run without a loss. Thus quantity bottle-necks in this system do not lead to a collapse of the whole system (which would take place with rigid production coefficients) but rather to price changes. Employment, final demand and prices are all brought into the picture provided that the main background assumptions are short run.

The change in the price indices will indicate the extent to which certain sectors are being asked to generate more income without relevant increase in the product. Thus supposing any particular sector is asked to have a higher profit or a higher employment but fails to increase its output in a corresponding way its receipts will exceed costs. Since it has been advised to cover costs it will be forced to raise prices. Thus the relative prices will show the extent to which the income generation programme is working in harmony with real output.

3.3

Goodwin[1] and others have shown that the Keynesian system may be treated as an aggregation of an input-output model. The aggregation in this case cancels all inter-firm transactions leaving only national income. Assuming that aggregated national consumption is related to national income in a non-homogeneous linear form we get the familiar Keynesian equation
$$(I-a) Y = I$$
relating income to investment.

[1] R. M. Goodwin: 'The multiplier as matrix.' *E.J.* LIX, 1949, pp. 537-55.

Aggregating on similar lines the present model is also reduced to the traditional Keynesian form. It only interprets the 'psychological propensity to consume' of a freely spending community as the 'allocation decision' of a non-economic authority. Suppose in a community under overall rationing 'a' is the marginal propensity to consume as desired by the community and 'α' is the marginal rate of consumption spending as determined by the authority. Then for a specific increment of investment ΔI the desired increment of income of the community will be $(1/1 - a)\,\Delta I$, while the actual rise of income of the community, as permitted by the authority, will be $(1/1 - \alpha)\,\Delta I$. If 'a' is greater than 'α' this will mean a larger desired income compared to the permitted income. $a\Delta y - \alpha.\Delta y$ may be considered as the involuntary saving of the community. Thus the allocation coefficient is a realistic concept relevant to income generation under an overall rationing system.

In an economy where demand is outstripping supply and some form of rationing and price control is operating the purchasers are forced to an involuntary saving, as far as spending money on a group of commodities is concerned. We define involuntary saving as the saving due to a situation where more demand is forthcoming in the market at a price higher than the present ruling price. Where such involuntary saving exists the basic assumption of a freely moving consumption curve is absent and therefore one can have no idea of the shape of such a curve from a study of the earnings, savings and consumption of the community. The consumption to output relation of the community in this case is represented by $\Delta o_c/(\Delta o_c + \Delta o_i)$ (where o_c and o_i are outputs of consumer goods and investment goods) which equals $\Delta c/\Delta y$, where Δc is the actual increment of consumption and Δy is the increment of income of the community but is not equal to $\Delta c'/\Delta y$, where $\Delta c'$ is the desired increment of consumption corresponding to that increased income. So long as $\Delta c = \Delta c'$ the stability of $\Delta c/\Delta y$ may be assumed as a community behaviour but otherwise these considerations will not make $\Delta c/\Delta y$ stable. So the division of income into spending and saving is determined not by the income earner but by the producer or the factors controlling the producer's decision.[1] Unlike the consumption function there is no simple way of determining the shape of the function relating the desired production of consumer goods to total output. In most economies of scarcity with large-scale controls the fundamental allocation between consumption and production is determined by a body of socio-economic forces. In the short period we can only accept the constants relating the two as institutional as a given datum and work with it—but to deny its existence in such situations and ignore constraints to economic behaviour can only lead us to wrong forecasts. The reaction mechanism itself thus ceases to be based on consumer's behaviour and becomes institutional.

[1] G. C. Mandal: 'An Aspect of Inflation in India, 1939–47.' *Bulletin of the International Statistical Institute*, vol. xxxii, part III.

CHAPTER 4

A NOTE ON LEONTIEF MODELS WITH NON-HOMOGENEOUS PRODUCTION FUNCTIONS

It is generally agreed that so far as economic theory is concerned the Leontief model is an oversimplified presentation of reality based on assumptions which are not acceptable in any rigorous sense. Its main claim to usefulness still may lie in its practical use for approximate predictions when a simplified model may be good enough for such purposes. For such a purely empirical success it is essential that the input coefficients should at least be a first approximation of the actual set.

Very little work, so far, has been done to test the production functions of the Leontief model. A paper by Cameron[1] shows that in the Australian economy over a representative sample tested, production functions seemed 'to be of a fairly simple form'. Cameron concludes 'The results of the investigation, however, show promise. It may well yet be that some modified variant of the Leontief system might provide a statisfactory model of short term change'.

The purpose of the present paper is to discuss such a slightly modified variant of the Leontief model which seems, on a number of grounds, to be more realistic and flexible than the Leontief model as originally conceived.

One highly controversial aspect of the Leontief production function is the validity of input coefficients derived from a single set of observations. This assumes that not marginal inputs but total inputs are proportional to outputs. Such an approach makes the Leontief coefficient matrix far more unstable, even for small actual changes. This aspect, however, can be remedied by considering the Leontief matrix not at a single point of time but as the net change occurring over an interval.

The original Leontief model consists of a set of accounting identities of the type

$$\sum_j X_{ij} = X_i \quad (i \neq j), \ (i,j = 1, 2, \ldots, n)$$

and a set of production functions of the form

$$X_{ij} = A_{ij} X_j.$$

We consider instead the set of identities

$$\sum_j (X_{ij}^1 - X_{ij}^0) = X_i^1 - X_i^0$$

[1] B. Cameron, *The Production Function in Leontief Models*, vol. xx, 1953, Review of Economic Studies, p. 63.

and the production functions

$$X_{ij}^1 - X_{ij}^0 = A_{ij}(X_i^1 - X_i^0),$$

where the superscript o and 1 indicate an initial and a subsequent accounting period. Instead, therefore, of the original closed Leontief system of

$$\Sigma A_{ij} X_j = X_i \quad (i, j = 1 \ldots n)$$

we get the system

$$\sum_j A_{ij}(X_j^1 - X_j^0) = X_i^1 - X_i^0.$$

Instead, thus, of using the present input proportions as the unique proportions for the future we assert that the relations existing between the input-changes and output-changes are the relations that will also remain in the near future.

This should be a significant improvement from the predictive point of view as the actual change taking place over a period is considered as the basis for the change likely to take place in the future rather than associating an actual ratio between input-output at a single point to the change in input-output that might come.

This departure implies that we accept production functions of the type

$$X_{ij} = C_{ij} + A_{ij} X_j$$

instead of

$$X_{ij} = A_{ij} X_j.$$

This involves a constant element C_{ij} which is independent of change in output along with a proportionality factor A_{ij} relating input to output. The introduction of an additional constant in the production function requires at least a pair of observations, instead of a single observation, for evaluation of the constants.

Taking, therefore, *two consecutive* input-output matrices of transactions we solve for both A_{ij} and C_{ij} and then associate the constants ΣC_{ij} with the bill of goods column in the open Leontief model.

Obviously where the constants are small, or non-existent, the difference matrix will be equal to the Leontief matrix.

We can now consider the statistical problems that are raised by considering a pair of observations rather than a single observation.

Statistically, Leontief production functions are based on one observed point in the input-output space and one arbitrary assumption, i.e. all production functions are linear through origin. It is obvious that while linearity may be generally accepted as a first approximation, the assumption of linearity through origin involves a complete knowledge of the slope of such approximate lines relating input to output. Actually it is quite conceivable that the production functions are non-linear, and if linear they will rarely oblige further by conforming to a simple proportionality. Given, therefore, a production function whose shape is not known and required to make a first approximation for a short range, a line through two observed points seems to be a more satisfactory approach than using a single point and the origin.

We can now consider the relative efficiency of a single point and a two-point approach to the question.[1]

Let the true production function be of the form

$$y_r = \alpha + \beta X_r + \epsilon_r$$

with
$$E(y_r) = \alpha + \beta E(X_r) \tag{1}$$

ϵ_r having 'o' mean and variance σ^2, where x_r is any random point in the output ordinate.

Let $A_{ij} + B_{ij} X_j$ be any line $(i < j)$ satisfying two observations on the input-output space such that

$$\left. \begin{array}{l} A_{ij} + B_{ij} X_j = \alpha + \beta X_i + \epsilon_i, \\ A_{ij} + B_{ij} X_j = \alpha + \beta X_j + \epsilon_j. \end{array} \right\} \tag{2}$$

Then it is obvious that,

$$B_{ij} = \beta + \frac{\epsilon_i - \epsilon_j}{X_i - X_j},$$

$$A_{ij} = \alpha + \frac{X_i \epsilon_j - X_j \epsilon_i}{X_i - X_j}$$

$$= \alpha + w\epsilon_j + (1 - w)\,\epsilon_i \quad \left(w = \frac{X_i}{X_i - X_j} \right).$$

It is easily seen that

$$E(B_{ij}) = \beta \quad \text{and} \quad E(A_{ij}) = \alpha,$$

also
$$E(B_{ij} - \beta)^2 = \frac{1}{(X_i - X_j)^2}\,2\sigma^2,$$

$$E(A_{ij} - \alpha)^2 = w^2 \sigma^2 + (1 - w)^2 \sigma^2$$

$$= \sigma^2 (2w^2 - 2w + 1).$$

Prediction of any point y_r is given by

$$y_r = A_{ij} + B_{ij} X_r$$

$$= \alpha + \beta X_r + \frac{X_i \epsilon_j - X_j \epsilon_i}{X_i - X_j} + \left(\frac{\epsilon_i - \epsilon_j}{X_i - X_j} \right) X_r$$

$$= \alpha + \beta X_r + \frac{(X_r - X_i)\,(\epsilon_i - \epsilon_j)}{X_i - X_j} + \epsilon_i,$$

$$E(y_r - \alpha - \beta X_r)^2 = \sigma_r \times \left[2\left\{ \frac{X_r - X_i}{X_i - X_j} \right\}^2 + 1 \right]$$

$$= 3\sigma^2 \quad [\text{for, } (X_r - X_i) = X_i - X_j].$$

The corresponding Leontief function with a single observation i may be written as
$$\beta_i X_i = \alpha + \beta X_i + \epsilon_i,$$

---

[1] I wish to thank Mr J. A. C. Brown of the Department of Applied Economics at Cambridge for some helpful suggestions on this point.

where prediction of y_r is given by

$$y_r = \beta_i X_r.$$

Since

$$\beta_i X_i = \alpha + \beta X_i + \epsilon_i,$$

$$E(\beta_i) = \frac{\alpha}{X_i} + \beta, \quad E(\beta_i - \beta)^2 = E\left(\frac{\alpha - \epsilon_i}{X_i}\right)^2 = \frac{1}{X_i^2}(\alpha^2 + \sigma^2).$$

Prediction of y_r by the Leontief function is

$$y_r = \beta_i X_r$$

$$= \left(\frac{\alpha}{X_i} + \beta + \frac{\epsilon_i}{X_i}\right) X_r,$$

$$E(y_r) = \alpha E\left(\frac{X_r}{X_i}\right) + \beta E(X_r).$$

Thus the bias in the prediction is

$$= \alpha \left\{ E\left(\frac{X_r}{X_i}\right) - 1 \right\}$$

and variance of the prediction about biased expectation,

$$= \sigma^2 \left(\frac{X_r}{X_i}\right)^2.$$

Taking an illustrative example we can explain the signficance of the comparative variances.

Suppose we are taking equi-distant intervals in output, i.e.

$$X_i - X_j = X_r - X_i$$

then variance in the non-homogenous case is

$$V(\beta) = 3\sigma^2.$$

If, therefore the point (X_r), for which the prediction is being made, has a ratio of $\sqrt{3}$ (roughly 1·7) to the earlier point x_i, i.e. if

$$\frac{X_r}{X_i} = \sqrt{3}$$

then the variances in the two cases become equal.

It seems, therefore, that if we are predicting future outputs for a period in which they are likely to differ from the earlier period by, say, 70 per cent, then the two-point estimate will be found to be generally more accurate for the coefficients. The longer, therefore, the interval the more consistently will be our prediction improved by two-point estimates. In a very short period estimation where production changes are less than 70 per cent it will depend on the size of the bias $\alpha(X_r/X_i - 1)$ and the variance σ^2.

In case, therefore, input-output tables become to some extent a routine work in any country it may be worth while to prepare such estimates for two consecutive years in succession at a time to study at a bird's eye view the actual slopes of the production functions however crude, rather than depending on the assumption of linearity through origin.

CHAPTER 5

A NOTE ON MULTI-SECTOR
GROWTH MODELS

5.1

Among the growth models on a multi-sector basis which are increasingly being discussed in connection with planning in many countries, are those that have grown from static input-output models and others that have grown from dynamic macro-models of the Harrod–Domar type. It is the object of this paper to review several variants of these growth models and their properties which are relevant in planning.

We shall introduce into the static input-output framework first a set of relations which may facilitate the transition to dynamic form and may be of interest by itself.

In using the open Leontief model for planning purposes we are required to make a projection for the required investment from the supply side. That is, we are required to estimate the future supply of certain commodities rather than the future demand.

Consider an open Leontief model where consumption by households of non-durable commodities is also set up as an intermediate sector and capital goods and durable consumers goods are the only exogenous elements. Let a be the augmented matrix of inter-industrial coefficients, including household consumption of non-durable goods, X the vector of outputs and S the final demand vector of capital goods and also durable consumer goods. Then we have

$$aX + S = X \quad \text{or} \quad X = (1 - a)^{-1} S.$$

Such a model is analogous to the Keynesian scalar multiplier in matrix form. But there is one important difference. In the Keynesian scalar multiplier, aggregated as it is for the whole economy, the capital goods supplied and the capital goods in demand are identical. In matrix form, S, the vector of capital goods supplied, is different from I, the vector of capital goods required, or purchased, though the sum of the two vector elements is equal.

In the Keynesian scalar multiplier this conceptual difference is not important. But in a multi-sector growth model for planning purposes this means fixing up the possible supply without reference to possible demands. In actual economic practice planning starts by fixing certain investment targets for different sectors and seeing if such targets can be fulfilled. One does not fix the total supply of motor-trucks first, one studies the demand for motor trucks of different sectors on the basis of their investment targets and then adds this up for the whole economy. Thus the Leontief model works with a vector S of the possible supply of investment goods by sectors, while planning operates with a vector I of planned investment for different sectors.

The simplest way to relate these two would be to assume a fixed structure of investment for each sector. That is, we assume that for any sector j an *investment* I_j (assuming no price change) in Leontief units can be broken down into components $C_{ij} I_j$, describing its distribution to other sectors. Thus investment I_j in the jth industry may mean $C_{ij} I_j$ units of trucks, $C_{2j} I_j$ units of implements and so on. Assuming such a set of coefficients for every sector we now write

$$S_{ij} = C_{ij} I_j,$$

where S_{ij} is the supply of ith type of goods to the capital account of jth industry.

The Leontief model in matrix notation,

$$a X + S = X$$

may be now written as $\qquad a X + C I = X.$

This gives us for the solution of vector X

$$X = (\mathrm{I} - a)^{-1} C I.$$

The convenience of this form is that I, the investment expenditure vector, is more readily available than S. If we use a matrix where the column vector of household consumption of non-durables and the *row* vectors of factor costs are also within the inter-industry matrix the above solution gives us the output by sectors corresponding to given targets of investment.

5.2

An advantage of this static formulation is the simple way in which we can proceed to give it a dynamic interpretation by formulating the accelerator vector for the system.

We have seen that S, the vector of investment goods supplied, may be written with the vector of investment targets as

$$S = C I.$$

Let us now assume that for the ith sector

$$I_i = g_i \frac{dX_i}{dt}.$$

We thus express investment demand by every sector as a fixed ratio of the rate of change of output of the sector concerned.

The dynamic equation system then becomes

$$a X + C \hat{g} \frac{dX}{dt} = X,$$

4-2

where $\hat{g}$ is a diagonal matrix and dX/dt a vector with elements dX_i/dt. In the present form this model has solutions of the form

$$x_i = \sum_j K_j e^{\lambda_j t} \quad (j = 1, 2, \dots, n),$$

where the λ's are obtained as roots of an nth order differential equation. This general formulation and its interpretations raise considerable difficulties and the system is not useful as a practical tool.

With special assumptions, however, this system may be easily reduced to simpler forms. We shall consider some of these forms.

Let us first investigate what happens to such a system under the special assumption that the investments allocated to the sectors will be a fixed proportion of the total investment $\sum_i I_i$ during the plan period. We then obtain

$$I_i = \lambda_i \Sigma I_i = \lambda_i I \quad \text{(say)}.$$

Any sectoral investment I_i may be written as related to I_j by a simple coefficient

$$\frac{I_i}{\lambda_i} = \frac{I_j}{\lambda_j} = I \quad \text{or} \quad I_i = \frac{\lambda_i}{\lambda_j} I_j.$$

This reduces the equation system in matrix form to

$$a X + C . \hat{g} . \hat{\lambda} \frac{d\overline{X}_j}{dt} . \frac{1}{\lambda_j} = X,$$

where $\left(\dfrac{d\overline{X}}{dt} . \dfrac{1}{\lambda_j}\right)$ is a column vector with every element $= \left(\dfrac{d\overline{X}_j}{dt} . \dfrac{1}{\lambda_j}\right)$ and $\hat{\lambda}$ is a diagonal matrix. It can be seen that the simultaneous differential equation has now been reduced to a simpler form involving only one differential element. Eliminating all the X's except X from the system we shall obtain

$$X_j = k \frac{dX_j}{dt},$$

where k is a function of the coefficients of the system of equations.

This leads to

$$X_j = X_j(0) \, e^{(1/k)t}.$$

It is obvious, therefore, that every X_j of the system will involve $e^{(1/k)t}$ in its solution along with other coefficients determined by the constants of the system.

It should be noted, however, that the growth in the model for each sector will move in a constant proportion to each other. That is, so long as λ's are kept constant the sectors will maintain a specific relation to each other and all will grow together, so to speak. This, of course, can be relaxed by making consumption exogenous or using a similar device, but basically this model destroys, during the constancy of λ, the simultaneous nature of the differential equation system.

A slightly different assumption making investments I_i a constant proportion of the gross output, i.e.

$$I_i = a_i X_i$$

again leads to the same form of relation, this time the growth being determined by the growth of gross outputs.

This model also maintains a constant proportionality in every sector and is thus of practically the same form as above.

Such models may have a use in periodic planning. If it is found that the allocation of investment cannot be changed every time and that certain overall growth rates are desirable, then, during the plan period, growth may be made to follow the above pattern.

5·3

In this section we consider a rather different approach to multisector growth. The aggregative dynamic approach of Harrod and Domar considers two fundamental relations in equilibrium. These are

Investments,
$$I(t) = g\frac{dx}{dt}.$$

Savings, $\quad s(t) = ax(t) \quad$ and $\quad I(t) = s(t).$

Let us consider a similar equilibrium condition for each sector of the economy.

Let P_i be the productive capacity of the ith sector such that

$$\frac{dP_i/dt}{I_i(t)} = \sigma_i.$$

Such a series of $\sigma_i s$ relates potential productive capacity of the ith sector to the investment in the ith sector.

Let $X_i(t)$ be the actual output at time t such that

$$\frac{dX_i}{dt} = k_i \frac{dP_i}{dt}.$$

The k_i's are thus the utilization coefficient for each sector. This gives us

$$\frac{dX_i/dt}{I_i} = k_i \sigma_i.$$

Let us define gross investment coefficients a_i for the ith sector such that

$$I_i = a_i X_i.$$

Then we have solutions for the output of each sector

$$X_i = X_i(0)\, e^{a_i \sigma_i k_i t}.$$

So far the above is a pure extension of the Harrod–Domar model to sectoral growth. We now bring in the static input-output relations.

$$\sum_j a_{ij} X_j + S_i = X_i \quad (i \neq j),$$

where S_i is defined as before.

Then we have, replacing X_j by its growth equation

$$\sum_j a_{ij} X_j(0)\, e^{a_j \sigma_j k_j t} + S_i = X_i$$

or $\qquad S_i = X_i(0)\, e^{a_i \sigma_i k_i t} - \sum_j a_{ij} X_j(0)\, e^{a_j \sigma_j k_j t}.$

This, therefore, gives us the final demand or the net output of each sector in terms of the growth rates and initial output of the sectors concerned and the other constants of the system. In matrix form this may be written as

$$S = (1-a)\, \hat{X}(0)\, e^{a\sigma k t},$$

where $\hat{X}_0$ is a diagonal matrix formed from the vector X_0 and $e^{a\sigma k t}$ a vector whose elements are $e^{a_i \sigma_i k_i t}$

$$X(0)\, e^{a\sigma k t} = (1-a)^{-1} S$$

$$e^{a\sigma k t} = [X(0)]^{-1} (1-a)^{-1} S$$

for given $S(0)$, $X(0)$, t and $1-a$, we have

$$e^{a\sigma k t} = \beta \quad \text{(a given vector)}$$

or $\qquad a\sigma k t = \log \beta \quad$ (another vector with elements $\log \beta_i$).

If, therefore, we assign values to some of the above we can get a determinate solution for the rest. Thus for given t, and $k = 1$ we get

$$a\sigma = \log \beta / t \quad \text{(a vector as above)}$$

with given σ's this gives us a determinate solution for a.

Thus we can find the investment ratios in a situation where the given conditions are fulfilled. Alternatively, if we impose arbitrary growth rates for the sectors, this gives us the determination of S and also for given σ and k, the corresponding a. It thus seems that we can think of planned growth during the planning period for various sectors and the investment requirements it will generate under given conditions. It may be noted that this approach does not involve any determination of the accelerator for every inter-sectoral cell in the input-output totals but only an accelerator for the sector as a whole since σ_i the investment productivity can easily be translated into sectoral level. This marriage of a static form of the input-output equations with a dynamic form of sectoral growth may be used to good purpose without going into complicated solutions of differential equations in several unknowns.

The time path of net output, then, involves knowledge of all the unknowns on the right-hand side, e.g. a, σ, k. For given values of these we can obtain growth rates, or for given S's we can obtain any one of them when others are given.

In this model, also, it may easily be seen that if we drop a and substitute investment allocation λ_j such that

$$I_i = \lambda_j I_j$$

we reduce the system to one of proportional developments. Thus all I_i's are then expressed in terms of only the jth sector and we get

$$\alpha X + \hat{k}\, dx_j/dt = X,$$

where dx_j/dt is a vector with elements $d\bar{x}_j/dt$ and $\hat{k}$ a diagonal matrix.

Introducing now α for the jth sector only such that $I_j = \alpha_j X_j$ we can reduce all the growth rates to one of strict proportionality to the jth sector, all growing exponentially. In all these examples, of course, the variable singled out may be the total investments ΣI_i as well.

We shall now discuss in the light of the above exposition one or two generalized forms of special models in connection with the problem of growth.

5·4

We saw that any extension of the Harrod–Domar type of model by introducing fixed allocation parameters leads easily to proportional growth of all sectors on the assumption that the allocation parameters, once found, are treated as constants to be retained in a subsequent period. Of course, if, after every fulfilment of the plan period, the constant λ's are changed arbitrarily then the situation will be different.

We now consider the four-sector model used by Mahalanobis[1] and some of its generalizations.

The four-sector Mahalanobis model is defined below. If y_i's and n_i's are the sectoral increases in income and employment respectively and λ_i are investment allocation ratios ($i = 1, 2, 3, 4$).

We have,

$$I_i(t) = \frac{1}{\beta_i}\,[y_i(t)], \quad I_i(t) = \frac{1}{\theta_i}\,n_i(t).$$

Then it follows that

$$I_i(t) = \lambda_i I(t) = \frac{1}{\beta_i}\,y_i(t), \quad I_i(t) = \lambda_i I(t) = \frac{1}{\theta_i}\,n_i(t),$$

also,
$$\Sigma\lambda_i = 1.$$

Introducing targets $\Sigma n_i = n$ and $\Sigma y_i = y$ and assigning a specific value to one of the λ_i's the remaining system is solved for y_i's, n_i's and the remaining λ_i's.

In the light of our previous discussions this model seems to be a half-way house. Thus sectoral investment productivity coefficients in Domar's sense are β_i's. Although no attempt is made to find a sectoral equilibrium condition in any form with a given rate of investments, with some further assumptions it leads, in one sense, to a proportional growth model.

Since y_i's are the increases in sectoral income we have

$$\text{total increase in income} = \Sigma y_i = y$$
$$= I\Sigma\beta_i\lambda_i$$
$$= I\beta,$$

[1] P. C. Mahalanobis, 'The approach of operational research to planning'. *Sankhya*, December 1955, pp. 26–37.

where β is the overall coefficient relating the increase of income to investment and I is total investment, $\sum_i I_i$.

Treating the increases as instantaneous we have

$$\frac{dy}{dt} = I\beta.$$

Here β plays the part of a weighted investment productivity coefficient. If, during the plan period, we also have I as a constant ratio α of y, we have

$$\frac{dy}{dt} = I\beta, \quad I = \alpha y.$$

This at once gives us Domar's form of the growth model,

$$I = I_0 e^{\beta \alpha t}.$$

Any sectoral increase $y_i = \lambda_i I \beta_i$

$$= \lambda_i \beta_i I_0 e^{\beta \alpha t}$$

and

$$\frac{y_i}{y_k} = \frac{\lambda_i \beta_i}{\lambda_k \beta_k}.$$

Thus it is seen that in the Mahalanobis model we cannot assume any overall β and an investment ratio without making the whole model more determinate. But both these coefficients are likely to be fixed by the planners before they go in for more detailed sectoral coefficients.

We now consider introducing input-output relations into this four-sector model. For this we redefine y_i as the increase in gross output rather than net output and β is now related to the gross output in place of net output.

Let y_i be the increase of gross output of the ith sector.

Let s_i be the increase in final demand in the ith sector.

Let us further have

$$I_i(t) = \frac{1}{\beta_i} y_i(t),$$

$$I_i(t) = \frac{1}{\theta_i} n_i(t).$$

Then, as before, we now have in gross terms

$$I_i(t) = \lambda_i I(t) = \frac{1}{\beta_i} y_i(t),$$

$$I_i(t) = \lambda_i I(t) = \frac{1}{\theta_i} n_i(t),$$

$$\Sigma \lambda_i = 1.$$

Let us now consider input-output relations involving y_i's

$$\sum_j \alpha_{ij} x_j + s_i = y_i \quad (i \neq j).$$

We further have targets

$$\Sigma n_i = n \quad \text{and} \quad \Sigma y_i = y.$$

We thus have unknowns y_i, s_i, λ_i, n_i, and for a four-sector model it leads to sixteen unknowns. We have eight equations relating I's with y and n, a definitional equation in λ and two targets $\Sigma n_i = n$ and $\Sigma y_i = y$. This gives us eleven equations. We have four input-output equations relating to y_i and s_i. This gives us fifteen equations. We now have to consider only one more unknown as given for the system to be solved. Giving an arbitrary value to a specific λ_i we get values of all the unknowns of the system, i.e. (1) changes in gross output; (2) changes in employment; (3) the allocation parameters; (4) the final demand.

The net incomes of the original model are now calculated as follows:

$$\text{net income} \quad y'_j = y_j - \sum_i \alpha_{ij} x_i,$$

which is calculated as a residual, the sum being over commodity sectors. Instead of assigning given values for λ_i we may do the same for s like, say, $\sum_i s_i = s$, making the total final demand, corresponding to a total gross output, fixed.

It will be found that λ's are now determined by the input coefficients of the system as are the investment productivity coefficients.

5.5

The four-sector Mahalanobis model, however, is a special case of a two-sector model, proposed by him,[1] based on investment and the consumption goods industry. If λ_i and λ_c are the allocation to the two industries' investment, α_0 the ratio of national investment to income, initially, and β_i and β_c are the output-capital ratios then

$$y_t = y_0 \left\{ 1 + \alpha_0 \frac{\beta_i \lambda_i + \beta_c \lambda_c}{\beta_i \lambda_i} [(1 + \beta_i \lambda_i)^t - 1] \right\},$$

where $I(t)$ the investment takes the form

$$I(t) = I_0 (1 + \beta_i \lambda_i)^t$$

and $c(t)$ the consumption in t takes the form

$$c(t) = y_0 \left[1 - \alpha_0 \left(1 + \frac{\beta_c \lambda_c}{\beta_i \lambda_i} \right) \right] + \alpha_0 y_0 + \frac{\beta_c \lambda_c}{\beta_i \lambda_i} (1 + \beta_i \lambda_i)^t.$$

It is interesting to note that in tracing the time path, in both cases, λ_i the investment allocation is sufficient. Further disaggregation, therefore, of $c(t)$ into $c_1(t)$ and $c_2(t)$ can be easily done so long as the basic allocation is not altered.

---

[1] 'The process of growth of national income' *Sankhya*, 1952. Domar has pointed out that the two-sector model on almost similar lines was first proposed by the Soviet economist Feldman as early as 1928.

Domar: *Essays in the theory of economic growth*, New York: Oxford University Press.

A slightly more generalized version of this can be obtained rather easily by splitting the investment goods sector into two, e.g. production of machine tools and production of machines which produce consumer goods. Then if X_1 is designated as the investment department which produces machine tools, X_2 as the investment department producing machines that produce consumption goods and X_3 the section that produces consumer goods, it is obvious that, for dynamic equilibrium, we must have

$$X_1(t) = I_1(t) + I_2(t), \quad X_2(t) = I_3(t).$$

That is, production of machine tools must satisfy the investment requirements of departments 1 and 2, and production of machinery which are capital equipment for department 3 must satisfy investment in that department.

As before, we assume accelerators such that

$$I_1(t) = \sigma_1 \frac{dX_1}{dt}, \quad I_2(t) = \sigma_2 \frac{dX_2}{dt}, \quad I_3(t) = \sigma_3 \frac{dX_3}{dt}.$$

Now, by the allocation principle, we have

$$I_1 = \lambda_1 I, \quad I_2 = \lambda_2 I, \quad I_3 = (1 - \lambda_1 - \lambda_2) I,$$

where I is total investment.

We can therefore write,

$$X_1(t) = I_1(t) + I_2(t)$$

$$= \left(1 + \frac{\lambda_2}{\lambda_1}\right) \sigma_1 \frac{dX_1}{dt}$$

or

$$X_1(t) = X_1(0) \int e^{\lambda_2/(1-\lambda_1-\lambda_2) \cdot 1/\sigma_2 \cdot t} \cdot dt$$

also,

$$X_2(t) = X_2(0)[e^{(1-\lambda_1-\lambda_2)/\lambda_2 \cdot 1/\sigma_2 \cdot t} - 1]$$

and for $X_3(t)$ we have

$$\frac{dX_3}{dt} = \frac{1}{\sigma_3} \cdot X_2(t),$$

$$X_3 = \frac{1}{\sigma_3} \int X_2(t) \, dt + \text{const.}$$

$$= \frac{1}{\sigma_3} \int X_2(0) \, e^{\lambda_2/(1-\lambda_1-\lambda_2) \cdot 1/\sigma_2 \cdot t} \cdot dt + \text{const.}$$

$$= \frac{1}{\sigma_3} X_2(0) \left[\frac{\sigma_2(1 - \lambda_1 - \lambda_2)}{\lambda^2} \cdot e^{(1-\lambda_1-\lambda_2)/\lambda_2 \cdot 1/\sigma_2 \cdot t} - 1 \right] + \text{const.}$$

We can, of course, also proceed by iteration with given initial values.

As can be seen in each the time path is now becoming slightly more complicated, involving, as it does, the investment in two sections rather than in one section.

We can now, of course, further expand the consumer goods sectors in more detail keeping the general consumer sector growth-rate fixed as above. Thus it can be seen that, by special classification and assumption of dynamic sectoral equilibrium, such a generalization can be made easily.

The differential equation system in this case is given by

$$X_1 = \sigma_1 \frac{dX_1}{dt} + \sigma_2 \frac{dX_2}{dt}, \quad X_2 = \sigma_3 \frac{dX_3}{dt}.$$

This gives us the relation between the delivery of investment goods of various types, e.g. X_1 and X_2 and the investment requirements of these groups. Any arbitrary allocation ratio now makes the rates of change dX_i/dt constant ratios of each other.

An alternative approach would be to bring in the consumption function at this stage. Let c_i be the consumption requirements of workers in the ith group and let $c_i = a_i X_i$. To fix the consumption as a ratio of output is to extend the concept of consumption by a group of workers to their income one step further, by relating their income to the output of the sector. Then we get X_3, the total consumption, as

$$X_3 = \Sigma c_i = a_1 X_1 + a_2 X_2 + a_3 X_3$$

or $$(1 - a_3) X_3 = a_1 X_1 + a_2 X_2$$

or $$\frac{dX_3}{dt} = \frac{1}{1 - a_3} \left[a_1 \frac{dX_1}{dt} + a_2 \frac{dX_2}{dt} \right].$$

We thus get the system,

$$X_1 = \sigma_1 \frac{dX_1}{dt} + \sigma_2 \frac{dX_2}{dt},$$

$$X_2 = \frac{\sigma_3 \sigma_1}{1 - a_3} \frac{dX_1}{dt} + \frac{\sigma_3 \sigma_2 \alpha_2}{1 - a_3} \frac{dX_2}{dt}.$$

The solution of this system can now be obtained along the usual lines.

It is to be noted here that no allocation is made, but a behaviour coefficient, a_i, is assumed for each sector. If $a_i = a_j = a$, then the second form is simplified further.

Another interesting approach follows from this model. Since X_3 is the consumption of the whole group we can assign a time path for X_3. Thus let

$$\frac{dX_3}{dt} = \phi(t),$$

then $$X_2 = \sigma_3 \phi(t), \quad \frac{dX_2}{dt} = \sigma_3 \frac{d\phi}{dt}$$

and $$X_1 = \sigma_1 \frac{dX_1}{dt} + \sigma_3 \sigma_2 \frac{d\phi}{dt}.$$

Corresponding to the shape we assign to $\phi(t)$, we get different time paths for X_1 and X_2. Thus we know what is the investment base for a consumption target. If there is no autonomous demand for investment in X_1, other than that induced by X_2, then in the above case we get

$$\frac{dX_3}{dt} = \phi(t), \; X_2 = \sigma_3 \phi(t) \quad \text{and} \quad X_1 = \sigma_3 \sigma_2 \frac{d\phi}{dt}.$$

This shows the sequence from the standpoint of consumer goods production.

Thus it can be seen that a large variety of multi-sector approaches are possible with varying assumptions. But unless we are prepared to have simplifying assumptions of different types we must ultimately face the solution of a high-order differential or difference equation.

CHAPTER 6

INFLATION IN A PLANNED
MULTI-SECTOR GROWTH PROCESS

6.1

Physical and financial balances are counterparts of the blueprints of a planned economy. Except in very special circumstances, for short periods, even the most centralized planning system has to conduct its business within a price framework, in spite of physical controls. This framework, in a free enterprise economy, is evolved through the operation of market forces and therefore, on the whole, equilibrates demand and supply for the commodities and factors in physical terms. In a planned economy physical allocation and distribution do not necessarily reflect market forces in the economic sense but rather the objectives of the planning authority. Therefore, the price system devised by the planning authority has to be such that it equilibrates the physical allocation with the financial allocation. This is necessary because, within the broad outlines of the physical allocation system, price plays an important part in every plan, in directing materials and factors towards desired goals without detailed directives from the central authorities. Thus, if there is a need to recruit more men for the mines, raising wages to attract more recruits may be resorted to more often than adopting an arbitrary conscription system. In a planned economy, though the demand mechanism as we understand it is often very weakly represented, much of the inter-play of demand and supply, at least on a lower plane, are still allowed to take place for the smooth functioning of the system. This means that the physical plan for the movement of men and material that the authority makes must be consistent with the price structure that has been fixed in order to implement the plan. The effective coordination of the two is an essential condition of the success of the plan.

In most planned economies the imbalance between the financial and physical counterparts, especially in the early years of development, comes in the shape of an inflationary pressure. This is because all such development is pushed through at a very high tempo. Such economies have very often an urge to grow at a rate which is not physically possible in the condition obtaining in such economies. It is often, therefore, seen that the physical plan faces shortages and bottle-necks which were not anticipated in the beginning. Since the financial plan precedes the actual physical execution it does not have the same rigid inhibitions and it often happens that, during the period of operation, the actual growth of the economy is smaller than its financial counterpart in the same period. This shows itself in a serious inflationary pressure, there being a more liberal flow of money than of goods or factors. This sometimes becomes so serious that it threatens the whole economy. It is a very important task of the planning authority to devise a consistent and balanced financial counterpart to the physical plan. To be forewarned of the possible dangers to the plan through a rising discrepancy between these counterparts and to provide adequate safeguards against such possibilities is a sound second line of defence for any ambitious plan.

In the present paper we shall study the application of input-output models in analysing this imbalance of the two counterparts in a planned multi-sector growth process. We shall assume that the economy does function as in an input-output model and that planning authorities have used such models for the purposes of preparing the plan-frame, but that imbalances arise because of the overestimation of labour productivity and waste of material inputs which emerge during the implementation of the plan itself.

6.2

Let the base period transaction matrix recording the deliveries and absorption of the different industrial sectors of the economy be denoted by the matrix x. Then we have the accounting identity

$$xi + F = X,$$

where x is the vector of intermediate outputs, i the unit sum vector, F is a vector of final demands on the economy and X is the vector of total deliveries to all the sectors including the final demands.

To proceed from such an essentially accounting type of identity to an economic model a highly simplified theory of production is assumed which states that
$$x = a\hat{X},$$

where $\hat{X}$ is a diagonal matrix formed from the vector X and a is the matrix of coefficients relating the inputs to the total deliveries.

The implication of such a set of production functions is well known. It denies in effect that there are economies of scale or the possibility of substitution at all. Without going into the controversies on these rather crude types of production functions we shall accept that the input coefficients, as defined here, are good enough approximations for reasonably short periods in planning models.

Proceeding from the above we can now write

$$X = a.\hat{X}.i + F,$$
$$= (I - a)^{-1} F,$$

where I is the unit matrix of order $n - 1$ and X represents the vector of outputs of material goods and is of the order $n - 1$.

By an almost analogous operation we can also construct a model which will express the financial framework of the economy.

Let the price per unit in any sector be broken up into the components of costs per unit paid to all the other sectors in the economy in the process of production and distribution. We can then rewrite the set of equations of the model in a price accounting identity.

$$a'.P + \hat{C}.\hat{X}^{-1}i = P,$$

$$P = (I-a')^{-1}\hat{C}.\hat{X}^{-1}i,$$

where P is the vector of price per unit, $\hat{C}\hat{X}^{-1}$ is the column of factors per unit of output consisting of elements like wages and salaries in each sector and a' the transpose of the matrix a. Solving for P in the usual way we get the determination of price per unit in terms of the factor costs per unit in the sectors.

From the relations between the inputs and deliveries in the first model we can also draw a further relation between final demand and factor costs in terms of a base period price. If C is the vector of factor costs then we have, according to our production function rules,

$$C = \hat{A}_n X,$$

where $\hat{A}_n$ is a diagonal matrix consisting of the proportions that factor costs are to outputs in each sector.

Then we have further

$$C = \hat{A}_n X$$
$$= \hat{A}_n (I-a)^{-1} F.$$

Corresponding, thus, to a final demand at constant price there is a unique vector of factor costs in the same price situation.

The price equation of the model gives us

$$P = (I-a')^{-1}\hat{C}.\hat{X}^{-1}i$$
$$= (I-a')^{-1} (\hat{A}_n \hat{X}) \hat{X}^{-1}i$$
$$= (I-a')^{-1}\hat{A}_n i.$$

So long as the actual output achieved by the system is identical with the output as projected by the model the relative prices will be unchanged if the factor costs are also planned according to the dictates of the model.

6.3

The most obvious procedure for the planning authorities is to formulate a vector of final demand over the time period t and to estimate from an input-output model the factor costs that must be generated in order to implement the same. This, then, gives us the size of the financial plan that has to be implemented in terms of the net national income at factor costs. We shall assume that the authorities are envisaging no change in the price levels.

Let the decision of the authorities regarding the growth rate of final demand at constant prices of the base period be such that

$$F(t) = (I+\hat{\delta})^t F(0),$$

where $\hat{\delta}$ is the diagonal matrix indicating the growth rate planned for the different sectors and $F(o)$ and $F(t)$ the final demand of the two periods. Then assuming input-output relations the growth of income will be given as follows:

$$
\begin{aligned}
C(t) &= \hat{A}_n \hat{X}(t)\, i \\
&= \hat{A}_n\, (I-a)^{-1} \hat{F}(t)\, i \\
&= \hat{A}_n\, (I-a)^{-1} (I+\hat{\delta})^t \hat{F}(o)\, i.
\end{aligned}
$$

We have already seen that the equilibrium price will be given by the relation as at the base period.

$$
P(t) = (I-a')^{-1} A_n.
$$

So long as the output, as projected by the planning model, keeps in step with the actual outputs, there will be no change in the relative prices of the base period, in terms of the factor costs of the base period.

We now assume that there are a series of shortfalls which were not properly visualized in the economy when fixing the levels of the growth of outputs. Let the growth rate ultimately attained by the economy be given by

$$
\begin{aligned}
{}_aX(t) &= (I+\hat{\beta})^t X(o) \\
&= (I+\hat{\beta})^t (I-a)^{-1} F(o),
\end{aligned}
$$

where the vectors X and F are in base period prices, and the diagonal matrix $\hat{\beta}$ is $\neq \hat{\delta}$.

Since however the authorities have made their financial plans on the basis of a growth rate $\hat{\delta}$, and have taken many steps like fixing the wage rates and the number to be employed by the sectors on the basis of that growth rate, they will not be able to retrace their steps in a financial sense. The national income, at factor cost, in a financial sense will then grow according to the rate

$$
C(t) = \hat{A}_n\, (I-a)^{-1} (I+\hat{\delta})^t F(o).
$$

But the actual output will be rising, as given by the growth rate of ${}_aX(t)$. This discrepancy between the actual growth of output and the growth of the planned financial outputs will cause a change in the price vector. This change will proceed along the following course over time t.

$$
\hat{P}(t) = (I-a')^{-1} \hat{A}_n\, (I-a)^{-1} (I+\hat{\delta})^t \hat{F}(o)\, [(I+\hat{\beta})^t (I-a)^{-1} F(o)]^{-1}.
$$

Depending on the discrepancy between $\hat{\delta}$ and $\hat{\beta}$ we shall have a different movement of the price vector over time. This is on the assumption that during this period the authorities do not change the financial plan or the number of workers they have planned to employ during the plan period. This will also mean that, since outputs cannot grow over a certain rate in different sectors, the number of workers employed, according to the plan, will produce a lower volume of output, that is, production per man will fall because of the refusal of the authorities to acknowledge the bottle-neck in time. The discrepancy between $\hat{\delta}$ and $\hat{\beta}$ need not be all in the same direction, that is, some elements of $\hat{\delta}$ may be greater and some less than the corresponding elements of $\hat{\beta}$. The price movement will be a compound of all the elements of $\hat{\delta}$ and $\hat{\beta}$ and the technical coefficients, and will vary from sector to sector. At any time the way in which a particular sectoral price will behave will depend on the discrepancies in all the sectors.[1]

In considering the above model we have deliberately assumed a certain rigidity of the financial plan, in the sense that price changes during the plan period are not allowed to affect the financial provisions of the plan at all. But when, due to the interaction of the discrepancies, the prices are rising fast, the authorities will find their income distribution plan and their accounting for the different sectors, distorted by the relative changes in prices. In order, therefore, to correct this distortion they will be forced to change their financial plans. The discrepancies, and therefore the price changes in the next period, will be more or less, depending on whether they made changes of a more realistic nature or not.

A simpler statement of the problem could be made if $\hat{\delta}$ is regarded as the planned growth rate for total output instead of that for planned final demand. That is, if the planned output in time t is defined as

$$X(t) = (I+\hat{\delta})^t X(\mathrm{o}).$$

The above formula then may be rewritten as

$$\hat{P}(t) = (I-a')^{-1}\hat{A}_n(I+\hat{\delta})^t \hat{X}(\mathrm{o})\,[(I+\hat{\beta})^t \hat{X}(\mathrm{o})]^{-1},$$

$\hat{\delta}$ and $\hat{\beta}$ being now the growth rates of planned and actual outputs respectively.

We shall now assume that when prices rise the authorities find it necessary to raise factor costs but do not think of reducing the size of their physical plan. That is, they continue their growth rate in the planning model to be the same as before and assume that there will be no more discrepancy between the planned and achieved rates. But they raise the factor costs proportionately with the average rise in prices to check the distortion in the plan due to the price changes in the earlier period. If we further assume that the actual growth rate again falls short of the planned rate as before then the price rise will now be having a spiral effect. The initial discrepancies in the physical and financial plans will first raise prices, and the latter in their turn will raise factor costs and so on. We shall illustrate the growth rate in this type of planning first for $t = 2$ and subsequently for any t as outlined below.

$$P(2) = (I-a')^{-1}\hat{C}(2)\,\hat{X}(2)^{-1}i$$
$$= (I-a')^{-1}\hat{A}_n\,\hat{X}(2)\,p(\mathrm{o})^{-1}p(\mathrm{I})\,_a\hat{X}(2)^{-1}i,$$

where $p(\mathrm{o})$ and $p(\mathrm{I})$ are scalar denoting the average prices in the two

[1] A numerical exercise carried out on failures of the Indian Plans to achieve targets and its inflationary effect by this formula is given in paper no. 14 in this volume.

periods, i.e. in other words the price index of period 1 with respect to period 0. This means that the price in the time period 2 will be affected both by discrepancies between the deliveries as actual and planned during this period and by similar discrepancies in earlier time periods. The general form for $P(t)$ according to this rule will be

$$P(t) = (I - a')^{-1} \hat{A}_n (I + \delta)^t \hat{X}(0) \, p(t) \, [p(t-1)]^{-1} X(0)^{-1} (I + \hat{\beta})^{-t} i.$$

Thus the revision factor at each stage involves all the prices at earlier time periods and, therefore, all the earlier discrepancies. The progress of inflation under such conditions will be far more accelerated than in the previous case.

6.4

In the two models considered in the earlier section we have worked on the assumption that the technical or production coefficients are stable and that there is no difficulty in moving materials or factors from one sector to another according to the changing structure of final demands from the economy. But it is very likely that if the final demands are changed rapidly, especially in an upward direction, so that shortages appear on a large scale in the economy, the unfettered movement of men and materials under a constant price system will break down and physical control, in a more direct sense, will be necessary. In planned economies of rapid growth, shortages and bottle-necks are very widespread, and, therefore, any freedom of movement that may be allowed to commodities and factors is likely to end in a mutual bidding up of the factors without substantially changing the allocation of an earlier period. As there is an almost unlimited demand for goods stimulated by development plans, which is undiminished by higher prices, such a situation can only be met by a more rigid plan of rationing on a detailed sectoral basis.

In economies of rationing, since every sector registers a high demand, the general tendency of the authorities is to preserve the stability of the allocation coefficients as far as possible, once it is arrived at by consideration of sectoral claims and counter-claims. Therefore we get an input-output type of model, with fixed allocation coefficients, instead of technical coefficients.

The allocation model may be defined with the allocation functions such that

$$X_{jk} = a_{jk} X_j$$

which implies that the supply of products of the jth sector to the kth sector is not determined by the need of the kth sector but the total available supply from the jth sector. We then obtain a system analogous to the input-output system:

$$E = a' . \hat{P} . X + C,$$

where E is the vector of total costs, a' the transpose of a, $\hat{P}$ the diagonal matrix formed from the price vector P and X the vector of outputs.

Assuming, as a condition of accounting balance, $E = P.X$, we get

$$\hat{P}.X = a'.\hat{P}.X + C$$

$$= (I-a)^{-1}C,$$

where C, the vector of factor costs, is interpreted as the net national income at factor costs generated in the different sectors. The movement of price is given by the formula following from the above equation:

$$P = (I-a')^{-1}\hat{C}.\hat{X}^{-1}i.$$

If, therefore, the planning authority has in mind the growth of income over time given by the following expression

$$C(t) = (I+\hat{\delta})^t C(o)$$

then we can write

$$P(t) = (I-a')^{-1}(I+\hat{\delta})^t\hat{C}(o)\,\hat{X}(t)^{-1}i.$$

If we assume once more that the planners have overestimated the growth rate such that the actual growth rate of the outputs is given by

$$_aX(t) = (I+\hat{\beta})^t X(o)$$

we get the movement of price given by

$$P(t) = (I-a)^{-1}(I+\hat{\delta})^t\hat{C}(o)\,(I+\hat{\beta})^{-t}X(o)^{-1}i.$$

Depending on the discrepancy between $\hat{\delta}$ and $\hat{\beta}$ we therefore get the movement of $P(t)$ determined by the above expression.

6.5

In the concluding section we shall try to discuss some possible uses of the present type of models in actual planning work. In order to do this we must begin first by pointing out that these models are all supply determined, in one sense. The model itself does not help us to determine the final demand but works with final demand as a datum. This means that a correct assessment of final demand is not a function of the model. Any mistake in the correct assessment of final demand from the side of demand will upset the model from a direction about which nothing can be done within the framework of the model itself. All that these models can do is to project total output for the given final demand. It is important to realize that lots of things can go wrong even in a fully controlled economy where demand had very little independent existence outside the decisions of the planning authorities. This is because of the fact that the decisions of the planning authorities depend partly on the demands of the community and partly on the estimates of the authorities about the capabilities of the economy. If the authorities are wrong about capabilities they are often unable to prevent a number of consequences from occurring precisely because they have already committed themselves financially to a number of expenditures. Suppose the authorities have fixed the factor costs of an industry on the assumption of a certain level of productivity or capital capability, they find, after operating the economy, that their anticipations are not going to be fulfilled. Since they have already employed the workers of that industry on the basis of that output this is going to add to the expenditure in the consumers market without adding to the product available to the economy. This kind of mistake therefore is quite independent of a mistake in assessing final demand correctly from the demand side. In our present series of models it is this kind of miscalculation and their effect over time that we have tried to study.

We shall now illustrate a method of using these models for the purpose of safeguarding ourselves from dangerous levels of inflation. Let us assume that there are two vectors of final demand that the planning body has fixed up. One of them is a kind of core or a desirable vector of final demand that the authority is quite sure is within the abilities of the economy, even if output does not reach expectation. Let us say this definitely achievable growth rate is given by the function

$$_aX(t) = (I+\hat{\beta})^t X(\text{o}).$$

Let us further assume that the maximum permissible inflation that the economy can stand during the plan period is given by the function,

$$P(t) = (I+\hat{\pi})^t P(\text{o}).$$

Then using the formula for growth of the inflationary pressure given in §6.3 we can write

$$(I+\hat{\pi})^t P(\text{o}) = (I-a')^{-1} \hat{A}_n \cdot (I+\hat{\delta})^t$$
$$\times (I-a)^{-1} F(\text{o}) [(I+\hat{\beta})^t (I-a)^{-1} \hat{F}(\text{o})]^{-1}.$$

As we know both $\hat{\pi}$ and $\hat{\beta}$, in the above equation we can find out the value of $\hat{\delta}$ which is determinate. This will give us the value of $\hat{\delta}$ which will be within the zone of calculated risk which the planners are ready to take. Even if things go wrong in such a case inflation will not be such as to raise prices higher than given by π. It is obvious that using this type of model with various assigned values it will be possible to know the different consequences likely from the action of the planners even if things go wrong. At least this will warn the authorities of the dangers likely to flow from certain blueprints.

CHAPTER 7

A PROGRAMMING APPROACH
TO DYNAMIC PLANNING PROBLEMS

The objective of this paper is to discuss some programming approaches to problems of perspective planning. The basic feature of perspective planning is that it imbeds a short-period plan for a specific period, say five years, in a sequence of plans covering a longer period of, say, fifteen to twenty years. Because of this the short-period problems of development are posed in a more dynamic setting. In a short-period plan many things can be viewed on a once for all basis with certain variables assigned exogenously. These exogenous variables of the short period become endogenous variables in the long period. Time enters into the determination of these variables and their mutual relationship in an essential way. A five-year plan may be characterized as a short-period static model for the purposes of considering alternative courses of action at a specific point in time. A perspective plan considers a dynamic model proposing alternative courses of action at different points of time. This brings in, as a direct consequence, the necessity of making choices about alternative time phasing together with alternative possibilities at the same time. There is, naturally, a large increase in the complexity of the planning procedures because of the introduction of time-marked variables. Instead of activities and items which have a constant definition throughout all time periods an activity must be specified separately for each period and each structural relationship elaborated.

In this paper we shall discuss some of the aspects of this increasing complexity which is brought into a programming model because of the introduction of time in an essential way and implying that the passage of time is changing the nature of the structural relationships of the variables in the problem and its solution. We shall do this with reference to concrete developmental problems involving industrial growth and the location of new units.

The paper falls into four parts. In the first part we consider, in general terms, the problems posed in a decision model of the programming type in a dynamic setting and the several approaches that are effective when facing such problems, e.g. static models with interval estimates through sensitivity analysis, or parametric programming, to consider possibilities for a wider range of alternatives over time. In the second part we consider elaborating a basically static structure to cover dynamic conditions that are also satisfied by the model.

In the third part, we consider some approaches developed in a successive programming sequence so that a sequence of decisions, all dynamically connected, can take place in an open or closed system of objective functions.

Finally we consider briefly dynamic programming techniques with their uses and limitations.

7.1

The decision process in perspective planning is dynamic because it is 'sequential'. That is the process is extended over time with decisions following each other and serving as initial conditions for those following after.

A feature of this sequence is that a number of uncertainties and imponderables have to be provided for. Further, the flow of information coming from past experience has to be used to make any necessary modifications to the sequence of subsequent decisions.

A short-cut approach is to partition a problem into several short-period problems of a static nature. But such approximations must not distort the main characteristics of the sequential decision problem.

The objective function for such short-range decision problems must ascribe a positive value to further information that may come even though the information is not used in immediate analysis.

One difficulty in perspective planning is that the objective function is not completely known. Such knowledge usually comes after the full sequential decision problem has been solved. The next problem must start with comparative ignorance, as, apart from some broad features, it is not known. Care has to be taken to ensure that the main problems of the sequential process are not missed.

Let us consider the following problem. During a five-year period the planning body aims for an increase in demand of a group of commodities and decides to expand existing units or establish new units. The objective of the planning authority is to maximize the output target at some point in time, e.g. the end of the period, given the initial resources available and the highest possible rates of growth in the different regions. Further, the development of the units is to take place in sequence, meeting certain inter-temporal consistency conditions; there are bottle-necks due to transport shortages, which, again, are changing over time.

The objective is to devise a chain of decisions to build in different regions while keeping to the boundaries of existing facilities and future facilities, keeping all consistency conditions over the entire period and maximizing the output, say, in the terminal year, or the years as a whole. This last hesitation shows us the dilemma regarding the objective. In a sequential problem there is no specific rule, on how growth is to be viewed at different periods. The nature of the objective function defines our attitude to the passage of time and any decision is based on the specific attitude we may have about the way to view time itself.

The fact that the optimization process extends over time here makes no difference at all. The same commodities may, at different time points, be treated as different commodities and dynamic optimization problems can be treated statically by elaborating the time periods involved and reproducing the special dynamic relations through such time periods. The use of timed variables for each time period formally reduces the problem to one of standard linear programming. But a dynamic problem has many features which are concealed by such static enumeration. The occurrence of physically identical commodities in time leads to a recursive structure. The recursive relations of similar commodities in time will be lost if similar commodities at different times are defined as different. No matter how rigid we make our assumptions about fixed coefficients of production, or fixed capital-output ratios, the introduction of a time dimension and stocks of capital will destroy the mechanical and determinate nature of the problem. It is no longer possible to dispense with the explicit device and optimization. Each commodity could be stored or produced later, capital could be held idle until some later knowledge made its use more advantageous. Thus the sequential nature of the decision, mutual conditioning, the existence of a structure over time can never be completely covered in any approximate decision involving a specific time period.

The other important point, from the standpoint of efficiency is that one period decisions may each be separately efficient but there may be no guarantee that such a sequence of one period decisions will be as efficient over the whole sequence. If a dynamic problem is to be programmed efficiently we should be conscious of the efficiency, as a whole, of the totality of our decisions.

7.2

We shall now consider a location problem in stages of varying complexity. Consider firstly a static formulation of the problem in a single commodity. During an interval it is anticipated that demand for it will increase. Since demand and production centres are dispersed, it is necessary to know how to locate additional centres that are required, so that costs may be minimized.

So we consider the problem of finding an optimal location pattern for future expansion. The major assumption we start with is that regional average costs are unaltered by the addition of new units.

It has been shown that a problem of this type can be formulated as a transhipment problem and is, therefore, similar to the transportation problem itself. We can start with the requirement equations as before. But the equation for delivery capacities must now be expressed as below:

$$\sum_j x_{ij} \leqslant k_i + n_i,$$

where n_i is the volume of capacity to be newly generated.

The regional requirement equations are as before. It is obvious that a new set of unknown variables has been introduced, which makes the problem different from the transportation model. This problem however can be changed into transportation form by a simple device. Assume initially a value for n_i which is sufficiently large to include the excess demand for all the regions together; thus making in fact

$$n_i = \sum_j r_j - \sum_i k_i.$$

It is easily seen that no region can now have a demand exceeding $k_i + n_i$.

It is strange that after having introduced n_i we now have to give a value of n_i sufficiently large so that n_i seems not to exist, but such apparent anomalies are common in convex sets.

Having given this upper bound value to all the new installations we can proceed in the conventional way. We now argue that of these extra capacities in each region the optimal solution will pick out and use capacities only where it is profitable to do so. All regions which will leave this new capacity unused are not suitable for expansion.

The question of selection of regions in an Indian context is not very easy. There are undoubtedly economies of scale in concentrating industries in a few regions. But in the long run this may lead to increasing costs, shortage of labour because of the comparatively small mobility in their case and suppression of many potentially important areas of industrial growth where necessary facilities exist for development in a more rudimentary form. From the standpoint of building up the nation as a whole again, the social cost of keeping several areas in a backward primitive state is very high. It encourages separatism. In a large country like India, there has to be therefore a continual balancing of the various factors before the location of industries are fixed.

Apart from the question of regions, the question of time phasing is also equally important in view of the scarcity of resources. While satisfying the growing demand, time phasing has to be done in such a way that over the period as a whole the scarce capital is used to maximum advantage. In principle one can think of solving all the elements of an economy in a programming problem within a single colossal computation—including simultaneously the details of space, time, technological choice and inter-industry relations. In practice, these interlocking details are not solved simultaneously but rather iteratively.

We shall now put in some more complications of a dynamic nature, but retain the single commodity character of the problem. Let us consider the following problem.

In a plan period of five years, the authorities want to provide for increased demand for a commodity, and decide to expand existing facilities with the objective of meeting this demand.

The authorities however have one criterion regarding possible location, e.g. minimum cost over the economy for its production and distribution. Introducing a set of simplifications we consider the production and transportation costs as given for each region. Installation cost is considered the same everywhere and dropped. An additional objective is to phase the programme so that total cost is minimized over the five year period as a whole.

The problem thus has two major objectives. The first consideration is that terminal total cost must be minimized. Location as a whole is fixed on that basis. In the second stage the phasing is done in such a way as to minimize the total plan period cost where the choice is now of the timing for each plant in a given location.

In defining the objective in this way we are assuming that as far as we are concerned the situation at the end of the plan period may be frozen at that stage. If at the end of the plan period the actual situation continues to change rapidly, then the advantage is lost. Hence the period of the plan leading to the terminal year becomes very important in defining optimality. We outline below the arrangement of a simple example of such a problem where the question of phasing and location has been taken up in sequence. We have introduced some drastic simplification in the formulation.

Let x_{ij} be the unit of shipment from any region i to a region j in time t. Let c be the production cum transportation cost which is treated as a constant.

The initial capacities are denoted by $_0C_i$ for the region and the requirement of the jth in period t by $_tR_j$.

Then the rule that the terminal demands must be met and regions selected optimally may be stated thus, if $_TC_i$ are the terminal capacities

$$\sum_j {}_TR_j = \sum_i {}_TC_i.$$

Let $_tC_i$ denote new capacities created in the tth period in region i. Then

$$_TC_i = {}_0C_i + {}_1C_i + {}_2C_i + \ldots + {}_kC_i,$$

where $t = 1, 2, \ldots, k$.

Let $_Tx_{ij}$ be the terminal shipments from i to j, then

$$\sum_j {}_Tx_{ij} \leqq {}_TC_i, \quad \sum_i {}_Tx_{ij} \geqq {}_TR_j.$$

Subject to the above, minimize,

$$\sum_i \sum_j C_{ij} \, {}_Tx_{ij}.$$

Since $_tC_i$ are not known excepting that

$$\sum_t {}_tC_i = {}_TC_i \quad \text{and} \quad \sum_i {}_TC_i = \sum_i {}_TR_i,$$

we have to devise a method to find out $_tC_i$ separately for each phase.

From the above programme we have determined how the new capacities to be created should be located. The next problem is to phase it over time so as to minimize total cost over the five-year period as a whole.

Let $_tC_i$ denote the new capacities to be created in the ith region in time t. Then minimize $\sum_t \sum_i \sum_j C_{ij} \, {}_tx_{ij}$ subject to,

$$(a)\ \sum_j {}_tx_{ij} \leqslant {}_0C_i + \sum_{t=1}^{t} {}_tC_i; \quad (b)\ \sum_i {}_tx_{ij} \geqslant {}_tR_j \qquad (t = 1, 2, \ldots, T).$$

This will ensure the optimality of the phasing decision up to the terminal period, given the location as fixed.

The problem of location and phasing is studied as a two-tier problem. The optimal plan location is decided on the basis of the terminal costs of operation. This of course does not mean that the optimality will be a function of the time horizon. No attempt is made to go into the length of the time horizon here at all. But given a fixed time period the phasing of the plant is considered independently of the location avoiding interactions of location and phasing.

We should at this stage point out the limitation of splitting the problem in this way. The correct approach theoretically would be to conceive of the programme considering the question of location and phasing over time in a single unified problem. This would have meant that the inter-relationship, if any, between phasing and location would have received due consideration in the optimal programme. But, treating them in this way is in effect implying that these two problems are not in any way interdependent and can be treated in isolation. In other words the optimality of the location problem is quite unrelated to the phase optimality. This however may not be so. While it is quite easy to accommodate phase optimality in our programme in theory, the size of the programme becomes unwieldy for any practical work. Hence our choice for an approximate but manageable sized problem.

A more complex situation may easily be created if we consider multiple sectors in the economy. The interdependence now is both sectoral and inter-temporal.

Consider an economy of three sectors, e.g. coal, engineering and iron and steel.

We can conceive of interdependence of the following types; machinery is required for capacity building in all the sectors, with a lag of say one year. Then there are current input requirements, e.g. coal is required by iron and steel, engineering, etc. We have some capital to output ratios, e.g. the machine requirement by all industries.

These are symbolically presented in the following system of equations for coal.

$$X_c(t-1) = x_{ci}(t) + X_{ce}(t),$$
$$X_{ci}(t) = a_{ci} \cdot X_i(t),$$
$$X_c(t) \leqq \sigma_c \cdot X_{ec}(t).$$

There will be similar equations for the other sectors.

We want to ensure that during the plan period the phasing will be aimed at reducing expenditure up to the terminal period as much as possible. Thus the problem of location and phasing over regions is split into two problems. One is the problem of terminal location which ensures that an optimal location is decided for the future and the other is regarding phasing.

Given the above system of constraints let us have, as an objective function, the maximizing of output of engineering from $t = 0$ to $t = 5$.

$$\text{maximize} \quad \sum_{t=0}^{5} X_e(t).$$

Now, it is obvious that the problem has entered into the dynamic field; first, there is an interdependence of a dynamic type and a necessary condition for the system is that the dynamic equilibrium conditions are met. The choice in this particular case is over the entire planning period; the optimization process will pick up such activity levels at different time periods as will lead to the total engineering output being at a maximum over the whole period.

We can easily extend this problem into a locational type by adding an additional set of regional interdependences superimposed on sectoral interdependence.

The balance equations are to be defined for the outputs of each region and the set of equations (11) will have to be framed in regional term. Thus, if r is the number of regions,

$$X_c(t-1) = x_{ci}(t) + X_{ce}(t)$$

can be written as,

$$\sum_r X_c^r(t-1) = \sum_r \left(X_{ci}^r(t) + \sum_r X_{ce}^r(t) \right)$$

denoting that all coal output in regions denoted by r in the $(t-1)$th period must equal the coal supplied to iron and engineering industries in the same regions. If there is a surplus of coal we can write,

$$\sum_r X_c^r(t-1) \geqslant \sum_r (X_{ci}^r(t) + \sum_r X_{ce}^r(t)).$$

Similarly, elaboration of all regional shipments could be quite easily done. An additional set of equations will now define production function for each region. Thus, the output of coal in region r depends on the total of engineering goods supplied to it and is a function of this, the coefficient being $_r\sigma_{ec}$.

The entire set is defined as below for region r.

$$_rX_c(t) = {_r\sigma_c} \cdot {_rX_{ec}(t)},$$

$$_rX_i(t) = {_r\sigma_i} \cdot {_rX_{ei}(t)},$$

$$_rX_e(t) = \sigma_e \cdot {_rX_{ee}(t)}.$$

In this case, the different regions have different output capital ratios for all industries, except engineering, which has a similar output capital ratio for all regions.

We further describe a set of constraints imposed by transport facilities as below:

$$_{12}X_c + _{12}X_i + _{12}X_e \leqq k_{12},$$
$$_{13}X_c + _{13}X_i + _{13}X_e \leqq k_{13},$$
$$_{23}X_c + _{23}X_i + _{23}X_e \leqq k_{23},$$

where 12 denotes shipment from 1 to 2 and so on.

These inequations describe the limits to which transportation of goods can be made from one region to another and will depend on r the number of regions.

Assuming equal weights for all regions we wish to maximize output over the plan period. Thus we have:

$$\text{maximize} \quad X = \sum_{t=1}^{5} \sum_{r} [_rX_e(t)].$$

Supposing there is one region where we want to push the engineering industries then we simply introduce a weighting system thus, (assuming three regions);

$$\text{maximize} \quad \sum_{t=1}^{5} [\lambda_1 \cdot {}_1X_e(t) + \lambda_2 \cdot {}_2X_e(t) + \lambda_3 \cdot {}_3X_e(t)].$$

These models determine the location of new installations for the five-year period. The optimal output of each year becomes part of the solution for the whole system and the Five-Year Plan is presented as a packet with certain optimal properties. The solution of each output is a separate figure with no specific link with the output achieved in the same field earlier.

7.3

In the previous section, we discussed models where time entered into the set of equations, the interdependence between two sets of time variables was procured through dynamic equilibrium conditions made necessary because of the dependence of the outputs of one period on the outputs of the next period. We could make this interdependence more realistic by expressing the technical possibilities of one period as depending on the actual achieved outputs of the earlier period say, generating a set of recursive programmes.

The simplest form of this model may be stated as follows:

$$\text{maximize} \quad (z_1(t)\, x_1(t) + \ldots + z_n(t)\, x_n(t)),$$

$$\text{subject to} \quad \left.\begin{array}{l} x_1(t) \leqq (1 + \lambda_1)\, x_1(t-1), \\ \dotfill \\ x_n(t) \leqq (1 + \lambda_n)\, x_n(t-1), \\ x_1(t) + x_2(t) + \ldots x_n(t) = k. \end{array}\right\} \quad (1)$$

This way of visualizing a programme is highly plausible. It has been generally seen that for most industries the maximum percentage rate of production expansion at any given time, after the start of the programme, depends on the type of activity but is relatively independent of the initial production level and it is generally a constant.

In such a sequence the solution of any one year, therefore, furnishes the boundary values for the next year.

During any one period, as soon as the constraint sets in (1) are known, the growth process becomes a difference equation of the form

$$x(t) = x(t_0)\, \gamma^{t-t_0}. \tag{2}$$

The flexibility constraint is defined by the difference equation. We can consider the family of difference equations as rails along which possible movements could take place. The maximizing of the objective function acts like 'a switch shutting the variables along one set of time paths', then switching it to a second set and so on indefinitely. Therefore we may say that these time paths describe different phases which are joined together at each critical period by the maximizing function. A perspective plan of fifteen years may consist of three phases of five years duration, passing from one phase to the next takes place by a maximizing function at the end of a five-year period.

Here we can consider in passing the general dynamic form of the Leontief system. It is generally recognized that a determinate solution of the Leontief system is obtained only under a special type of initial configuration which in planning models may not always be achieved in practice. In case such an initial configuration does not exist additional rules of choice must be described and the dynamic Leontief form could be described as a programme of the type given below:

$$\text{maximize} \quad x_2(t+1),$$

$$\left.\begin{aligned}
(1 - a_{11})\, X_1(t) - a_{12} X_2(t) &\geqslant X_1(t+1) - S_1(t), \\
- a_{21} X_1(t) + (1 + a_{22})\, X_2(t) &\geqslant X_2(t+1) - S_2(t), \\
b_{11} X_1(t) + b_{12} X_2(t) &\leqslant S_1(t), \\
b_{21} X_1(t) + b_{22} X_2(t) &\leqslant S_2(t), \\
X_1(t) \geqslant 0, \quad X_2(t) &\geqslant 0,
\end{aligned}\right\} \tag{3}$$

where X_1 and X_2 are sector outputs, S_1 and S_2 are savings level, the b's are capital coefficients, etc.

Under such conditions, we can consider a solution of this system by some optimizing principle which pushes the economy from one phase to another at crucial points, where questions of choice arise, while in between phases the solutions are generated by the dynamic system itself.

The recursive set up shown in (1) will generate a system of simultaneous difference inequations and for the solution of these a set of objective functions which could, in the beginning, be considered as exogenously supplied. Thus perspective programming may be described as recursive programming with equations tracing time paths for five years, say, while the objective function works every fifth year switching the path from one to another five-year plan.

A linear programme can always be represented (if a solution exists) by a system of equated constraints.

Thus, our system in (1) may be written up

$$x_1(t) = (1 + \lambda_i)\, x_i(t-1) \quad \text{for binding } i \text{ in (1),}$$

$$\text{and} \qquad x_j = 0 \qquad\qquad \text{for all non-binding equations.} \tag{4}$$

If a solution exists then we can always formally represent the solution as above.

A phase of a recursive programme can now be described as a system of such equated constraints and the equated constraint system will describe the time path of the variables for the duration of the phase.

The multiple phase behaviour of the system is then determined by a dynamic system of equated constraints.

We consider the following system as a model for recursive programme planning. Let us say that there are two sectors x_1 and x_2 and that there is a preference system for the phases and w_1 and w_2 weights attached to the sectors.

Let us further suppose that while increasing output we can never expand any year's output by more than a certain percentage of the previous year. Then we have the following system:

$$\text{maximize} \quad w_1 x_1(t) + w_2 x_2(t),$$

$$x_1(t) \leqslant L_1 = (1 + \beta_1)\, x_1(t-1), \quad x^2(t) \leqslant L_2 = (1 + \beta_2)\, x_2(t-1). \tag{5}$$

Consider β_1, β_2 constants denoting the limits imposed by the gestation period for training up skilled labour. Let w_1 and w_2 be exogenous. Then this gives a recursive programme.

Now consider the following:

$$\text{maximize} \quad w_1 x_1(t) + w_2 x_2(t),$$

$$x_1(t) \leqslant L_1 = \psi_1[x_1(t-1), x_2(t-1)],$$
$$x_2(t) \leqslant L_2 = \psi_2[x_1(t-1), x_2(t-1)], \tag{6}$$

where the restraint may be due to technical rigidities of some kind operating along with skilled personnel scarcity. There is a certain level of production in the first sector which fixes a limit to the capacity that could be achieved in the second sector. Consider the first sector as the fabrication of machines for building other machines, the second sector as the fabrication of machines for the consumption goods industry and the consumption goods industry itself. Then it may be said that a certain level of the first sector will automatically settle what we can do for the second sector in the next period. Three sectors will make this even clearer. Thus:

$$\text{maximize} \quad w_1 x_1(t) + w_2 x_2(t) + w_3 x_3(t),$$

$$x_1(t) \leqslant \psi_1(x_1(t-1)),$$
$$x_2(t) \leqslant \psi_2(x_1(t-1), x_2(t-1)),$$
$$x_3(t) \leqslant \psi_3(x_2(t-1), x_3(t-1)). \tag{7}$$

Now we formulate this in equated constraints. They become a set of difference equations for each phase.

The above model can be described in equated constraints, assuming they are all binding, thus

$$\left.\begin{aligned}
x_1(t) &= \psi_1 x_1(t-1), \\
x_2(t) &= \psi_2[x_1(t-1), x_2(t-1)], \\
x_3(t) &= \psi_3[x_2(t-1), x_3(t-1)], \\
x_1 &\geqslant 0.
\end{aligned}\right\} \tag{8}$$

These constraints describe the output levels in t as a function of the output levels in $(t-1)$ in a system of simultaneous difference equations. The solution in a linear set up may be written as,

$$\left.\begin{aligned}
x_1(t) &= \alpha_{11}\pi_1^t + \alpha_{12}\pi_2^t + \alpha_{13}\pi_3^t, \\
x_2(t) &= \alpha_{21}\pi_1^t + \alpha_{22}\pi_2^t + \alpha_{23}\pi_3^t, \\
x_3(t) &= \alpha_{31}\pi_1^t + \alpha_{32}\pi_2^t + \alpha_{33}\pi_3^t,
\end{aligned}\right\} \tag{9}$$

depending on π_1, π_2 and π_3, the roots of the characteristic equation respectively. This is the growth path as prescribed by the constraint system, which is binding.

In considering the above group of programmes we took the preference function as exogenously given for each phase. We now consider a closed dynamic model which will generate its own objective function through a self-adjusting growth process. Consider for example an objective function:

$$\text{maximize} \quad \sum_i w_i x_i(t),$$

where w_i is described by,

$$w_i = w_{0i}[\alpha + \beta_i.t + \gamma_i.t^2] \tag{10}$$

so we have:

$$\text{maximize} \quad \Sigma w_i x_i(t) = \Sigma w_{0i}[\alpha_i + \beta_i.t + \gamma_i.t^2]x_i(t)$$

$$x_i \leqq L_i \quad \text{(as before).}$$

Now, such a weight system will automatically generate new sequences over time with varying t.

Consider again as follows:

$$\text{maximize} \quad w_1 x_1(t) + w_2 x_2(t),$$

subject to
$$\left.\begin{aligned}
x_1(t) &\leqslant \psi_1(x_1(t-1), x_2(t-1)), \\
x_2(t) &\leqslant \psi_2(x_1(t-1), x_2(t-1)), \\
w_1(t) &= \phi_1[L_1(t-1) - x_1(t-1)], \\
&= \phi_1[fx_1(t-2), x_2(t-2) - x_1(t-1)], \\
w_2(t) &= \phi_2[fx_1(t-2), x_2(t-2) - x_2(t-1)].
\end{aligned}\right\} \tag{11}$$

Here the weights are generated by the same process as the constraints but with a lag increased by one. If the limits of the coming year's outputs are functions of last year's output, then the weights of the current year are a function of the gap in the first year (deficit or surplus) and therefore functions also of the last but one year's outputs. This generates an infinity of objective functions and boundaries in sequence, weights being automatically adjusted to gaps.

Consider this model for a location problem similar to one described before. Let us have $x_{ij}(t)$ as the amount transported from i to j and let $R_i(t)$ be the requirement of the ith region in t. Let $C_{ij}(t)$ be the cost of transporting from i to j. Let us assume that transportation capacities cannot be increased by more than a certain percentage each year in any particular area. Then, the following programme may be constructed:

$$\text{minimize} \quad \sum_i \sum_j C_{ij} x_{ij}(t),$$

$$\sum_i x_{ij}(t) = R_i(t), \quad \sum_j x_{ij}(t) \leqslant (1 + \beta_i) \left(\sum_j x_{ij}(t-1) \right). \tag{12}$$

In a system of equated constraints there will be some equations among the latter group that will become equalities giving

$$\sum_j x_{ij}(t) = \lambda_{0i} \left[\sum_j x_{ij}(t-1) \right]. \tag{13}$$

The model will give for equalities new installations which will be utilized depending on the values of β_i.

If a set of equations is binding then it will indicate a full utilization of potential capacity on these terminal points, consider the effect of a change in costs. Let the cost trends be defined by the equation

$$C_{ij} = C_{ij}^0 + (\beta_{ij} t + \gamma_{ij} t^2). \tag{14}$$

Denoting the polynomial in bracket by λ we have, thus:

$$\text{minimize} \quad \Sigma(C_{ij}^0 + \lambda) x_{ij}(t), \tag{15}$$

$$\sum_i x_{ij}(t) = R_i, \quad \sum_j x_{ij}(t) = (1 + \beta_i) \left[\sum_j x_{ij}(t-1) \right]. \tag{16}$$

An obvious generalization will be to express C_{ij} as functions of the gap between capacity and utilization in the previous year. If additional capacities have to be built up this can also be done by introducing inequations,

$$\sum_j x_{ij}(t) \geqslant [1 + \theta_i] \sum_j x_{ij}(t-1). \tag{17}$$

To close the model dynamically C_{ij} may be made specific functions of t in some way. Thus the C's may be made functions of the gap between last year's consumption and capacity giving in the ith region,

$$P_i = \psi_i[L_i - x_i], \tag{18}$$

and

$$C_{ij} = P_i + T_{ij},$$

where P_i is the production cost in the ith region and T_{ij} is the cost of transportation from i to j per unit. Then the model will again be dynamically closed.

In all the above discussions we have considered only the primal form of the programme. It should not be difficult to formulate and interpret the dual corresponding to these forms.

In this connection a small note on integer programming will not be out of place. All the problems stated above have been formulated in terms of quantities of outputs. But new installations have definite sizes attached to them which are indivisible and discrete. Thus a factory can be designed to produce 10,000 tons or 20,000 tons and so on but not for all values between 10 and 20,000 tons. Therefore, capacity in discrete integral size is included as additional constraints on the system. Such problems are approached by the so called integer programming techniques or by dynamic programming. Thus a typical problem may be stated as follows:

$$\text{maximize} \quad \Sigma b_{ij} x_{ij},$$

subject to
$$\left.\begin{aligned} &\Sigma C_{ij} x_{ij} \leqslant C_t, \\ &0 \leqslant x_{ij} \leqslant 1, \\ &x_j \text{ has integral values only.} \end{aligned}\right\} \tag{19}$$

The integer solution due to Gomory uses Simplex methods but adds new restrictions in the form of cutting planes to the original set. This involves the addition of supplementary linear restrictions which cut away part of the original feasible region without disturbing so-called lattice points of feasible integer-solution. By successive cuts a new programme emerges whose solution is an integer solution to the original problem. The restriction cannot be stated in the beginning but emerges with the computation.

7.4

In the concluding section we briefly discuss dynamic programming.

It must be said at the outset that in the present state of dynamic programming most economic problems could not be numerically solved with this technique. But the approach of dynamic programming does offer us a powerful tool which will definitely have many applications to planning problems in future. The best way of demonstrating the logic of the technique is to start from an illustration. Let us suppose that there are different types of industrial projects which are to be developed in a particular area. Now suppose that the available capital is limited and therefore a choice has to be made to put in those units that will give the maximum net return to our capital. The problem is how to choose the projects with the maximum net return and how to decide the size of each unit given the capital cost per unit size, the net return per unit size by type and the size of the capital budget.[1]

If n_i denotes the number of projects of the ith type and if x_i and r_i are the capital cost and net return per unit of the ith type and no fractional

---

[1] See Bellman's *Applied dynamic programming*.

Table 7.1

Type Number of project	Capital Cost per unit	Net return per unit
1	20	72
2	18	60
3	14	40
4	12	27
5	10	20
6	16	50
7	22	85
8	24	96

Table 7.2. *Solutions for some values of the capital limit*

Capital Limit	Total return	Size of unit by Project	
		Project No.	Size of Unit
100	384	8	4
95	373	7	1
		8	3
91	351	7	3
		8	1
89	340	7	4

projects are permitted then our object is to:

$$\text{maximize} \quad \Sigma r_i n_i,$$

subject to $\Sigma x_i n_i = K$, where n_i is integral and non-negative.

If the last restriction on integer values were not included the problem would have been of the straight forward linear programming type but the integer condition makes this unapproachable by the standard linear programming technique. An available powerful technique is the approach of dynamic programming.

The basic approach in dynamic programming is to look at these problems as if it were indeed a sequential decision problem in time but in the reverse order.

In the ordinary linear programming approach this difficulty is faced if the variable takes distinct values only. In the functional equations technique of dynamic programming the whole situation is considered comprehensively and a choice is made by enumerating all possible efficient combinations.

We restate the specific allocation problem we are considering.

Let x_i denote the cost allocation to the ith activity then total funds available lead to the constraint

$$\Sigma x_i = x \text{ (say)} \quad \text{with } x_i \geqslant 0.$$

We want to maximize the function $R(x_1, x_2, ..., x_N)$, when N is a non-negative integer.

We write,

$$R(x_1, x_2, ..., x_N) = g_i(x_i) + g_2(x_2) + ...g_N(x_N).$$

We thus embed it in a family of allocation processes. Instead of a particular quantity of capital and a number of projects we consider the entire family of projects N. In a static process we introduce, artificially, a time-like property by requiring the allocations to be made one at a time. An arbitrary amount is assigned to the last activity first—that is the dynamic process is looked at from the reverse side up. We consider the Nth activity first, the $(N-1)$th activity next and so on.

Now, depending on the value of N consider the sequence of function

$$f_N(x), \quad N = 1, 2, ..., x \geqslant 0;$$
$$f_N(x) = \max_{x_i} [R(x_1, x_2, ..., x_N)] \quad \text{with} \quad x_i \geqslant 0, \sum_{i=1} x_i = x,$$

where $f_N(x)$ defines the optimal return from allocating x amount of resources to N activities. Now $f_N(x) = 0$ when N is 0 and $f_1(x) = g_1$.

Whatever choice is made for x_N let us consider the remaining resources $x - x_N$ which have to be used for $N-1$ activities.

Define an optimal return for $(N-1)$ activities with $x - x_N$ amount of resources as $f_{N-1}(x - x_N)$ so that the total return from Nth and $(N-1)$th activity is $g_N(x_N) + f_{N-1}(x - x_N)$.

We thus obtain

$$f_N(x) = \max_{0 \leqslant x_N \leqslant x} [g_N(x_N + f_{N-1}(x - x_N)], \quad N = 2, 3, ..., x \geqslant 0,$$

with $f_1(x) = g_1(x)$.

This is the well known 'principle of optimality' which says that given any decision, whatever it is, later decisions should always be optimal for the state resulting from the first decision.

The process thus consists of picking up the set of optimal policies of the $(N-1)$th stage corresponding to the whole set of decisions regarding the Nth stage. From this enumeration we now try to pick up the maximal sum of the combined decision resulting from any Nth and the corresponding optimal $(N-1)$th decision.

The method is thus enumerative. That is, we can think in terms of determining the maximum value by a shear enumeration of cases. The principle of optimality tells us that having chosen an initial x_N we do not examine all policies but only those which are optimal for an $(N-1)$ process.

'The dynamic programming approach automatically imbeds the original problem in a form of analogous problem in which the basic parameter x and N assume sets of values which permit us to respond to this fundamental question.' In the allocation process, for example, solutions are found for activities ranging from 1 to N and for quantities of resources from 0 to x. So that the solution gives us an immense variety of sub-problems.

The difficulties of the process, however, as the dimensions increase put it out of practical use in most planning problems except those of a simpler type.

This approach does become powerful in capital budgeting and similar problems, that is problems where there are alternative projects at different points of time and where maximization of some type is to be carried out with constraints on capacity and no fractional projects being permitted.

7.5. CONCLUSION

With the development of programming techinques many of the normative models of economic theory can now be given in empirical content for the first time. Further, programming offers a set of tools which are very flexible and which could be adjusted, or suitably formulated to answer diverse types of problems. Further, these tools are still in their very early stage of development and the tool box is expanding fast. With the simultaneous development of the super-fast electronic computers most of the problems which formerly could not be even handled empirically can now be solved. Therefore we are, fast approaching a phase where programming and econometric techniques will combine to make the science of prediction and guidance in economics a matter of practiced skill and training rather than of intuition and the inspiration of a genius.

CHAPTER 8

THE INTER-DEPENDENCE
OF CAPITAL IN AN INPUT-OUTPUT
FRAMEWORK

8.1

The conventional form of the Leontief model deals with current production. It involves (i) a matrix of transactions representing the flows of commodities between different industrial sectors engaged in current production; (ii) a vector of final demands placed on producing sectors by the non-producing sector, and (iii) a matrix of coefficients relating flows in sectors with total transactions of the inter-industrial blocks. Representing the transaction matrix in partitioned form we can write:

$$\begin{bmatrix} x & f \\ \hline y^1 & 0 \end{bmatrix},$$

where x is a sub-matrix of order $n-1$, f a vector of final demands, y^1 a row vector representing net factor costs and 0 a scalar. If X is a vector of total outputs of $n-1$ industries the accounting identity may be written in matrix notation as

$$X = xi + f, \tag{1}$$

where f is a column vector with $n-1$ elements and x is the matrix of intermediate outputs and i the unit sum vector. The assumption that inputs are related to outputs can be expressed as

$$x = a\hat{X}, \tag{2}$$

where a, the coefficient matrix, is of the order $n-1$ and $\hat{X}$ is a diagonal matrix whose elements are the elements of X.

By substitution, we obtain

$$X = (I-a)^{-1}f, \tag{3}$$

where I is a unit matrix of the order $n-1$. This gives us the so called Leontief open model connecting the total output vector X with the final output vector f by means of the matrix multiplier.

The matrix multiplier $(I-a)^{-1}$ shows, in each column, the supplies directly and indirectly required from every industry to satisfy a unit of final demand for the product of the industry named at the top of the column.

The matrix multiplier throws light on the structure of industry by showing the indirect relationship existing between different branches of production.

This description of the Leontief model shows that the use of the model is mainly restricted to current production levels and their structure.

In many countries, under different levels of planning, however, quick description and prediction is required of capital implications and inter-sectoral capital relationships of given final demand targets. That is, planners are interested in a simple concept relating final demands with capital capacities directly and indirectly required, as is given in the case of the matrix multiplier which provides a simple expression of the direct and indirect current outputs associated with given levels of final demands. In such cases the Leontief model is used initially to discover the current output levels associated with a unit of final demand. Subsequently this is translated into capital through the use of some familiar device like the *output-capital* ratios. These are defined by

$$X = \hat{\lambda}K, \tag{4}$$

where X is a vector of outputs, K a vector of capital employed in sectors and $\hat{\lambda}$, a diagonal matrix relating capital to output. In this case capital is defined as a composite commodity evaluated at some base period price, assuming there is no change in its composition, of the different components entering into it during the period under consideration.

It is suggested here that instead of using these two models in sequence we may develop a matrix describing the capital relationship between different sectors by combining these two steps into a single step defined by a single coefficient. Thus if x_{ij} is the flow from i to j and if we have

$$x_{ij} = a_{ij} X_j$$

defining the level of input of type i to the output of type j we can multiply into this relationship from (4) giving

$$X_j = \lambda_j, K_j$$

so that we have $x_{ij} = a_{ij} \lambda_j K_j = \beta_{ij}, K_j$ (say).

β_{ij} then gives us the amount of the ith commodity directly required to keep a unit of capital of the jth type in activity. Assuming, therefore, that a vector of capital output ratios exists, as in (4), we can substitute this into (3) to obtain $X = \hat{\lambda}K = (\mathrm{I} - a)^{-1}f,$

or $K = \hat{\lambda}^{-1} (\mathrm{I} - a)^{-1} f = \beta^{-1}f,$

where β^{-1} is the matrix obtained by matrix multiplication from

$$\hat{\lambda}^{-1}(\mathrm{I} - a)^{-1}.$$

The elements of β^{-1} define the direct and indirect capital requirements of a specified level of final demand.

The advantage of integrating the capital output ratios into the matrix, instead of considering them in sequence, is that the inverse matrix β^{-1} now gives the sectoral capital repercussions of final demands directly and indirectly involved in a single expression.

Probably this approach has no new theoretical implications but it may have its uses in practical operations where capital implications of different types of programmes may have to be compared.

We may demonstrate, by a simple illustration, the practical use of this approach. Let the input coefficient matrix $(1-a)$ be denoted by the following:

$$\begin{matrix} 1 & -0.6 & -0.2 \\ -0.1 & 1 & -0.2 \\ -0.5 & -0.2 & 1 \end{matrix}$$

Further, let output-capital ratios be denoted by the following diagonal matrix.

$$\begin{matrix} 2 & & \\ & 3 & \\ & & 3 \end{matrix}$$

Then the matrix multiplier $(1-a)^{-1}$ is given by the following matrix:

$$\begin{matrix} 1.3043 & 0.8696 & 0.4348 \\ 0.2717 & 1.2228 & 0.2989 \\ 0.7065 & 0.6793 & 1.2772 \end{matrix}$$

and matrix β^{-1} is denoted by

$$\begin{matrix} 2.6086 & 1.7392 & 0.8696 \\ 0.8151 & 3.6684 & 0.8967 \\ 2.1195 & 2.0379 & 3.8376 \end{matrix}$$

We are already familiar with the use of the matrix multiplier which tells us, in effect, that for a unit of final demand of type 2 the direct and indirect consumption of output of sector 1 in sector 2 is 0.8696. If we now turn to the second matrix denoted by β^{-1} we can say that the direct and indirect capital requirement of type 1 to produce a unit of final demand of a commodity of type 2 is 1.7392. If we are interested, for example, in the question what is the capital implication of type 1, 2, and 3 in a bill of goods of unit 1, of type 1 respectively, this is given by the vector 2.6086, 0.8151, and 2.1195.

The matrix β^{-1} thus gives us a convenient way of summarizing the capital implications of any bill of goods, just as the matrix multiplier gives us the total output implications of a given bill of goods.

8.2

To pass from this static study to the dynamic form of the Leontief model we first expand the final demand into its components, e.g. consumption and capital goods supplied by the different sectors in the accounting identity given in (1). Expanding (1) we can write

$$X = xi + C + I(s),$$

where $I(s)$ denotes the vector of supply of capital goods from different sectors.

Let us now define a matrix of capital input ratios which gives the composition of a unit of capital used in the different sectors. Let this matrix be denoted by B. Since $I(s)$ gives the vector of capital goods supplied, breaking it up into the components with the help of the matrix B, we can write

$$I(s) = B I(d),$$

where $I(d)$ is the vector of investments in different sectors.

With the above two sets of equations, we can now write

$$(1 - a) \lambda K(t) = C + B I(d) = C + B[K(t) - K(t-1)].$$

This gives, for assigned consumption levels, the dynamic form for the growth of capital in all sectors.

8.3

The present model can be usefully extended into the field of inter-regional planning studies. Its use is specially assured by the fact that in most planning economies capital shortage and the problem of the regional location of specific types of capital makes it necessary to study alternative ways of fixing targets so that the capital existing in different regions is best utilized in the course of producing the given final output for the nation. We shall, in the present case, first formulate a conventional type of regional model which combines input-output with some form of linear programming and then show how, by translating it into the terminology of capital, we can make more significant use of it for developmental purposes. Let the balance equations for the nth region be written in the form

$$\sum_j {}_n a_{ij} X_j + \sum_m {}_{mn} X_i + {}_n C_i + {}_n I(s)_i = {}_n X_i,$$

where the first subscript refers to the region of origin and the second subscript to that of destination, other symbols being interpreted for the same variables, as before, but as scalars.

The constraints on the transport available from region to region may be expressed by the following equations:

$$\sum_m \sum_j W_j \cdot {}_{mn} X_j \le T_{mn},$$

where W_j denotes the weight per Leontief unit of a commodity of a particular jth type and T_{mn} denotes the total weight that can be carried from m to n—the assumption being that it will be used in full.

Using the above two sets of equations as constraints we can now use the linear programming format to minimize an objective function defining total costs (labour and transportation) as follows:

$$\sum_m \sum_n \sum_i {}_{mn} X_i ({}_m P_i + {}_{mn} P'_i) + \sum_m \sum_n \sum_i ({}_m X_i - {}_{mn} X_i) {}_m P_i.$$

P denotes production costs and P' denotes the cost of transportation from m to n. Other symbols are defined as before.

Into the above set we now bring the capital-output ratios and the capital-input ratios defined earlier. The balance equations are reformulated for the regions, in terms of capital in productive use, as follows:

$$\sum_j {}_n a_{ij}\,{}_n\lambda_j\,{}_nK_j + \sum_m {}_m\lambda_i \cdot {}_{nm}K_i - \sum_m {}_n\lambda_i \cdot {}_{nm}K_i + {}_nC_i + \sum_j {}_nb_{ij} \cdot \Delta K_j = {}_n\lambda_i \cdot {}_nK_i.$$

I have assumed here that the output capital ratio λ differs in both regions and industries.

The transportation constraint can be recast in capital terminology as below:

$$\Sigma W_j \cdot {}_{mn}\tau_{ij}\,X_j = {}_{mn}\tau\,\chi_{mn},$$

where χ is capital employed to carry a volume of transport T and τ is the ratio of capital to output. We thus have

$$T = \tau \cdot \chi.$$

We now define the objective function as follows:

$$\text{minimize} \quad \sum_n \sum_j {}_nK_j + \sum_m \sum_n \sum_j {}_{mn}\chi_j.$$

Here λ and τ represent the capital on production, other than transportation and transportation activities, respectively.

The objective function thus gives us an expression for capital employed to produce in all regions for all sectors and the transportation capital employed to carry goods of all types to different destinations.

Minimizing this objective function, subject to the two sets of equations given before, we arrive at the regional production and distribution pattern that makes the best use of available capital in different regions and also fulfils final demand targets.

Note that investment targets for the next period are arbitrarily fixed so that the optimization procedure is strictly at one point of time. Thus the present employment of capital is a subject of optimization, in the present model, but not investment allocation for a future period.

This optimization procedure gives the regional flow pattern that can be used most effectively at present to produce the required final demands.

This is only one way in which the problem can be formulated for planning purposes. There may be others, depending on the objectives of the planners, but in many of them this simultaneous use of the capital-output ratios or labour-output ratio and input coefficients together, may lead to many quick procedures for efficient planning, where considerations of capital or labour are important to the planners.

CHAPTER 9

INTER-REGIONAL MODELS
AND THE PROBLEM OF SUBSTITUTION[1]

9.1

Studies of models in inter-regional input-output analysis often suffer from a lack of economic realism. The general trend of such models is to assume, in some way or other, constancy of trading patterns, for which no adequate economic reasons are produced. The possibility of substituting one regional flow for another is not given the importance it deserves.

The problem of the substitution of different inputs is present in a similar, though less pronounced way. When elaborate tables are prepared and models constructed for them it is often found that many sectors become potential substitutes amongst which choice must lie on grounds other than those of the technical rules of production. Thus, while consumption of energy by some specific sector may be subject to technical ratios of production, there may not be any strict reason, other than an economic one for taking to coal, or oil, or atomic energy to meet this.

Several models have been proposed to deal with the problem of regional flows. Some of these models pay attention to substitution possibilities and some do not. The object of this paper is to review a number of these models and also to present some alternative constructions to handle the substitution problem. We shall confine our discussion to the problem of regional substitution though it will be obvious that technical substitutions can also be handled by similar types of models.

The present series of models will be tested for their efficacy in describing or predicting flow pattern in only one particular type of economy. This is the economy of the Indian Union during the last ten years or so. Such economies are different in an important respect from the more mature economies of the West. They are characterized by rapid structural changes through substitution due to the growth of industries in regions where previously almost no industrial units existed. Any model describing the problems of such economies has to be specially devised to meet this aspect of quick change. Adequate handling of the substitution problem, particularly in such models, becomes essential for a realistic approach. We can characterize the two most important features of such economies

[1] This paper was prepared by the author as a Rockefeller Fellow in Harvard Economic Research Project during 1963. It was presented to a seminar and the author acknowledges comments he had on it from Professor W. W. Leontief.

which bring out the scope of substitution in inter-regional model building work as follows:

1. The economy is rapidly changing; new demand units and supply sources are coming up all the time, leading to constant revisions of the existing pattern of flows.

2. The sectors, in most regions, in important commodites are working at full capacity so that, to some extent, regional distribution at any point of time is determined by available supplies at that time only, a situation similar to rationing.

The result of these limitations of inter-regional models is naturally very great. The structure of distribution is subject to rather violent fluctuations frequently due to large scale substitutions. Models suitable for a more stable type of economy may not necessarily fit this kind of economy.

In the following section, we shall review models with rigidly fixed coefficients introduced by Moses and Isard, in their pioneer work in the formulation of regional flow models. We shall subsequently discuss a fixed coefficient model developed by Leontief and some flexible changing coefficient models, allowing substitution, developed as a more suitable mechanism for describing regional flows in a changing economy.

9.2

The original approach, due to Isard,[1] considered the same industry in two regions as two distinct industries and proceeded with the analysis in the traditional Leontief style.

Subsequent refinements suggested by Moses[2] consisted of a set of trading coefficients along with the usual set of input coefficients. Thus Moses defined the production function, of the nth region as

$$_na_{ij} = \frac{_nx_{ij}}{_nX_j}. \tag{1}$$

He then assumed a regional coefficient so that if $_nx_{ij}$ denotes the inflow of the ith type of goods from m to all industries in n then, we have,

$$_{mn}t_i = \frac{_{mn}r_i}{_nR_i}, \tag{2}$$

where $_nR_i$ is the total commodity of type i imported from all regions. We then have the assumption that if $_na_{ij}$ is the requirement of industry of type i in region j then, of this, $_na_{ij} \cdot {}_{mn}t_i$ units will be coming from region m. Thus the individual inputs are replaced by the corresponding expressions $_{mn}t_i \cdot {}_na_{ij}$. These are then substituted into the balance relations.

[1] Inter-regional analysis and regional development. Walter Isard, *American Economic Review*, vol. 43, May 1953.

Inter-regional and regional input-output analysis—Walter Isard, *Review of Economics & Statistics*, 1951.

[2] The stability of inter-regional trading pattern and input-output analysis. Leon. N. Moses, *American Economic Review*, vol. XIV, no. 5.

A somewhat similar formulation was made by Leontief. Commodities are broadly classified as regional or national according to the inter-regional flow of the commodity using the model for the entire economy. Then the regional commodities, as they are contained within the regions, could be tackled separately and solved. Using the usual notations the system was as follows:

technical coefficients,
$$a_{ik} = \frac{x_{ik}}{X_k};$$
(3)

regional coefficients for national industries,
$$m_j^r = \frac{{}_m X_j}{X_j};$$
(4)

for the regionally balanced group the equations were
$$_m X_i - \sum_j {}_{mi} a_{ij} \cdot {}_m X_j = {}_m Y_i;$$
(5)

for the entire economy, the equations were
$$X_i - \sum_k a_{ik} X_k = Y_i;$$
(6)

for regional economies we get, therefore,
$$_m X_i = \sum_j B_{ij} \cdot {}_m X_j + \sum_k C_{ik} \cdot {}_m Y_k.$$
(7)

Regional requirements of national commodities are given by the first term on the right and local requirements by the second.

B_{ij} are obtained from the input coefficients and regional coefficients while C_{ik} are obtained from input coefficients.

Obviously in these approaches a set of pure trading coefficients for regional flows have been assumed constant. We do not have any economically valid reason for assuming that inputs which are substitutes must come from one area rather than another area. It is obvious that if a commodity is produced in many regions the source of supply chosen by any unit which is using it will be dictated by many circumstances. The most important are likely to be price, transportation facilities, time, etc. The supplies from different regions are always potential substitutes and sources of supply may be changed if these conditions change.

We may now take up a fixed coefficient model, subsequently developed by Leontief,[1] for the purpose of determining regional flows.

It has been described as a gravity model in the sense that the structure of the model is not unlike the usual gravity models of the physical sciences. The gravity model of Leontief may be defined as below:

$$_{mn} x_i = \frac{{}_n R_i \cdot {}_m X_i}{\sum\limits_m X_i} {}_{mn} Q_i,$$
(8)

[1] Wassily Leontief with Alan Strout, Multi-regional input-output analysis, in *Structural interdependence and economic development*. Editor: T. Barna.

where the symbols are as before. Q_i being a constant estimated from data, with respect a base year, $_{mn}x_i$ denoting input from m to n of commodity i and $_mX_i$ denoting output of commodity i in region m and

$$_nR_i = \sum_m {}_{mn}x_i.$$

The Leontief gravity model tries to explain regional flows by considering the attraction of a volume of demand at a point and the sales push of a volume of supply from a given centre. All other forces are estimated through a coefficient evaluated from one set of observed values of the system. The coefficient thus may include the effect of distance, cost and other factors. The basic limitation, once more of the model, is that it does not allow regional substitutions. The result is that once, in a given situation, a coefficient has been determined, the coefficient, as in the Leontief input-output system, is fixed once and for all. In a problem of regional flows, where technical factors are of less importance and particularly in areas of rapid change, the rigidity of the model becomes apparent.

Models similar to the Leontief gravity model, but more explicit in defining other variables rather than leaving it to a coefficient evaluated empirically, were also tried out by the author. Two strictly formal types of gravity models tried out are given below:

$$_{mn}x_i = \frac{_nR_i \cdot {}_mX_i}{_{mn}d^2}, \tag{9}$$

$$_{mn}x_i = \frac{_nR_i \cdot {}_mX_i}{_{mn}d\sqrt{_{mn}d}}, \tag{10}$$

other symbols being defined as before, $_{mn}d$ denoting the average distance of region m from region n.

The main difference between these models and that of the Leontief type is the explicit treatment of distance in a non-linear form. This was done because it was found that distance has a more than proportional effect on the pattern of flow. Slight variation of these substituting costs of transportation were also tried out as follows:

$$_{mn}x_i = \frac{_nR_i \cdot {}_mX_i}{_{mn}C_i}. \tag{11}$$

It was seen that the limitation of the cost approach was that the cost figures were not sufficiently sensitive to all the implications involved in transportation problems arising in long distance flows. Long distance transportation is not only more expensive, it is also uncertain, time consuming and imperfectly known. The cost of transport is often a poor underestimate of all these various factors involved.

Finally, we tried out a regression model of the form given below:

$$_{mn}x_i = (_nR_i)^\alpha \cdot (_mX_i)^\beta \cdot (_{mn}d)^\gamma. \tag{12}$$

This model was tried out first for the area as a whole and subsequently for each specific region separately. The prefixes α, β, γ were evaluated from a single set of observations at one point of time. The common feature of all the models described above is that they are continuous rather than discrete. This continuous form, it was seen, places us at some disadvantage. An increase in the volume of supply or demand seems to transcend the limitations of distance and other factors, and there is no way of distinguishing between supplies from a distance and from a neighbourhood which always has the same influence as it had in the beginning. This is to say that the coefficients which are found once are perpetuated, even though the basic supply of sources and demand centres have changed considerably. This rigid approach to regional flow problems is unrealistic, particularly in a developing area. Regional flows are rather more sensitive to cost and distance and transportation factors. This is even more so in a changing industrial structure. Therefore it is necessary to bring the aspect of substitutions, both in theory and in application, into the model more explicitly.

9.3

Keeping in mind the limitations of the approach so far suggested, we shall now try to introduce models in which the substitution possibilities of one region for another, or of one input for another, are given full play. Sectoral or regional substitutions are to be treated here, not as two distinct phenomena, but as aspects of the problem of substitution itself.

In introducing this new concept it may be useful to start with the idea of the ring structure introduced by Frisch.[1] The idea of a ring structure can be easily explained by an example. Let us say that there are sectors supplying coal and oil respectively. Let us further assume that both coal and oil are available in both regions A and B in a system containing A, B, and C. An industry in region C has a specific requirement of energy which may be supplied either from coal, or oil, or both.

If one uses a short period model with a large number of industrial sectors, then one may assume that a particular sector has a well defined energy coefficient which is a fraction of its total product in a suitable unit. In such a case a fairly well defined energy coefficient may not be unrealistic as a first approximation.

But we cannot go on from that to assume that each specific kind of energy can be expressed in the same way. Often the first given problem is to make a choice from a variety of energy sources in the cheapest way. Thus an industry may well have to choose between imported oil, domestic hydro-electric power, coal or atomic energy. It would be unrealistic to take them altogether in one single sector called energy production. These sources have to be considered separately.

But if all these energy sectors are kept separate there are many receiving sectors for which it would be absurd to assume that each sector

---

[1] Oslo Channel Model. Ragnar Frisch (unpublished).

needs a fixed quantity of each of these specific types of energy. While it is realistic to assume that the total energy requirement is a fixed fraction it would be artificial to rigidly divide it up into requirements for specific types of energy.

Similar considerations apply to many other types of deliveries to production sectors. Sometimes it may, for instance, be a question of replacing one kind of raw material for another, or of replacing a certain item of complementary import by a similar kind of product from the domestic sector, though it may not be equally satisfactory. In this we are facing the general problem of substitution.

If a certain sector, say j, requires a certain kind of input, such as energy, it should not be assumed that it is always one of the other sectors, or other delivering categories, in particular, that is supplying this input to j, but rather that there may be a 'ring' of other sectors or other delivering categories such as $i+1$, $i+2$, etc. from which the supply may come. We will assume that the individual sectors within the ring are equivalent, in the sense that a specific quantity of the input from one of these sectors, can replace a certain fixed quantity of the input from one of the other delivering categories in the ring. We will assume that sector j has a technologically well defined requirement of this ring product as a whole rather than for components within the ring.

We shall take up the problem of the substitution of one regional source by another in the model with reference to a base period configuration caused by changing prices. This can be generalized easily to include sectors as well. The price system will be exogenous data to be fed into the system as the final demand is fed into the model. This, obviously, means that for our purposes changes in the price system in the short period will be taken to be the factor determining changes in the regional pattern itself.

In the base period, let $_{mn}x_{ij}$ denote the flow of a specific input from region m to n and from sector i to j.

In the sense of Frisch, let there be a ring structure in the requirement, the ring being defined for regions from $m_1, ..., m_r$. Thus, let there be a production coefficient defined for the ring including $m_1, ..., m_r$ from any one of which the technical requirements may be met.

Then the inputs in the ring are given by

$$\sum_R {}_{mn}x_{ij},$$ (13)

where all flows from regions $m_1, ..., m_r$ forming the region are summed, R denoting a summation over $m_1, ..., m_r$.

The production functions for the structure of the ring as a whole are defined as

$$_{R.n}a_{ij} = \frac{\sum_R {}_{mn}x_{ij}}{{}_nX_j}.$$ (14)

Further, let $_mP_i$ denote the price index of the ith commodity in the mth region. Let us define the index in the sense of Pasche, that is, we take the period 1 as the base and the period 0 as the reference period for which the index is being calculated. The price index in our sense is defined as follows:

$$_mP_i = \frac{\text{Price of commodity } i \text{ in region } m \text{ in base period 0}}{\text{Price of commodity } i \text{ in region } m \text{ in current period 1}}. \quad (15)$$

In the base period (0) let us define $_{mn}K_{ij}$ as the ratio of the input of m going to n of commodity i going to j such that

$$_{mn}K_{ij} = \frac{_{mn}x_{ij}}{\sum\limits_R {_{mn}x_{ij}}}. \quad (16)$$

Let $_RP_i$ be the mean of the price indices defined in (15) for the ring with weights given by the corresponding K such that $_RP_i$ is given by

$$_RP_i = \sum\limits_R {_{mn}K_{ij}} \cdot {_mP_i}. \quad (17)$$

The base period coefficient for any region is related to the ring coefficient as below:

$$\frac{_{mn}x_{ij}^0}{_nX_j^0} = {_{Rn}a_{ij}} \cdot {_{mn}K_{ij}}. \quad (18)$$

Then the expression we suggest for the reference period for the same region is given by

$$\frac{_{mn}x_{ij}'}{_nX_j'} = {_{Rn}a_{ij}} \cdot {_{mn}K_{ij}} \cdot \frac{_mP_i}{_RP_i}. \quad (19)$$

It should be noted that if there is no price change for the current period the above expression reduces to (18).

This means that so long as there is no relative price change there will be no change in the position regarding the regional flows. That is to say there will be no substitution of one region by another, or of one sector by another.

If there is a change in the relative price there will also be changes in the coefficient structure. In the case of such changes, the component flowing in from a region, or from a sector, in a particular region will decrease, if the ratio of the relative price index to the average increases, and will increase if this price ratio decreases.

It should be noted that the change in a particular flow may be a sectoral substitution or a regional substitution, or both. For us there is no distinction between the two in the model. Thus, coal from region A to region C may have declined because there has been a substitution of oil from A, or of coal from B, or of oil from B.

Summing up over the regions in the ring which are all part of the ring structure we get:

$$\frac{\sum\limits_R {_{mn}x_{ij}'}}{_nX_j'} = \frac{_{Rn}a_{ij}}{_RP_i} \sum\limits_R {_{mn}K_{ij}} \cdot {_mP_i} = {_{Rn}a_{ij}}. \quad (20)$$

This satisfies the basic equation for the ring over the regions inside the ring.

The introduction of the parameter involving the price constellation requires that more information is fed into the model before a solution can be obtained. It should be pointed out, however, that one can project relative price ratios along with projecting the final demand vector and find out the different patterns for alternative price constellations.

Although we have discussed this model only for regional substitution it may be easily extended to sectoral substitution by summing for substitute sectors, also in a ring.

9.4

The price model discussed in the earlier section is one of the models in which coefficients are allowed to change because of the change of relative price. But a region may not take from another region if it has not been taking from the very beginning. Similarly, it cannot give up importing from a region whatever the price change. It can only diminish the quantity.

The logical form for a really effective substitution model is the programming form. The usual programming model for our purposes can be formulated as follows:

given the production functions for the sectors,

$$\sum_m {}_{mn}x_{ij} = {}_na_{ij} \cdot {}_nX_j \tag{21}$$

and given the balance relations for the regions,

$$(1) \quad \sum_n \sum_j {}_{mn}x_{ij} + \sum_n {}_{mn}f_i = {}_mX_i, \tag{22}$$

$$(2) \quad \sum_m \sum_j {}_{mn}x_{ij} + \sum_m {}_{mn}f_i = {}_nR_i, \tag{23}$$

where R denotes requirements, also given the transport costs for each of these regional flows, ${}_{mn}C_{ij}$.

Find a set of flows which will minimize the total transport costs (say) given by,

$$\sum_m \sum_n \sum_i \sum_j {}_{mn}C_{ij} \cdot {}_{mn}x_{ij}. \tag{24}$$

The main difficulty in this approach is that while, for planning purposes, it may be useful to be given an idea of the direction in which to move to attain an optimal goal, it is no use for any prediction purposes, as this will not bring out the effect of prices, except in a static sense. That is, an optimal set will remain optimal only so long as the given price system does not change. Therefore, for any given change in prices, the optimal set has to be recalculated. Secondly, and still more importantly in a real economic world, various rigidities operate and one does not move from optima to optima but from one position historically given to another position in the direction of the optima.

9.5

We come now to the question of testing the models, demonstrated analytically in the previous sections, to determine their applicability in a particular situation. This situation is one of rapid change in a growing, but still largely under-developed, economy. The success of a particular model, is shown better against this type of economic background than a general failure. It may be quite possible that a model suitable in these conditions may fail in the more stable conditions represented by the industrialized economies of the West. But for economic applications all models have to be adjusted to local situation. Economic models are rarely of such general types that they fit all countries irrespective of their distinctive features.

It is also true that inter-regional flows can only be estimated, for any region, for all industries as a whole. There is no way of isolating the different regional elements going into different industries. The maximum that one can do is to find out some rule for the regional-flows of a commodity and then redistribute it, according to some assumptions, into the various industrial sectors.

Before presenting the results, it may be useful to give a brief discription of the data for the present experiment.

The data relate to the flow of cement into various regions in India from different producing regions for the four years 1950, 1954, 1957 and 1959. The figures relate mainly to railbound trade. The regions consist of groups of separate states where they are small or unimportant. Where they are large or important they have been retained as separate units.

Isard's fixed coefficient model has been defined in (1) and (2). The inflows into a region in the model are strictly proportional to the total inputs of the consuming regions. The Leontief model, as defined in (3) to (7), is also of a similar type analytically except that it treats the sectors in two distinct clusters, one of which must be determined separately before the other can be determined but has not been computed separately.

Table 9.1 gives the observed and computed values in the fixed coefficient form of the model as given by Isard.

It may be seen that the fixed coefficient model, starting as it does with a rigid initial production situation, fails to respond to changes. When new industries come up in different regions, where there was no such industry previously, the situation changes very drastically in reality but is not reflected by the model.

The next series of similar rigid models are the gravity models discussed by the author as defined in section 9.2.

Table 9.2 gives the results of the Leontief gravity model described in (8), and Table 9.3 gives the alternative gravity model described in (10). Other models discussed in the section were subsequently dropped as they were found to be of inferior performance.

From the results it may be seen that while generally doing better than the fixed coefficient models they are also not able to reflect the impact of

Table 9.1. *Inflows of cement in* 1000 *mds into*

From	West Bengal Observed	Computed	Uttar Pradesh Observed	Computed	Punjab Observed	Computed	Bombay Observed	Computed
				1954				
West Bengal	—	—	4	312	3	146	—	—
Bihar	7340	8442	1320	719	100	67	1	—
Orissa	919	38	1	1	116	6	—	—
Uttar Pradesh	—	18	—	—	13	2	2	14
Punjab	47	176	2205	4055	—	—	917	934
Bombay	—	—	24	121	39	321	—	—
Madras	381	—	270	1	118	3567	214	63
Rajasthan	—	13	3442	2055	2859	1575	572	938
Hyderabad	—	—	—	1	2452	—	1006	752
				1957				
West Bengal	—	—	1	229	—	290	—	—
Bihar	6880	7340	506	528	6	134	1	1
Orissa	1159	33	—	1	499	11	—	—
Uttar Pradesh	3	15	—	—	11	3	2	2
Punjab	—	153	367	2978	—	—	14	1028
Bombay	1	—	28	89	66	635	—	—
Madras	—	—	7	1	1	7063	86	240
Rajasthan	2	11	4428	1570	9035	3119	47	666
Hyderabad	—	—	—	1	1068	—	2891	1128
				1959				
West Bengal	—	—	1	411	4	293	2	—
Bihar	10380	11541	96	947	12	135	7	—
Orissa	1472	52	—	2	584	11	—	—
Uttar Pradesh	—	24	—	—	10	3	—	38
Punjab	—	241	1747	5338	—	—	32	2582
Bombay	2	—	34	159	100	641	—	—
Madras	—	—	—	2	567	7132	23	173
Rajasthan	—	17	7688	2706	8711	3149	1045	2590
Hyderabad	—	—	—	2	1406	—	6384	2079

change in a realistic sense. An area, however far from a centre of consumption, still remains a centre of supply only if it is big enough. This may be acceptable, so long as nearby centres of supply do not operate, but are bound to fail when centres are closer together.

The third set of models tried out was of the regression type where a function was fitted involving both distance and volume of production.

The equations fitted were as follows:

Indian Union $\quad x = R^{0.5463} X^{1.4531} D^{-1.8911}$

Uttar Pradesh $\quad x = X^{1.3839} D^{-0.9143}$

Bombay $\quad x = X^{1.4724} D^{-1.0491}$

Table 9.4 gives results for the two regions Uttar Pradesh and Bombay—the other two regions were dropped as the fit was literally a failure.

Table 9.2. Inflows of cement in 1000 *mds into*

From	West Bengal		Uttar Pradesh		Punjab		Bombay	
	Observed	Computed	Observed	Computed	Observed	Computed	Observed	Computed
				1954				
West Bengal	—	—	4	222	3	10	—	—
Bihar	7340	9176	1320	782	100	78	1	—
Orissa	919	1111	1	41	116	164	—	—
Uttar Pradesh	—	9	—	—	13	—	2	7
Punjab	47	94	2205	2173	—	—	917	503
Bombay	—	—	24	88	39	234	—	—
Madras	381	—	270	1	218	2835	214	50
Rajasthan	—	18	3442	2949	2850	2261	572	1351
Hyderabad	—	—	—	2	2452	—	1006	37
				1957				
West Bengal	—	—	8	27	—	34	1	—
Bihar	6880	5891	506	—	6	107	1	—
Orissa	667	1192	—	—	499	401	—	—
Uttar Pradesh	3	18	—	—	11	2	2	19
Punjab	—	16	367	316	—	—	14	112
Bombay	1	—	28	123	66	885	—	—
Madras	—	—	7	1	1	3452	86	34
Rajasthan	—	28	3442	3833	9635	7921	47	2681
Hyderabad	—	—	—	2	1068	—	2891	45
				1959				
West Bengal	—	—	1	15	4	10	2	—
Bihar	10380	8991	96	738	12	105	7	—
Orissa	1472	1069	—	60	584	360	—	—
Uttar Pradesh	—	7	—	—	10	—	—	11
Punjab	—	44	1747	980	—	—	32	476
Bombay	1	—	34	94	100	381	—	—
Madras	5	—	—	2	567	5546	23	135
Rajasthan	2	37	7668	5780	8711	6729	1045	5557
Hyderabad	—	—	—	4	1406	—	6384	156

The model fitted for India as a whole was a failure as it meant averaging the supply conditions and volume of supplies in different regions. This failed for the specific region because of the wide disparity between regions. The curves fitted separately for the regions are also unsuccessful because of the same difficulties. It would have been better to fit separately for each region over different time periods. But the data for such a type of fitting is hard to come by.

In the tables 9.1 to 9.4 we have tried out the models which are essentially of a fixed coefficient type. We shall now demonstrate the price model with varying coefficients. This model has been discussed in details in § 9.3.

Table 9.5 gives the main results of the demonstrations.

It may again be seen that a price index of this type is not a sufficiently sensitive instrument for forecasting change in regional flows in this area. It is possible that if some suitable indicator of the changing distance from

Table 9.3. Inflow of cement in 1000 *mds into*

From	West Bengal		Uttar Pradesh		Punjab		Bombay	
	Observed	Computed	Observed	Computed	Observed	Computed	Observed	Computed
				1950				
West Bengal	—	—	220	13	26	17	—	139
Bihar	5317	4859	507	1112	12	143	—	1370
Orissa	24	112	1	3	1	1	—	5
Uttar Pradesh	11	5	—	—	3	36	27	18
Punjab	111	284	2859	2979	—	—	1823	1538
Bombay	—	14	85	41	57	20	—	—
Madras	—	40	1	74	634	14	122	483
Rajasthan	8	148	1449	902	280	769	1829	1436
Hyderabad	—	60	1	—	—	16	1468	270
				1954				
West Bengal	—	—	4	16	3	5	—	5
Bihar	7340	7471	1320	2048	100	669	1	757
Orissa	919	461	1	151	116	59	—	70
Uttar Pradesh	—	4	—	—	13	17	2	5
Punjab	47	215	2205	2707	—	—	917	419
Bombay	—	14	24	50	39	28	—	—
Madras	381	101	270	100	218	49	214	195
Rajasthan	—	301	3442	2194	2850	4775	572	1048
Hyderabad	—	120	—	—	2452	98	1006	194
				1957				
West Bengal	—	—	8	28	1	10	1	85
Bihar	6880	6048	506	1635	6	602	1	580
Orissa	667	624	—	202	499	88	—	89
Uttar Pradesh	3	10	—	—	11	47	2	11
Punjab	—	47	367	579	—	—	14	86
Bombay	1	29	28	104	66	66	—	—
Madras	—	68	7	66	1	40	86	125
Rajasthan	—	585	3442	4196	9635	10307	47	1925
Hyderabad	—	143	—	—	1068	130	289	218
				1959				
West Bengal	—	—	1	16	4	4	2	7
Bihar	10380	9519	96	3018	12	692	7	1443
Orissa	1472	901	—	341	584	93	—	203
Uttar Pradesh	—	4	—	—	10	14	—	7
Punjab	—	131	1747	1907	—	—	32	382
Bombay	1	20	34	84	100	33	—	—
Madras	1	175	—	200	567	69	23	508
Rajasthan	2	798	7668	6716	8711	10272	1045	4156
Hyderabad	—	328	—	—	1406	219	6384	792

which different amounts of supplies are made available could be found, it would be a better variable for explaining the change in the pattern in the regional flows. Models of this type may work better in more stable situations where more or less unlimited amounts may be made available at certain prices in the different regions. But in an area where capacities

Table 9.4. Inflow of cement in 1000 mds into

From	Uttar Pradesh		Bombay	
	Observed	Computed	Observed	Computed
		1954		
West Bengal	4	—	—	—
Bihar	1320	923	—	469
Orissa	1	38	—	18
Uttar Pradesh	—	—	—	—
Punjab	2205	538	917	155
Bombay	24	8	—	—
Madras	270	46	214	51
Rajasthan	3442	750	572	466
Hyerabad	—	81	1006	157
		1957		
West Bengal	1	3	1	—
Bihar	506	745	1	378
Orissa	—	61	—	30
Uttar Pradesh	—	—	2	—
Punjab	367	70	14	18
Bombay	28	24	—	—
Madras	7	29	86	35
Rajasthan	4428	2032	47	1343
Hyderabad	—	111	2891	221
		1959		
West Bengal	—	—	2	—
Bihar	96	122	7	638
Orissa	—	92	—	46
Uttar Pradesh	—	—	—	—
Punjab	1747	251	32	70
Bombay	34	13	—	—
Madras	—	93	23	122
Rajasthan	7688	2729	1045	1837
Hyderabad	—	308	6384	652

are limited and where new industries are growing capacity limits are changing all the time and models of this type are not adequate to describe the drastic revisions taking place continuously.

Finally we come to the programming models defined in §9.4. The programming model takes into account the capacity and requirement changes occurring all the time. It takes each such situation as discrete. In this respect it is realistic. Where it is not realistic is in assuming that a minimization of total cost is the objective. This would be a realistic situation if we had conditions of perfect competition and each region had minimized its own procurement costs. One may assume that each regional unit is trying to achieve a local minimum. Conditions of perfect competition do not exist. Thus the minimization of a global optimum does not automatically lead to a local optimum.

Table 9.6 gives a demonstration of this model.

Table 9.5. *Inflow of cement in* 1000 *mds into*

From	West Bengal		Uttar Pradesh		Punjab		Bombay	
	Observed	Computed	Observed	Computed	Observed	Computed	Observed	Computed
				1954				
West Bengal	—	—	4	400	3	130	—	—
Bihar	7340	8456	1320	749	100	71	1	—
Orissa	919	31	1	1	116	5	—	—
Uttar Pradesh	—	13	—	—	13	13	2	11
Punjab	47	175	2205	4078	—	—	917	917
Bombay	—	3	24	123	39	327	—	—
Madras	381	—	270	2	218	3732	214	62
Rajasthan	—	12	3442	1912	2850	1394	572	849
Hyderabad	—	—	—	2	2452	—	1006	887
				1957				
West Bengal	—	—	8	2	1	6	1	—
Bihar	6880	6090	506	1016	6	194	1	1
Orissa	667	1067	—	1	499	288	—	—
Uttar Pradesh	3	—	—	—	11	26	2	2
Punjab	—	38	367	1617	—	—	14	969
Bombay	1	—	28	20	66	81	—	—
Madras	—	382	7	231	1	468	86	262
Rajasthan	—	—	3442	2449	9635	4975	47	580
Hyderabad	—	—	—	—	1068	5247	2891	1229

Generally, however, it can be seen that the programming model gives a better approximation to reality than the other models in spite of the limitations pointed out.

In Table 9.7 we give the comparative performances by presenting the total absolute deviations in the different methods.

Table 9.6. *Inflow of cement in* 1000 *mds into*

	West Bengal		Uttar Pradesh		Punjab		Bombay	
From	Observed	Computed	Observed	Computed	Observed	Computed	Observed	Computed
				1950				
West Bengal	—	—	220	—	26	—	—	—
Bihar	5317	5471	507	—	12	—	—	354
Orissa	24	—	1	—	1	—	—	—
Uttar Pradesh	11	—	—	—	3	—	27	58
Punjab	111	—	2859	4727	—	—	1823	30
Bombay	—	—	85	396	57	—	—	—
Madras	—	—	1	—	634	—	112	842
Rajasthan	8	—	1449	—	280	1013	1829	2553
Hyderabad	—	—	1	—	—	—	1468	1432
				1954				
West Bengal	—	—	4	—	3	—	—	—
Bihar	7340	7827	1320	1626	100	—	1	—
Orissa	919	860	1	—	116	—	—	—
Uttar Pradesh	—	—	—	—	13	41	2	—
Punjab	47	—	2205	3626	—	—	917	—
Bombay	—	—	24	388	39	—	—	—
Madras	381	—	270	400	118	—	214	—
Rajasthan	—	—	3442	1226	2859	5659	572	—
Hyderabad	—	—	—	—	2452	—	1006	2712
				1957				
West Bengal	—	—	1	—	—	—	1	—
Bihar	6880	6394	506	1717	6	—	1	—
Orissa	1159	667	—	—	499	—	—	—
Uttar Pradesh	3	—	—	—	11	—	2	—
Punjab	—	—	367	—	—	—	14	—
Bombay	1	—	28	784	66	—	—	—
Madras	—	—	7	—	1	—	86	—
Rajasthan	2	—	4428	2836	9635	11286	47	—
Hyderabad	—	—	—	—	1068	—	2891	3042
				1959				
West Bengal	—	—	1	—	4	—	2	—
Bihar	10380	11346	96	—	12	—	7	—
Orissa	1472	530	—	1455	584	—	—	—
Uttar Pradesh	—	—	—	—	10	39	—	—
Punjab	—	—	1747	1464	—	—	32	—
Bombay	23	—	34	540	100	—	—	—
Madras	1	—	—	—	567	—	23	—
Rajasthan	—	—	7688	6107	8711	11355	1045	—
Hyderabad	—	—	—	—	1406	—	6384	7493

Table 9.7. Total deviation (absolute value) from observed

Year	Region	Isard	Leontief Gravity	Gravity (2)	Price Model	Regression	Pro-gramming	Observed
1950	West Bengal	—	—	1027	—	—	308	5471
	Uttar Pradesh	—	—	1600	—	—	4358	5123
	Punjab	—	—	1336	—	—	1466	1013
	Bombay	—	—	3759	—	—	3668	3269
1954	West Bengal	2524	2483	1476	2539	—	974	8687
	Uttar Pradesh	4514	5102	2871	4738	5119	4439	7266
	Punjab	7764	5942	4890	7976	—	5656	5700
	Bombay	800	2331	2639	1475	2358	3411	2712
1957	West Bengal	1761	1574	1753	1614	—	984	7553
	Uttar Pradesh	5898	1069	2546	2991	3132	3933	5337
	Punjab	15529	7296	2701	9741	—	3301	11286
	Bombay	3553	5647	5422	3327	4440	301	3042
1959	West Bengal	2865	1884	2885	—	—	1931	11876
	Uttar Pradesh	9965	3434	4641	—	6994	3922	9566
	Punjab	15066	8983	4488	—	7340	5346	11394
	Bombay	8577	11314	11228	—	—	2218	7493

CHAPTER 10

THE CEMENT INDUSTRY IN
INDIA UNDER FIVE-YEAR PLANS

10.1

With the rapid growth of industries the character and pattern of inter-regional exchange has become very important in India. Because modern industrial complexes often have to gather their component materials from great distances and markets are far more dispersed these factors bring the location and transport aspects of development into great prominence.

Broadly there are two aspects, the static and the dynamic, from which this problem should be studied. The static aspect of the problem can be stated rather simply. On the assumption that present regional requirements and capacities are fixed how is a distribution system achieved which minimizes total costs, including transport costs, to the consumer of the product.

The answer to this problem can be sought in two ways. We can try to find out the ideal flow pattern that minimizes total costs and attempt to achieve it by direct control of distribution. Alternatively, we can ask for a pricing system which will force the producers and distributors to adopt the ideal pattern in order to avoid loss.

The dynamic aspect of an inter-regional study goes deeper into the problem of regional growth and poses the question given regional requirement-levels for the future, what should be the optimum locational pattern such that future cost to the consumer of the product will be minimized. In this paper an attempt will be made to study these problems in connection with the cement industry.

10.2

It is well known that, like international trade, inter-regional trade is subject to various extra-economic pressures. Thus, in big countries, regional interests may often go against a decision to cut down production in a particular region even if it is nationally most efficient to do so. Regional government and regional business groups often support specific regional products over products from other region, even if it is less efficient to do so from a national standpoint.

We have, therefore, to study first how far the present system of inter-regional trade is optimal from a national standpoint.

If c_{ij} represents the production and transport cost for moving a unit from the ith to the jth region, x_{ij} represents the total unit moved from the ith to jth region then obtain a plan such that

$$\sum_i \sum_j c_{ij} x_{ij} = \text{minimum},$$

$$\sum_j x_{ij} \leqq k_i, \quad \text{where } k \text{ is actual output and } i \neq j,$$

$$\sum_i x_{ij} \geqq r_j.$$

Table 10.1 (see pp. 108–9) gives the results of the programming for 1950, 1954 and 1957. The saving per unit may be seen in Table 10.2 below:

Table 10.2

Year	Actual	Optimal	Savings	Savings as % of actual
1950	1·41	1·32	0·09	6
1954	2·16	1·89	0·27	12
1957	1·83	1·76	0·07	4

It was realized that such a national optimum might go against genuine regional interests and produce undesirable consequences. Therefore the problem was, solved in alternative ways, by assuming certain restrictive movements on regional targets and intra-regional movements.

In one of these solutions it was assumed that regional production targets cannot be tampered with nor can intra-regional movements be changed.

In the second solution it was assumed that production targets can be changed but that intra-regional movements cannot be interfered with.

Collecting together the per unit saving in the different methods over different years we get the following table.

Table 10.3. Total saving per unit

Year	Intra-regional fixed (no excess)	Intra-regional fixed but (excess allowed)	Intra-regional movement and excess are both allowed
1950	0·11	0·14	0·09
1954	0·14	0·21	0·27
1957	0·04	0·07	0·07

The last method is not strictly comparable with the other because of the change in the cost structure induced by the zero cost diagonal entry in the solution, but even then it may be seen that intra-regional delivery is much more efficient in the second method and still more in the third method when computed on the same basis.

Table 10.1. *Inter-regional transportation of cement (9 months) for 1950, 1954 and 1957 in '000 mds with average distance in miles with corresponding optimal amounts in brackets*

Regions	Year					Months					Total
		1	2	3	4	5	6	7	8	9	
1. West Bengal	1950	(805)	481	67	220	26	—	2	9	—	305 (805)
	1954	—	61	6	4 (77)	3	—	2	0·8	—	77 (77)
	1957	—	118	19	0·8	0·1	0·5	—	6	0·9	146 (—)
		156	156	254	623	903	1223	1082	1094	1254	
2. Bihar	1950	5317 (4666)	4993 (5658)	643 (795)	507 (505)	12	(759)	—	0·5	—	11473 (12383)
	1954	7340 (8687)	6682 (7113)	689	1320 (154)	100	1	4	9	—	16145 (15954)
	1957	6880 (5010)	13061 (13787)	715	506 (66)	6	1	—	3	—	21172 (18863)
		156	266	266	596	876	1068	1044	1067	1266	
3. Orissa	1950	24	5	(31)	1	1	—	0·3	—	—	31 (31)
	1954	919	176	2921 (3784)	1	116	—	2	—	—	4135 (3734)
	1957	667	569	4116 (4863)	—	499	—	2	2	—	5855 (7406)
		254	266	862	862	1131	1334	778	1322	1000	
4. Uttar Pradesh	1950	11	14	—	— (58)	3	27	0·6	2	—	58 (58)
	1954	—	—	—	655 (4713)	13	2	—	26	—	697 (4713)
	1957	3	26	—	4431 (4712)	11	2	—	66	—	4539 (4712)
		623	596	862		269	840	1640	460	1862	

Region	Year	1	2	3	4	5	6	7	8	9	Total
5. Punjab, etc.	1950	111	155	6	2859 (4560)	—	1823	32	281	—	12995 (13301)
	1954	47	65	14	2205 (2977)	—	917	79	461	4	16036 (16637)
	1957	—	5	—	367	—	14	—	479	6	17215 (18401)
		903	876	1131	269	861	861	1828	191	1606	
6. Bombay	1950	0·2	10	—	85	57	5718 (6875)	2	216	26	6114 (6875)
	1954	—	0·4	—	24	39	12779 (14116)	9	311	5	13167 (14116)
	1957	1	0·5	—	28	66	18609 (20237)	14	668	83	19470 (20237)
		1223	1068	1334	840	861	967	967	695	745	
7. Madras, etc.	1950	—	—	110	1	634	122	11249 (11646)	1	1100	13217 (11646)
	1954	381	129	104	270	118	214	16569 (16665)	8	877	18670 (16665)
	1957	—	—	12	7	0·6	86	20539 (20953)	—	1394	22039 (20953)
		1032	1044	778	1640	1828	967	1662	695	222	
8. Rajasthan, etc.	1950	8	—	—	1449	280	1829	—	727 (1237)	—	4293 (4590)
	1954	2	—	—	3442	2859	572	—	4825 (5641)	2	11700 (11700)
	1957	—	7	0·6	4428 (9229)	9635 (9229)	47	—	327 (1553)	2	14449 (15772)
		1094	1067	1322	460	191	695	1662	1440	222	
9. Hyderabad and Mysore	1950	—	—	—	1	—	1468	360	—	1962 (3088)	3791 (3088)
	1954	—	—	—	—	2452	1006	—	—	3660 (4548)	7113 (4548)
	1957	—	—	—	—	1068	2891 (1414)	398	2	5377 (6863)	9736 (8277)
		1254	12666	1000	1862	1606	745	222	1440		
Total	1950	5471	5658	826	5123	8741	10987	11646	1237	3088	52777
	1954	8687	7113	3734	7921	17944	15491	16665	5641	4548	87745
	1957	7553	13787	4863	9768	27630	21651	20953	1553	6863	114621

The general conclusion, therefore, seems to be that in the cement industry the allocation has been becoming more efficient since 1954, while, earlier it probably operated at moderate levels of efficiency.

Since the State Trading Corporation took up the allocation of cement this improvement has been generally maintained.

One would like more conclusive evidence, over a large stretch of years, before finally assessing the comparative efficiency of the private and public management of the inter-regional transportation of cement, but in general, during 1950–9 the State Trading Corporation seems to have been rather more efficient.

10.3

We now consider the problem of trading an optimal set of prices leading to the same optimal distribution.

This solution is obtained by imputing delivered values for each regional requirement and attaching royalty payments to each location so that the net revenue, e.g. the sum of the delivered values × requirement less the imputed royalty × capacity is maximized. Such a price system conforms to the price system obtainable under perfectly competitive equilibrium and forms the normative system against which we can study the actual official price policy as also the market price ruling at the time.

We consider here the solution, without restrictive assumptions about the volume of regional production and consumption, etc., with costs which include both production and distribution charges. Table 10.4 gives the optimal prices and royalties for the complete solution.

Table 10.4

Regions	Optimal costs			Royalties		
	1950	1954	1957	1950	1954	1957
1. West Bengal	1·94	2·01	2·11	0·37	0·49	0
2. Bihar	1·58	1·65	1·75	0	0	0
3. Orissa	2·18	2·16	1·54	0·58	0	0·06
4. Uttar Pradesh	2·58	2·65	2·75	1·36	0·60	0·70
5. Punjab, etc.	1·98	2·05	2·37	0·84	0·80	0·91
6. Bombay	2·95	2·70	2·45	1·20	0·80	0·64
7. Madras, etc.	1·72	1·81	1·57	0	0	0
8. Rajasthan	1·87	1·62	1·90	0·64	0·08	0·06
9. Hyderabad and Mysore	1·93	1·54	1·34	0	0	0

The Punjab is the only area which shows a rising royalty and a rising delivered value. Most states in 1957 show a declining or zero royalty showing the existence already of excess in the optimal programme. Since, in our programme, the existence of a zero royalty indicates the presence of unutilized surplus, this obviously implies that in 1957 in the frame-work of demand there is excess capacity in most areas.

We now consider the problem of finding an optimal location pattern for future expansion. The main assumption that we have is that regional average costs are unaltered by the addition of new units.

Using present techniques we may put the present problem in the linear programming form as below:

Let x_{ij} indicate regional deliveries, r_j the requirement of the jth region, k_i existing capacities in the ith region and n_i additional capacity installed in the ith region.

Given regional requirements

$$\sum_i x_{ij} \geqq r_j$$

and given regional delivery capacities

$$\sum_j x_{ij} \leqq k_i + n_i$$

such that total requirements > total capacities of the old installations denoted by k_i. If c_{ij} is the associated total cost, find the deliveries x_{ij} such that the expression
$$\sum_i \sum_j c_{ij} x_{ij} \quad \text{is minimum.}$$

An obvious way out of this would be to solve this problem for all proposed location sets and select the cheapest from among them.

While being a tractable programme this is not practicable and the enumeration of all possible sets of location will not be feasible. Therefore we must try an indirect way of solving this problem.

For a more efficient approach we can rewrite the capacity equation in the form

$$\sum_j x_{ij} - n_i \leqq k_i.$$

Since n_i does not enter into the objective function, arbitrary values of the n_i may be taken, subject only to the fact that we do not require excess capacity to be more than the amount $\sum_j r_j - \sum_i k_i$. Therefore, to start with, we can make all $n_i = \sum_j r_j - \sum_i k_i$.

Since we have to minimize the objective function involving the x_{ij}'s then the requirement equation will ultimately determine the effective levels of excess capacity that should be utilized in the regions.

First let us assume the future regional requirement targets as given. We assume that these requirements will exceed existing capacity and assess this excess, calling it Δ, the excess of planned requirements over existing capacity. We have already said that production of this excess will not change any regional costs per unit. Let us now assume that there are unused resources of the size Δ in every regional unit. This makes the capacity equations

$$\sum_j x_{ij} \leqq k_i + \Delta \quad \text{when} \quad \Delta = \sum_j r_j - \sum_i k_i.$$

On the assumption that unused capacity of magnitude Δ exists in every region all that we need now is to find out an optimum programme on the basis of the increased requirements, as planned, and see which of the assumed excess capacities are really used in the new optimal flow, and which are left unused. It is argued that if capacity is left unused somewhere then there is no point in increasing its capacity as the increased capacity in that region will not be needed in the optimal solution. If, in more than one region, use is made of this excess it indicates that these regions benefit from an expansion of capacity in the optimal solution. That is, their expansion will be consistent with a reduction of total costs.

We now consider a demonstration of this problem.

It may be seen that the excess requirements

$$\Delta = R_{57} - K_{54} = 21 \cdot 949, \quad R = \sum_j r_j, \quad K = \sum_i k_i.$$

Let us assume that all regions have reserve capacity equal to 21,949.

Let us further assume that there is no restriction on the movement in the diagonal cells, i.e. self consumption is also considered free to move in any direction like other variables.

Therefore we solve, the following linear programming problem:

$$\sum_i \sum_j c_{ij} x_{ij} = \text{minimum},$$

$$\sum_j x_{ij} = k_i + \Delta,$$

$$\sum_i x_{ij} = r_j.$$

Note that the requirements are those of 1957 while the capacity is equal to that of 1954 plus Δ in each region. We thus increase total capacity by eight, since eight regions are being considered. West Bengal has been omitted because it has no factory and the production costs could not be calculated.

The solution is given in Table 10.5.

Some interesting features of the relative cost components of the cement industry now become obvious. If there is no change in the cost of production then the lowest cost would be for each unit except Uttar Pradesh to produce its own requirements. That is proximity to consumers, under the present cost structure, is rather more important than the proximity of raw materials in considering expansion provided that the relative cost structure does not change. This is probably due to the fact that power and several other important cost components are obtained more cheaply close to the centres of consumption. This makes the cost of production differential smaller than the transport cost differential.

It is worth noting that the cement industry in Uttar Pradesh is the only unit for which the cost of production differential exceeds the cost of importation to Uttar Pradesh.

What happens, however, when all intra-regional supplies are once

Table 10.5

Region of Destination → / Region of Origin ↓		1	2	3	4	5	6	7	8	9	Excess	Total
1. West Bengal	(1)	·	·	·	·	·	·	·	·	·	77	77
	(2)	·	·	·	·	·	·	·	·	·	77	77
2. Bihar	(1)	·	13787	·	·	·	·	·	·	·	4553	18340
	(2)	·	726	747	·	·	·	·	·	·	23699	24446
3. Orissa	(1)	7553	·	4863	·	·	·	2500	·	·	11168	26684
	(2)	7553	·	·	·	·	·	·	·	·	10907	19186
4. Uttar Pradesh	(1)	·	·	·	·	·	·	·	·	·	4712	4712
	(2)	·	·	·	·	·	·	·	·	·	19449	19449
5. Punjab, etc.	(1)	·	·	·	9768	27630	·	·	·	·	788	38186
	(2)	·	·	·	5337	·	·	·	1226	·	12497	19060
6. Bombay	(1)	·	·	·	·	·	21651	·	·	·	14414	36065
	(2)	·	·	·	·	·	·	·	·	·	14674	14674
7. Madras, etc.	(1)	·	·	·	·	·	·	17850	·	·	—	17850
	(2)	·	·	·	·	·	·	·	·	1486	15812	17298
8. Rajasthan, etc.	(1)	·	·	·	·	·	·	·	1553	·	10147	11700
	(2)	·	·	·	·	11286	·	·	·	·	19254	30540
9. Hyderabad and Mysore	(1)	·	·	·	·	·	·	603	·	6863	—	7466
	(2)	·	·	·	·	·	3042	414	·	·	17800	21256
Total	(1)	7553	13787	4863	4768	27630	21651	20953	1553	6863	45859	160480
	(2)	7553	726	747	5337	11286	3042	414	1226	1486	134169	165986

Note: Figures (1), (2) indicate different levels of excess capacity. For (1) the excess capacity of 21949 was tentatively given only for Orissa, Punjab and Bombay which showed possibilities of expansion then; for (2) excess capacity to the extent of 19167 was taken for all states except West Bengal.

more fixed arbitrarily and the only variables of the problem are exports to other regions?

In that case we have to solve the same problem with a different type of restriction. This restriction is, again, on self consumption which has a 'zero cost' of transportation. Let us assume that the actual increase in self consumption from self production is fixed, as was actually the case in 1947. That is let us once more take the diagonals out of the picture. Then we solve again the reformulated problem as follows:

$$\left.\begin{aligned} \sum_i \sum_j c_{ij} x_{ij} &= \text{minimum}, \\ \sum_j x_{ij} &= K_i + \Delta, \\ \sum_i x_{ij} &= r_j, \end{aligned}\right\} \quad (i \neq j).$$

The solution is given in Table 10.5, solution set 2. It can be seen that when the diagonal cells are taken out of the picture the locational criterion picks out the regions in the order given in Table 10.6. For comparative purposes we have also given actual increases in production in 1957 side by side.

Table 10.6

Regions	Actual absolute level of increase in 1957 over 1954 in '000 mds	Actual rank by increase of output	Optimal level of increase in 1957 over 1954 in '000 mds	Optimal rank by increase of output
1. West Bengal	*	*	*	*
2. Bihar	10322	1	−8532	8
3. Orissa	3271	4	+8260	1
4. Uttar Pradesh	0	8	+ 281	6
5. Punjab, etc.	2163	7	+6669	2
6. Bombay	6120	3	+4492	3
7. Madras, etc.	6628	2	+3355	4
8. Rajasthan, etc.	2845	5	− 87	7
9. Hyderabad and Mysore	2448	6	+1367	5

* No production, only re-export.

With suitable simplification it is possible to use simple programming techniques even to obtain optimal solutions for further expansion policies.

A more realistic solution could be secured if we could also have the upper bounds of regional expansion clearly stated. In a case where such limits were known it might be possible to discard the restriction on the diagonal cells found necessary earlier.

Any change, however, in the cost structure, when the industry expands will take us out of the usual format of linear models.

Within certain narrow limits, therefore, linear programming techniques may be usefully employed to determine the best location for new industry.

AN INTER-INDUSTRIAL PROGRAMMING MODEL FOR THE PRODUCTION AND TRANSPORTATION OF COMMODITIES FOR DIFFERENT REGIONS OF INDIA[1]

II.I INTRODUCTION

This paper is an exploratory study into the optimal pattern of regional production and exchange of commodities in India. The process of economic development in India as a whole has raised quite urgent problems concerning the kind of dispersal of industries that should be made in order to ensure that the different regions have satisfactory rates of growth without loss of efficiency. At the same time the operation of the industries as a whole must also be efficient in both production and transportation. This is especially important in India, because an important part of the total industrial investment is in the public sector and therefore is guided by ideas of national welfare in so far as they are consistent with certain norms of efficiency.

The scope of this paper is comparatively limited. It is an investigation into the optimal regional production and exchange patterns for a number of commodities produced and exchanged between regions in India. The production processes of the commodities are assumed to be interdependent and conform to a Leontief-type technology. No attempt has been made to go into the problems of the allocation of investments. The aim here is to test the efficiency of the present trading patterns between different regions of India, viewed against some theoretically optimal flow that could be achieved with certain simplifying assumptions.

II.2 A REVIEW OF EARLIER MODELS AND THE PRESENT MODEL

It is obvious that in a broader framework of national planning targets and capacity levels for any specific commodity cannot be regarded in isolation as independent data. They become part of a set of interdependent variables. In this sense the regional requirement for coal, for example, is partly determined by the regional output of, let us say, steel. Therefore

---

[1] Part of the work for this paper was carried out by the author as a Rockefeller Foundation Fellow in the Harvard Economic Research Project. The completed paper was discussed in the fourth Econometric Conference in Hyderabad, India in 1964. The author was assisted by Sri. A. Chakravarti in the preparation of this paper.

a comprehensive plan must be based on an understanding of the inter-relations between different industrial sectors in a region, as much as on the inter-regional flows in the country as a whole.

The accounting frame-work for a model of this type will require the flows of the commodity from region p to region q and also the flow from the ith industrial sector of the pth region to the jth industrial sector in the qth, a typical unit of the flow being denoted by $_{pq}x_{ij}$.

The analysis can be carried out along two distinct lines. One of the lines of approach is the traditional input-output frame-work in fairly rigid form, assuming both a set of input coefficients for the industrial sectors and a set of regional coefficients to relate the inter-regional flows. The simplest method, and possibly the most illustrative of this approach is to assume that an industry in one region is different from the same industry in another region and then to assume a simple Leontief type of structure of production.

The delivery of the output of an industry e.g. sector i in region p to all sectors and all regions can be described as below:

$$_pX_i - \sum_q \sum_j {}_{pq}x_{ij} = \sum_q {}_{pq}f_i \quad (p, q \quad 1, \dots, n \text{ regions},$$
$$i, j \quad 1, \dots, m \text{ sectors}), \quad (1)$$

where $_{pq}f_i$ denotes the final demand of industry i in region q met from region p, and $_{pq}x_{ij}$ denotes the delivery from sector i in region p to sector j in region q.

Assuming constant production coefficients, i.e. a fixed amount of each input required per unit output of each commodity, the coefficient for a specific cell, say sector, j, may be expressed as

$$_{pq}a_{ij} = \frac{{}_{pq}x_{ij}}{{}_qX_j}, \quad (2)$$

where $_qX_j$ is the total output of the commodity produced by industry j in region q.

Substituting technical input coefficients into the balance relation we get,
$$_pX_i - \sum_q \sum_j {}_{pq}a_{ij}\,{}_qx_j = \sum_q {}_{pq}f_i. \quad (3)$$

The solution of equations for the required output of each industry of each region in terms of the bill of goods is developed as below:

$$_pX_i = \sum_q \sum_j {}_{pq}A_{ij} \sum_q {}_{pq}f_i, \quad (4)$$

where $_{pq}A_{ij}$ are the elements of the inverse of the matrix of coefficient in the left-hand side of the system (11.3).

Instead of considering distinct technical coefficients for each industry in each region two sets of coefficients have been proposed by some economists. These are the technical coefficients relating input to outputs and regional coefficients which assume some form of constancy in regional ratios of outputs.

Thus, Moses[1] has considered a variant, where regions have separate input coefficients so that if $_qx_{ij}$ is the input from the ith industry to the jth in region q, consisting of inputs procured from all the regions for this industry in region q, then

$$_qa_{ij} = \frac{_qx_{ij}}{_qx_j}, \tag{5}$$

where $_qX_j$ is the jth of output in region q.

We, then, define a regional coefficient so that if $_{pq}x_i$ denotes the ith type of commodity imported from p to q summed over all using industries then

$$_{pq}t_i = \frac{_{pq}x_i}{_qR_i}, \tag{6}$$

where $_qR_i$ is the total commodity of type i imported by region q from all the regions (the regional requirements being summed for both industries and regions).

We now have the further assumption that if $_qa_{ij}$ is the requirement of industry j per unit of output of type i goods in region q, then of this $_qa_{ij}$, $[(_qa_{ij}) \times (_{pq}t_i)]$ units will be coming from region p. Thus, if the steel requirement in the motor-car industry in Bihar is 0·2 per unit of car produced and if Bihar imports 10 per cent of her total steel requirements from Bengal, the assumption is that the motor-car industry in Bihar per unit of car gets 0·2 × 0·1 = 0·02 units of steel imported from Bengal.

Once these individual inputs $_{pq}x_i$ are replaced by the corresponding expressions $_{pq}a_{ij} = (_qa_{ij}) \times (_{pq}t_i)$ these are substituted into the balance relations given earlier from which a solution of the levels of regional outputs immediately follows.

The assumption of an unchanging regional pattern is unsatisfactory for many purposes. It is obvious that if a commodity is produced by several regions many circumstances will dictate the source of supply chosen by the user unit. The most important is likely to be price. Supplies from different regions are always potential substitutes and sources of supply may be changed when prices change. From our standpoint subject to the technical requirements of production, sources of supply for the nation as a whole should be fixed according to some cost minimizing principle.

We first formulate a programming model for a multi-sectoral economy assuming that production coefficients are similar for the same industry in different regions but that the regional flow pattern is determined subject to these coefficients and according to the objective of minimum national cost.

The balance relation for the output of any specific cell may be written as

$$\sum_q \sum_j {}_{pq}x_{ij} + \sum_q {}_{pq}f_i = {}_pX_i. \tag{7}$$

This indicates that all inter-industrial deliveries and final demand deliveries to all other regions from any region must equal that region's production excluding any re-exports.

[1] L. N. Moses, The stability of inter-regional trading patterns and input-output analysis, *American Economic Review* (December, 1955).

The second balance equation relates to the regional inputs and may be stated thus:

$$\sum_p \sum_j {}_{pq}x_{ij} + \sum_p {}_{pq}f_i = {}_qr_i. \tag{8}$$

We now introduce Leontief type technical coefficients, as below, and further assume that they are similar from region to region.

$$\sum_p {}_{pq}x_{ij} = a_{ij} \cdot {}_qX_j. \tag{9}$$

Therefore, we write the earlier balance requirement as

$$\sum_j a_{ij} \cdot {}_qX_j + \sum_p {}_{pq}f_i = {}_qR_i. \tag{10}$$

Thus we now have two balance relations and the technical coefficients in the picture. With these constraints, if ${}_{pq}c_{ij}$ is the cost of the delivery from the ith sector in region p to the jth sector in region q, the objective, obviously, is to minimize

$$\sum_p \sum_q \sum_i \sum_j {}_{pq}c_{ij} \cdot {}_{pq}x_{ij}. \tag{11}$$

The model finally used was slightly altered because of the type of available data.

Thus, the balance relation (7) showing the output and its deliveries to all sectors in all regions requires that we know how the output of any sector goes to the various sectors in other regions. This kind of detailed information is not available. The usual technique of transforming inputs into functions of output cannot be applied separately for inputs produced locally and imported. In this case the only balance relation that could be constructed depends on regional input-output data, where supply sources are aggregated, as in (11.13).

A regional balance equation is written for the ith sector, as

$$\sum_j {}_qx_{ij} - \sum_p \sum_j {}_{pq}x_{ij} - \sum_p {}_{pq}f_i + {}_qf_i + \sum_p {}_{qp}x_i = {}_qX_i \quad (p \neq q), \tag{12}$$

which means that the inter-industrial absorption in the qth region from all regions plus final deliveries from all regions to the qth plus export from q to other regions must equal the home production of the qth region plus imports from all other regions to the qth region. The absorption by industries in the qth region is aggregated over all supplying regions including itself.

Since any ${}_qX_j$ absorbs ${}_qa_{ij} \cdot {}_qX_j$ units of the ith commodity, irrespective of its origin, we can replace the elements ${}_qx_{ij}$, which denote the total absorption in the jth sector of q region of the ith commodity by ${}_qa_{ij} \cdot {}_qx_j$ where ${}_qx_j$ is the output of the jth sector in region q.

Then, the balance relation can be rewritten as,

$$\sum_j {}_qa_{ij} \cdot {}_qX_j + \sum_p {}_{qp}x_i - \sum_p \sum_j {}_{pq}x_{ij} - \sum_p {}_{pq}f_i + {}_qf_i = qX_i, \tag{13}$$

where, as before, the symbols pq and qp indicate the direction of the flow from p to q and from q to p respectively.

With the use of separate regional input-output tables, showing flows from all regions to one particular region, we obtained a set of equations relating inputs, outputs, exports and imports.

But there is still one form of limitation that may be considered which was not considered in the first model. This is the limitation in the transportation capacity from one region to another. One way of using transportation would, of course, be to make it a sector. This has not been done because of difficulties in obtaining data. In the present model transportation is considered exogenous and its requirements are included with others in final demand.

The transportation limits are considered in the following way. Let a 'Leontief' unit of material, (in the accepted sense) of any type i be associated with a weight w_i so that $w_i x_i$ denotes the weight of x_i units, in the Leontief sense. Then the model requires that a balance is kept between the transport availability from region p to region q and the total material transported, as in the following equations:

$$\sum_j w_j \cdot {}_{pq}x_j \leqq T_{pq}, \tag{14}$$

where T_{pq} is the maximum weight that could be transported from p to q with existing transport facilities. It is assumed that T_{pq} are independent constants.

We now come to the minimizing function. Since we have considered gross production, to avoid duplication in the production costs, the minimization may be done with respect to labour costs of achieving the same together with the transportation costs. We thus minimize the following function:

$$\sum_p \sum_q \sum_i {}_{pq}x_i({}_{pq}\Pi_i + {}_p\Pi_i), \tag{15}$$

where ${}_p\Pi_i$ denotes the labour costs of producing ith commodity in pth region and ${}_{pq}\Pi_i$ transportation cost from p to q of the same.

11.3 Empirical Implementation of the Model

The empirical implementation of the model is based on data relating to the Indian Union in 1954. A regional input-output table, which has been prepared by Sri R. Dhar,[1] has been used as the basic table from which this aggregation has been done. In the original table Dhar has considered sixteen sectors and five regions. In this model the dimension has been reduced for preliminary experimentation.

The regions were demarcated as follows:

Region 1	Region 2	Region 3	Region 4	Region 5
West Bengal Orissa Assam	Bihar, Uttar Pradesh	Punjab, Madhya Pradesh, Delhi, Rajasthan, Pepsu, Ajmir, Himachal Pradesh, Vindya Pradesh	Madras Andhra Mysore Kerala	Bombay Saurashtra

[1] The complete regional input-output table on which this is based forms a part of a doctoral thesis by Sri R. Dhar, prepared under my supervision in Jadavpur University.

Since we are considering only a few sectors explicitly the balance relation makes it imperative that one sector, comprising all the other industries should be considered exogenous along with final demand or be included as a composite group. The 'others' column was supplied exogenously on the basis of aggregated 'others' output and a set of sector-coefficients as given in column 7 of the input-output tables.

The input-output tables constructed for the current experiment are given in Tables 11.1 to 11.5 for the five regions.

Table 11.1. Region (1)

1.	0·064001	0·000315	0·153603	0·001806	0·008150	0·019984	0·00323
2.	—	0·001093	—	—	—	—	0·00023
3.	—	—	—	—	0·000404	—	—
4.	—	—	—	0·089991	0·003717	0·002320	—
5.	—	0·003347	0·137262	0·000600	0·00431	0·063343	0·00040
6.	—	—	—	—	—	0·110191	0·00973

Table 11.2. Region (2)

1.	0·064001	0·003092	0·114234	0·001352	0·012826	0·110191	0·00150
2.	—	0·030068	—	—	—	—	0·00023
3.	—	—	—	—	0·000337	—	—
4.	—	—	—	0·061454	0·000675	—	—
5.	—	0·018675	0·131862	0·000546	0·000675	0·001609	0·00034
6.	—	—	—	—	—	0·120500	0·000384

Table 11.3. Region (3)

1.	0·063999	0·001060	0·153603	0·005121	0·040072	0·068837	0·00058
2.	—	0·018354	—	—	—	—	0·00006
3.	—	—	—	—	—	—	—
4.	—	—	—	0·001985	—	—	—
5.	—	0·006753	0·135679	0·001135	0·010173	—	0·00015
6.	—	—	—	—	0·522451	—	0·00193

Table 11.4. Region (4)

1.	—	0·013340	0·052131	0·001451	0·024362	0·093165	0·00055
2.	—	0·005780	—	—	—	—	0·00016
3.	—	—	—	—	—	—	—
4.	—	—	—	0·208800	0·001070	—	—
5.	—	0·004086	0·134640	0·001197	—	0·017549	0·00027
6.	—	—	—	—	—	0·366194	0·00109

Table 11.5. Region (5)

1.	0·007388	0·001343	0·153603	0·012177	—	0·004938	0·00260
2.	0·030631	0·005570	—	—	—	—	0·00040
3.	—	—	—	—	—	—	—
4.	—	—	—	0·540219	—	—	—
5.	0·042458	0·007721	0·137262	0·003599	0·000177	—	0·00067
6.	—	—	—	—	0·507497	—	0·00038

11.4 THE PRICE PROBLEM

Before going on to the other basic tables it is necessary to clear up the problem of price variations and their effect on the inter-regional tables.

The problem arises because of local variations in the price of the same commodity in different regions. The input-output flow tables, compiled from the usual official statistics, generally reflect local costs. But, the inter-regional flow tables in physical quantities and the transportation costs are usually given in money per physical unit, i.e. it is more or less uniform from region to region in India. To make the whole model come into the same unit we have either to reduce them to physical quantities or to a common Leontief unit based on a suitable price system.

To do this we make the following assumptions: (i) in most regions, the input-output flow tables reflect the local paid costs of input and the value of the product at local prices; (ii) the inputs are in rates of the biggest producers of commodities, or if, there is more than one big producer, an average of them. This means that any region using ith commodity, which it mainly imports, will pay a price for ith type of input, as determined by a big producer of i. This means that inputs are already in dominant All-India prices. Small producers who use them pay what the big producers of these commodities declare to be their price. The outputs, however, are in local prices, and have to be transformed into an All-India price by a suitable index. This means, in effect, that input values are accepted as they are but outputs are expressed in terms of All-India ruling prices.

The consequence of using this method is that the coefficients of any big producer of a commodity will not be changed. His inputs are in All-India prices and his outputs are also in dominant All-India prices. For small producers output values will be changed, leading to changes in the local coefficient.

Tables A (1) to A (3) in the Appendix give the local output prices and the All-India prices, as assumed in the current study, the transport costs and the labour costs for the sectors in each region.

The following figures are given for the final demand and 'others' output as estimated for sectors not included in these six.

Table 11.6. ('000 *Rs.*)

Sectors	Region 1	Region 2	Region 3	Region 4	Region 5
Coal	29849	50298	29926	18933	14650
Sugar	186240	797798	362363	461192	322932
Cement	0	504	0	0	0
Cotton	1104880	2058132	1213985	1758483	1051002
Jute	1152438	0	0	0	0
Iron	146279	249070	0	0	0
'Other output'	11264086	17742000	17024137	12934545	8872307

It can be seen that I have assumed that cement is not included in final demand except in region 2 where there are some exports. Jute is not included in final demand in any region other than the first, as it is either exported or has inter-industrial use, and it is exported only from region 1. Similarly iron and steel is exported as a final output from regions 1 and 2 only.

The transport constraints (T_{pq}) are given below in tons:

Table 11.7. (*'000 tons*)

	Region 1	Region 2	Region 3	Region 4	Region 5
1.	—	1971	1012	227	136
2.	4458	—	590	429	1010
3.	27	329	—	691	1642
4.	30	22	41	—	58
5.	22	37	222	49	—

These constraints were determined on the basis of present actual load carried and other considerations.

We are now in a position to formulate the model in numerical terms from the set of equations or inequations and the minimizing function in (11.13) to (11.15).

11.5. THE SOLUTION

As has been noted before the present experiment was conducted on the flow table for 1954 and the regional input-output table prepared for the same year.

In the first experiment the assumption was made that a capacity limit on production does not exist in any sector or any region. This implied that an optimal solution will only have to conform to the restrictions stated in (11.13) to (11.15).

Table 11.8 gives the result of this experiment, along with the corresponding actual data. Some useful conclusions may be drawn from this very preliminary experiment.

Table 11.8. (*'000 Rs.*)

Region	Sector			Region			
			1	2	3	4	5
1	Coal	i	(196699)				
		ii	177776	2447	12539	2231	1496
	Sugar	i	(188726)				
		ii	231217	49798	1732	403	24
	Cement	i	(50661)				
		ii	171135	981	483	6	—
	Cotton	i	(1219268)				
		ii	1206052	16197	2502	1549	119

i Optimal.   ii Actual.

Table 11.8. (cont.)

Region	Sector		1	2	3	4	5
	Jute	i	(1088498)				
		ii	1202684	20296	16580	3668	3287
	Iron and	i	(267113)				
	steel	ii	325796	51071	37258	21102	9289
2	Coal	i		(178114)			
		ii	55123	262259	13836	7450	13400
	Sugar	i		(826691)			
		ii	10818	928177	114993	95	48825
	Cement	i		(57475)			
		ii	32652	64954	602	28	12
	Cotton	i		(2578264)			
		ii	6552	2446420	11437	1072	2740
	Jute	i	(65826)				
		ii	1906	41472	22108	1906	4479
	Iron and	i		(269472)			
	steel	ii	68255	470870	36561	13162	7815
3	Coal	i			(112113)	(7227)	
		ii	248	319	86641	9810	1985
	Sugar	i			(247524)		
		ii	71	2230	197119	1044	10130
	Cement	i			(55833)		
		ii	419	23130	86675	2177	18098
	Cotton	i			(1554160)		
		ii	1007	35620	1457289	3931	59089
	Jute	i					
		ii	715	1668	4442	572	2835
	Iron and	i	(8500)	(102245)	(272070)	(67099)	
	steel	ii	423	4044	28996	2308	3256
4	Coal	i				(47752)	
		ii	—	—	19	32307	192
	Sugar	i				(442069)	
		ii	1115	—	4413	479197	9585
	Cement	i				(62954)	
		ii	1972	1624	1458	66889	1137
	Cotton	i				(2222551)	
		ii	9173	5837	30259	22173021	23469
	Jute	i					
		ii	619	775	3192	14194	905
	Iron and	i	(9380)	(6969)			
	steel	ii	446	171	1017	16240	2399
5	Coal	i					(78329)
		ii	—	1	63	3	63073
	Sugar	i			(120459)	(23815)	(475769)
		ii	—	24270	62277	474	346835
	Cement	i					(51404)
		ii	766	95	11440	46	51405
	Cotton	i					(2538216)
		ii	6469	87919	152139	66356	2780599
	Jute	i	(28395)	(96526)	(45053)	(15397)	(214569)
		ii	47	48	8052	1763	24620
	Iron and	i					(119429)
	steel	ii	—	2593	15573	7918	28144

i Optimal.   ii Actual.

It can be seen that the deviation between optimal and actual is not very large as far as production is concerned, but there are large discrepancies between the actual and the optimal for the inter-regional flows. For two reasons this should not immediately be interpreted as a sign of the inefficiency of the trade pattern.

First, in this experiment, the real capacity levels are bound to affect inter-regional flows. Therefore the situation is bound to change once realistic capacity limits are introduced.

But this unrestricted flow and its direction, still gives us some useful information. Note that some regions are producing more than the actual in the optimal. Such cases show the comparative advantages of producing more in the regions in the existing cost and transport situation. In a later experiment, however, this assumption of unlimited capacity has been withdrawn, and some capacity limits have been imposed in some sectors of some regions to study a more realistic situation.

The second reason for the large difference between the actual and the optimal is however due to a more difficult technical hurdle. It can be seen that in our regional classifications each of the regions is a substantially large area of two or more states combined. In such cases the distance between two points on the border of two states which may be quite small has still been taken to be the average distance between the centres of the two regions, in an economic sense. Naturally, therefore, many flows between two such neighbouring points in the two regions look, in the aggregated solution, like inefficient cross-hauling while in effect this is not so. The programming model, in such cases, has eliminated all such extensive border trade between the regions because of our failure to give a proper definition of distance.

The remedy for this is to increase the number of regions in a more realistic fashion and to do the experiment on a more elaborate basis.

Table 11.9 gives the results of the subsequent experiment where a number of limits to capacity were introduced based on *a priori* knowledge of the various regions and their products. Where an area is known as a small producer it was assumed that it was already working to full capacity. The limits considered were:

Table 11.9. *Production Capacity Limits* ('000 *Rs.*)

		Region 1	
$_1X_1$	$\leqslant$	177776	(Coal)
$_1X_2$	$\leqslant$	188726	(Sugar)
$_1X_3$	$\leqslant$	17135	(Cement)
$_1X_4$	$\leqslant$	1206052	(Cotton)
		Region 2	
$_2X_4$	$\leqslant$	2446420	(Cotton)
		Region 5	
$_5X_2$	$\leqslant$	346835	(Sugar)

The result of the experiment is given in the following Table 11.10.

Table 11·10. ('000 *Rs.*)

Region	Sector		Region				
			1	2	3	4	5
1	Coal	i	(177775)	—	—	—	—
		ii	177776	24447	—	—	—
	Sugar	i	(188726)	—	—	—	—
		ii	188726	49798	—	—	—
	Cement	i	(17135)	—	—	—	—
		ii	17135	981	—	—	—
	Cotton	i	(1206051)	—	—	—	—
		ii	1206052	16197	—	—	—
	Jute	i	(1184390)	(5548)	—	—	—
		ii	1202684	20296	—	—	—
	Iron and steel	i	(278003)	—	—	—	—
		ii	325796	51071	—	—	—
2	Coal	i	(13527)	(197200)	—	—	—
		ii	55123	262259	—	—	—
	Sugar	i	—	(810271)	—	—	—
		ii	10818	928177	—	—	—
	Cement	i	(29468)	(86955)	—	—	—
		ii	32652	64954	—	—	—
	Cotton	i	—	(2446419)	—	—	—
		ii	6552	2446420	—	—	—
	Jute	i	—	(32681)	—	—	(3977)
		ii	1906	41472	—	—	4479
	Iron and steel	i	—	(282968)	—	—	—
		ii	68255	470870	—	—	—
3	Coal	i	—	—	(112197)	(7606)	—
		ii	—	—	86641	9810	—
	Sugar	i	—	—	(370236)	—	—
		ii	—	—	197119	—	—
	Cement	i	(2274)	—	(58108)	—	—
		ii	419	—	86675	—	—
	Cotton	i	—	(51094)	(1605356)	—	—
		ii	—	35620	1457289	—	—
	Jute	i	—	—	(46274)	—	—
		ii	—	—	4442	—	—
	Iron and steel	i	—	97344	(274921)	(58940)	—
		ii	—	—	28996	2308	—
4	Coal	i	—	—	—	(47525)	—
		ii	—	—	—	32307	—
	Sugar	i	—	—	—	(466023)	—
		ii	—	—	—	479197	—
	Cement	i	—	—	—	(62954)	—
		ii	—	—	—	66889	—
	Cotton	i	(12409)	(72670)	—	(2330105)	—
		ii	9173	5837	—	22173021	—
	Jute	i	—	—	—	(15624)	—
		ii	—	—	—	14194	—
	Iron and steel	i	(8190)	—	—	—	—
		ii	446	—	—	—	—

i Optimal.   ii Actual; where not mentioned it is the same as in Table 11.8.

Table 11.10. (*cont.*)

| | | | \multicolumn{5}{c}{Region} | | | |
			1	2	3	4	5
5	Coal	i	—	(718)	(3194)	(703)	(82607)
		ii	—	1	63	3	63073
	Sugar	i	—	(15926)	—	—	(346834)
		ii	—	—	—	—	346835
	Cement	i	(1822)	(24270)	—	—	(53227)
		ii	766	24270	—	—	51405
	Cotton	i	—	—	—	—	(538216)
		ii	—	—	—	—	2780599
	Jute	i	—	—	—	—	(24620)
		ii	—	—	—	—	24620
	Iron and	i	—	—	—	—	(23030)
	steel	ii	—	—	—	—	28144

i Optimal.   ii Actual; where not mentioned it is the same as in Table 11.8.

It can be seen that the introduction of a number of constraints does improve the nature of the agreement between the actual and the optimal flow. But there have been no startling changes.

By comparing our solution, in these cases, with the type of solution that was obtained in the study of the cement industry,[1] where more than nine regions were defined, it was surmised that the very large size of the regions was the main reason behind this divergence between the actual and the optimal flows.

This difficulty, however, cannot be easily handled. The construction of input-output tables becomes increasingly difficult and meaningless when regions are made smaller and more compact in size. Inter-regional flows, however, can be studied more and more realistically when regions are made smaller and smaller. Somewhere along the lines between these two the size of the regions must be delimited. These and other problems are being taken up in later phases of the experiment.

[1] A. Ghosh, *Efficiency in location and inter-regional flows: The Indian Cement Industry during the five year plans 1950–1959*. North Holland.

APPENDIX

Regional price per ton with corresponding All-India prices.

Table A(1)

Commodities	Regions (in Rs.)					
	1	2	3	4	5	All-India
Coal	15·27	13·67	14·88	21·52	—	14·41
Sugar	680·60	619·81	680·60	697·90	740·66	644·69
Cement	—	—	—	—	—	—
Cotton	3699·20	2662·40	2956·40	3238·40	3302·40	3237·26
Jute	1294·69	1181·20	1113·59	1153·42	—	1294·69
Iron and steel	279·50	310·32	472·31	472·01	422·14	429·89

Transport costs from one region to another per Leontief unit are given in the following tables.

Table A(2)

Region	1	2	3	4	5
	Coal (in Rs.)				
1.	0·3872	1·8972	3·0272	2·8972	3·2872
2.	1·9269	0·4169	2·3169	3·5669	2·8269
3.	2·8856	2·1456	0·2456	3·6556	2·4156
4.	2·8886	3·5286	3·7886	0·3786	2·6386
5.	2·9000	2·4100	2·1700	2·2600	0
	Sugar (in Rs.)				
1.	0·0953	0·1290	0·1543	0·1514	0·1602
2.	0·1221	0·0884	0·1310	0·1588	0·1423
3.	0·0910	0·0746	0·0320	0·1083	0·0805
4.	0·1410	0·1553	0·1612	0·0849	0·1355
5.	0·1397	0·1287	0·1233	0·1254	0·0748
	Cement (in Rs.)				
1.	0·1218	7·2318	12·5618	11·9418	13·8118
2.	7·1939	0·0839	9·0639	14·9239	11·4539
3.	12·5332	9·0732	0·0932	16·1732	10·3132
4.	11·9037	14·9237	16·1637	0·0837	10·7437
5.	13·7980	11·4780	10·3280	10·7680	0·1080
	Cotton (in Rs.)				
1.	0·2503	0·2570	0·2620	0·2614	0·2632
2.	0·2087	0·2020	0·2105	0·2160	0·2127
3.	0·2390	0·2358	0·2273	0·2425	0·2369
4.	0·1846	0·1875	0·1887	0·1735	0·1835
5.	0·2642	0·2620	0·2609	0·2613	0·2513

Table A(2) (cont.)

Region	1	2	3	4	5
		Jute (in Rs.)			
1.	0·1837	0·2005	0·2130	0·2116	0·2160
2.	0·2563	0·2395	0·2607	0·2745	0·2664
3.	0·3109	0·3088	0·2876	0·3255	0·3117
4.	0·2281	0·2352	0·2381	0·2002	0·2253
5.	0·0323	0·0269	0·0241	0·0251	0
		Iron and steel (in Rs.)			
1.	0·2511	0·3211	0·3736	0·3675	0·3858
2.	0·2816	0·2116	0·3000	0·3578	0·3236
3.	0·2956	0·2615	0·1731	0·3315	0·2737
4.	0·3159	0·3457	0·3579	0·1995	0·3045
5.	0·3808	0·3581	0·3467	0·3511	0·2461

The labour costs per Leontief unit are given in the following table (in Rs.).

Table A(3)

Region	Coal	Sugar	Cement	Cotton	Jute	Iron
1.	0·3872	0·0953	0·1218	0·2503	0·1837	0·2511
2.	0·4169	0·0884	0·0839	0·2020	0·2395	0·2116
3.	0·2456	0·0320	0·0932	0·2273	0·2876	0·1731
4.	0·3786	0·0849	0·0837	0·1735	0·2002	0·1995
5.	—	0·0748	0·1080	0·2513	—	0·2461

ON A MODEL FOR THE PROJECTION OF EXPENDITURE AND INCOMES OF THE UNION GOVERNMENT IN THE THIRD FIVE-YEAR PLAN PERIOD[1]

12.1 INTRODUCTION

An attempt has been made in this paper to project the likely trends of income and expenditure of the Union Government during the period of the third Five-Year Plan. A five-year plan is, in itself, a projection of expenditure in the next five years. It is a projection that an official agency, e.g. the Planning Commission, has made in pursuing the declared objective of the Government to direct economic growth in a particular way, keeping in mind the various factors that may affect the national economy in the next five years. Since the Government holds, in this case, an immense driving force behind it, it is obvious that the Plan itself is likely to be one of the basic indicators of the future trends of income and expenditure for the next five years.

The task of this exercise, by an external agency other than the Government, in making a set of projections, is, in essence, a reassessment of the intentions of the authorities and the likely impact on them of factors beyond their control, which may lead to a deviation of the actual situation from that envisaged in the Plan.

The most obvious use of such an exercise is to check official expectations against a similar appraisal of factors through a non-official angle. Alternative projections, provided that the assumptions on which they are based are clearly stated, are warnings of possible lines of deviation, of hidden dangers which could give a greater touch of realism to the Plan itself. In this sense, alternative projections may be usefully discussed in order to spread the consciousness that a plan itself is a projection of possibilities under given assumptions, economic and institutional.

The question naturally arises as to how far such exercises are, or should, be used as guides to official policy-making. In the present stage of econometric model-building it must be admitted that many relations that are assumed, many variables that are measured, involve various crudities, approximations and errors. Naturally, therefore, to rely on such projections one must be cautious and be prepared for a wide margin

---

[1] This article is based on a more detailed exercise by the author published under the heading 'Union budget and prices', Asia Publishing House.

of error. As is said, economic models are more easily compared to meteorological models than to those in physics. But just as meteorological forecasts are of great use in understanding the weather and antici-pating rough weather so econometric model-building is of use in under-standing the economic future and the possible 'low pressure' areas in the economic horizon.

The choice of Projection Technique

It must be stated at the outset that a good 'rule of thumb' projection is an extremely difficult thing to make. In 'rule of thumb' projections one goes by what may be called a 'hunch' or a guess. A good guess, however, involves a very close understanding of the forces involved and a sensitive appreciation of likely prospects. In the matter of government expendi-ture a 'rule of thumb' projection, if it is to be good, can only be made by people closely in touch with official reactions. For any one depending mainly on published data such an institutional approach is bound to be rather dangerous. Apart from this, the 'rule of thumb' approach, right or wrong, often fails to state clearly the underlying assumptions on which such 'hunches' are based, simply because no conscious exposition can be made of an unconscious weighing of pros and cons. While, therefore, 'rule of thumb' approaches should not be brushed aside one should remember the peculiar limitations of such an approach. For a non-official economist such a 'rule of thumb' approach may often be wide of the mark.

The problem of projection has been approached by setting up a macro-model which will delineate the main variables we consider essential, the data on which we base our observations and the inter-relationships we assume to exist between them. When we speak of a macro-model we particularly emphasize the fact that price, public income and expenditure are all inter-related and only a system of simultaneous equations, rather than a single isolated equation for each, can adequately handle the problem.

Basic assumptions of the Model

We formulate the following fundamental assumptions before setting up our model.

(1) There will be no outbreaks of war on Indian borders, though the military situation will continue to be tense, in the next five years.

(2) There will be no basic changes in the political approach of the Government of India regarding planning and development through a mixed economy with the Government directly taking a large share in development efforts.

(3) The tempo of expansion of the economy and of government expenditure and income will generally be similar to that of the second Five-Year Plan.

(4) Foreign aid will continue to flow into the economy more or less as planned by the government.

These assumptions amount to saying that the general economic and political circumstances will be of the type prevalent during the second Five-Year Plan. The present set of projections will not work if some completely unexpected factors distort the picture. As may be seen when the work was done, situation (1), on the question of border troubles, was assumed to be one of 'cold war'. Since then active border conflicts have taken place and this has shaken the most important basic assumption of the model. It will considerably affect the validity of the model in several important respects.

The Data and its Sources

The main data for our model relates to the income and expenditure incurred by the Union Government. The Union Government expenditure passes through several stages. The first is the planned expenditure announced by the Government at the beginning of a five-year plan. This expenditure relates only to new developmental items and is only a part of the total expenditure. This, however, gives the earliest indicator of the level of expenditure the Government proposes to incur, as a whole, in the next five years. But the Plan is not a sanction to spend.

The official sanction to spend for a particular year is first announced in the budget. The budget differs from the Plan in many ways. The budget gives sanction for only one year, it covers all types of expenditure, new and old, developmental and non-developmental. Only a part of the budget can be identified as originating from the Plan of the period. Though the original budget is presented and passed officially it does not constitute actual expenditure, as many of the items are revised later on.

The next stage is the saction given to the revised budget which makes a closer approximation to actual expenses by increases, or cuts, as the original budget is operated. Even this, however, does not give actual government expenditure. For that, we have to turn to the Accounts or Actuals which generally give a much more definite, though not always a complete, picture of the expenses of the Government.

12.2 CHOICE OF VARIABLES FOR THE MODEL

The first task in setting up a model is obviously to choose the set of variables we are interested in projecting. As I explained before, we have chosen to solve for these variables through a macro-model which will depict the working of a whole related system. In such a system, apart from the problem variables, we must bring in variables which are so-called independent or exogenous to the system. The main distinction is drawn on the criterion of whether a variable depends for its movement on a set of variables included in the model or not. If these are variables which influence, but are not influenced by the variables already in the model, they are called exogenous, or externally determined variables.

In depicting a coherent picture economically, however, some additional variables may have to be brought in relating the problem variables with the exogenous or independent variables. So long as the total number of variables does not exceed the number of equations in the system, these incidental variables can be solved along with the problem variables.

A word on the choice of these variables. Problem variables are, of course, chosen for us by the problem setter which may be a political or economic authority. The other variables depend on the discretion of the econometrician and can only be selected through a trial and error process based on a general understanding of the working of the system by the econometrician.

One big limitation in choosing what might seem to be the most effective system of variables is the limitation of data. In fact, the non-availability of data often forces us to choose a set of variables which may be a second best set. Econometric models, thus, for their validity and correctness ultimately depend heavily on the availability of raw data as much as on technical ingenuity.

Single Equation versus a Simultaneous System

The variables then—that is the set to be projected and the associated set —are presented in a system of simultaneous equations defining the relationship between them. The method, in this approach, is to set up a system of equations with these variables and estimate them all together, rather than singly. Any attempt at approaching inter-dependent variables and estimating them separately by single equations involving these variables may lead to bias. Thus, government income and expenditure are mutually inter-dependent and the single equation approach for this estimation may lead to bias.

Various devices have been suggested to by-pass this difficulty. We shall briefly discuss one of these techniques. It is possible, in many cases in such systems, to manipulate the variables in such a way that all the endogenous variables are expressed as functions of purely exogenous variables. Since the exogenous variables are assigned from outside and are not probabilistic, it becomes possible to obtain estimates of the endogenous variables as functions of the exogenous variables by a simple least square approach.

The difficulty in this approach is that while predictions of the values of the variables can be carried out easily it is not always possible to estimate the parameters of the original system from that of the reduced form. The cases in which such an estimation of the parameter is possible are usually known as identified systems.

In one particular case of the reduced form it is always possible to identify the parameters of the original system. This is the case known as a recursive system. In such systems it is possible to proceed step by step by first expressing one equation of the system in terms of the exogenous variables and then using the variable thus evaluated through the exogenous variables to obtain a solution for the next and so on. The variables occur in such a sequence, in recursive systems, that a step by step approach in this way is possible so that at no stage does an endogenous variable enter into the estimation procedure except the one to be determined. The estimates of the parameter, in such cases, are consistent and unbiased.

The model we have set up here is of the recursive type. We could have estimated the parameters by proceeding step by step from the first equation of the system onwards. However in the present case it is not our intention to establish the values of the parameters but to obtain predictions for the variables in the system. We have, therefore, used the formal procedure of the reduced form in fitting the parameters and predicting the value of the variables for the future.

Demonstration of a Condensed Form of the Model

We want to project future government expenditure (E) and income (Y). These are, therefore, our 'projection' variables.

We know that government expenditure (E) largely depends on developmental capital expenditures $(E^{c.dev.})$; routine type of expenditures on revenue account (E^r); and defence expenditures (E^d). Government earning (Y) depends largely on governmental requirements for finance and on the previous level of government earnings over time, depending on long-term factors like institutional efficiency, response to taxation, or loans, etc. We now construct the following system:

1. $E^{c.dev.} = a_M^{c.dev.} \cdot M + a_{I_g}^{c.dev.}, \quad I_g + a_t^{c.dev.} \cdot t + \lambda^{c.dev.};$

2. $E^{c\Sigma} = a_E^{c\Sigma} \cdot E^{c.dev.} + a_t^{c\Sigma} \cdot t + \lambda^{c\Sigma};$

3. $E^{r\Sigma} = a_E^{r\Sigma} \cdot E^{c\Sigma} + a_t^{r\Sigma} \cdot t + \lambda^{r\Sigma};$

4. $E^d = a_t^d \cdot t + \lambda^d;$

5. $E = E^{c\Sigma} + E^{r\Sigma} + E^d;$

6. $Y = a_E^Y \cdot E + a_t^Y \cdot t + \lambda^Y;$

7. $P = a_E^P \cdot E + a_Y^P \cdot Y + a_t^P \cdot t + \lambda^P;$

where

$E^{c.dev.}$ = expenditure on capital account of developmental type;

$E^{c\Sigma}$ = total capital disbursement excluding defence;

$E^{r\Sigma}$ = total revenue disbursement excluding defence;

E^d = total defence expenditure on revenue and capital accounts;

Y = earned income of the government, i.e. excluding foreign aid and deficit spending;

M = total imports;

I_g = planned expenditure by government as proposed in Five-Year Plans;

t = time;

P = general price level.

The variables above may be classed as:

(1) projection variables: E, Y;
(2) associated endogenous variables: $E^{c\Sigma}$, $E^{r\Sigma}$, E^d, $E^{c.dev.}$, P;
(3) associated exogenous variables: M, I_g, t.

In the above model, we have seven equations and ten variables. Of these we are assuming that total imports (M), planned expenditure (I_g) and time (t) are exogenous to the system.

Total imports are taken as exogenous as it is largely determined nowadays by our export level and our foreign aid receipts and is almost equal to the sum of those two, both of which are determined largely by factors outside our direct control.

The second specific assumption is that relations between these ten variables are linear, at least in the short run.

I_g is taken as exogenous, as it is the announced intention of the Government to spend on development, and is of an autonomous nature.

Coming now to the equations, equation (1) states that total government capital expenditure on development is largely determined by planned outlay (I_g), important availability (M), and by time (t), which accounts for a part of other influences on the growth of capital outlay.

Equation (2) states that total capital disbursement largely depends on capital development, and on time, as there are various maintenance and replacement type expenditures which are outside the developmental category.

Equation (3) states that expenditure on revenue account is partly determined by the size of the capital budget as the revenue account usually follows up by providing for various routine types of expenses associated with development; it is also determined partly through a trend, which gives the growth of revenue expenditure over the years through salaries, administrative and other routine expenses. It would have been more reasonable to assume a lag here but this has not been done for a first approximation.

Equation (4) states that defence expenditure has only a secular trend.

The next equation (5) is an identity relating total expenditure to its three components.

Equation (6) states that government income is partly determined by government expenditure and partly by the effect of time. It thus assumes that to a large extent government income may be increased or decreased according to whether government expenditure is expanded or contracted. It is thus used as a broad indicater of total national activity.

Equation (7) states that price is determined by the level of government expenditure and income and partly by a time trend.

It may be useful to elaborate the basic logic of the system.

The most important assumption about income is that it depends on the requirements of the Government indicated by its expenditure level. The other factor which influences it is a smaller component which shows the effect of time, indicating that there are other factors operating which slowly work over time.

The components of income, like excise, income tax, small savings are determined through the level of expenditure and time. The underlying assumption here is that, when government expenditure increases, there is a certain ratio by which the Government succeeds in raising its income. This may, of course, be done by increasing rates of taxation or by other measures. However, we are not concerned with the effect of specific tax increase, etc. We are assuming that the net results of these measures will tend to increase income in a certain way which will keep in line with the past, relations of government income with expenditure and time.

Government expenditure has a twofold effect on the income of the Government. First, higher levels of government expenditure stimulate the income of the country directly and indirectly by stimulating production, thus expanding the base of the taxation system.

Secondly, larger government expenditures lead to an effort on the part of the Government to raise more revenue by increasing taxation rates, encouraging savings and so on. We generally assume that these efforts lead to a certain resultant response in government income which tend to move with its expenditure.

This indicates that government efforts to increase income directly or indirectly leads to a result which, however, tends to move in its own way. This is not necessarily the way the Government originally thinks it will move. In fact the Government tends to anticipate rather higher incomes by raising tax rates and so on. But, given the present social and institutional set-up, such efforts tend to lead only to a specific pattern of rise. The marginal return from additional government efforts, once this pattern is reached, tends to fall to zero.

Once these assumptions of relations specific to the model are accepted as giving a realistic picture of the interplay between the variables, we are on the way to establishing a determinate model.

The Fitting Procedure

We have already explained the logic behind the reduced form technique.

We now rewrite the system by separating the exogenous and endogenous variables and eliminate the constants by measuring from the mean. The system can now be rearranged and written in matrix notation as follows:

$$
\begin{bmatrix}
1 & & & & & & \\
a_E^{c\Sigma} - 1 & & & & & & \\
& a_E^{r\Sigma} - 1 & & & & & \\
& & & 1 & & & \\
1 & & 1 & 1 & -1 & & \\
& & & & & a_E^Y - 1 & \\
& & & & & a_E^Y & a_Y^P - 1
\end{bmatrix}
\begin{bmatrix}
E^{c.\,dev.} \\
E^{c\Sigma} \\
E^{r\Sigma} \\
E^d \\
E \\
Y \\
P
\end{bmatrix}
=
\begin{bmatrix}
a_M^{c.\,dev.} & a_{I_g}^{c.\,dev.} & a_t^{c.\,dev.} \\
& & -a_t^{c\Sigma} \\
& & -a_t^{r\Sigma} \\
& & a_t^d \\
& & O \\
& & -a_t^Y \\
& & -a_t^P
\end{bmatrix}
\begin{bmatrix}
M \\
I_g \\
t
\end{bmatrix}.
$$

Symbolically, it may be written as

$$A . \epsilon = B . \eta.$$

Where A represents the coefficient matrix and ϵ is the vector of variables to be determined on the left side and β is the coefficient matrix associated with the exogenous variables and λ the vector of exogenous variables on the right.

Solving the above system in matrix notation we get all the endogenous variables in terms of the exogenous variables as below

$$\epsilon = A^{-1} B . \eta.$$

It is now seen that all the endogenous variables are expressed as functions of only the exogenous variables. We can now apply the least square technique to evaluate the coefficients without the possibility of bias in the estimate.

12.3 Projecting a Model for Expenditure, Income and Price

The following equations were obtained for E, Y, and P by the method described earlier.

$$E = 340.5483 + 0.0331M + 0.6978I_g + 45.3969t$$

$$Y = 537.77 - 0.2004M + 0.2203I_g + 63.1397t$$

$$P = 58.102 + 0.01315M + 0.002146I_g + 4.776349t$$

The projections were made separately under three sets of assumptions.

(1) The first projection is made on the basis of the assumption that the import and foreign aid target as envisaged by the government will be maintained and that, even if there is a price rise, no upward revision will be made of the financial targets announced in the plan.

(2) In the second set, it is assumed that, while the import and foreign aid targets are as before, the Government makes an upward revision each year of the financial targets, on the basis of the price rises of the preceding year, in order to maintain the physical targets intact

(3) In the third case, it is assumed that the Government holds on to a deficit of the order of Rs. 550 crores, as announced, and makes such alterations in the Plan as are necessary for this purpose, the data on import and foreign aid remaining unaltered.

Table 12.1 below gives the estimated and observed values for the last ten years on the basis of the present model and projection of expenditure, income and price from the model for the period of the third Five-Year Plan on the basis of the first set of assumptions.

Table 12.1. (*In crores of Rs.*)

$$E = 340 \cdot 5483 + 0 \cdot 0331M + 0 \cdot 6978I_g + 45 \cdot 3969t$$

| Year of Plan | At 1952–3 price | | | | At 1960–1 price |
| | First Five-Year Plan | | Second Five-Year Plan | | Projection for third Five-Year Plan |
	Observed	Expected	Observed	Expected	
1	597·19	581·30	1035·72	1068·29	1828·88
2	554·68	642·60	1360·15	1279·37	2172·54
3	700·75	718·23	1318·57	1398·14	2357·14
4	980·12	883·83	1446·87	1446·54	2419·63
5	985·51	991·25	N.A.	1537·81	2554·39
Total	3818·25	3817·21	5161·31	6730·15	11332·58

$$Y = 537 \cdot 77 - 0 \cdot 2004M + 0 \cdot 2203I_g + 63 \cdot 1397t$$

1	600·47	482·55	822·39	806·52	1398·73
2	499·37	574·17	895·76	916·73	1560·19
3	640·14	671·63	1116·69	1026·16	1714·50
4	959·26	733·57	1312·13	1109·62	1824·59
5	823·93	805·33	N.A.	1148·93	1870·54
Total	3523·17	3267·25	4146·97	5007·96	8368·55

$$P = 58 \cdot 102 + 0 \cdot 01315M + 0 \cdot 00215I_g + 4 \cdot 77635t. \text{ Base } 1952\text{--}53 \ (= 100)$$

1	—	—	105·30	103·87	131·69
2	—	—	108·40	109·48	137·57
3	—	—	112·90	113·05	140·92
4	89·60	88·22	117·10	116·64	144·25
5	92·50	94·54	—	—	152·07

As may be seen the observed and estimated are reasonably close, particularly in the last five years and as we expect the third Plan to follow the lines of the second, the closeness of the fit of the last five years gives us greater confidence.

Though not clearly stated in the plan price rises will necessarily occur in our model. It is obvious that such price rises will depreciate the Plan. The achievement of the physical target and the deficit spending consequent on carrying it out will be as below:

Table 12.2. (*In crores of Rs.*)

Year	Original Plan target (at 1960–1 price)	Plan target as depreciated by price rise during 1961–5 (at 1960–1 price)	Excess of expenditure over income excluding foreign aid
1961–2	1032·00	978·01	430·15
1962–3	1441·50	1307·72	612·35
1963–4	1632·75	1445·93	642·64
1964–5	1647·75	1425·63	595·04
1965–6	1746·75	1433·93	683·85
Total	7500·75	6590·82	2964·03
Deficit spending assuming foreign aid as in the plan			764·03

Reliability of Projections

How reliable is the above picture presented in our projection? The following table gives the standard error of estimates of our projections. The standard error has been calculated from the formula,

$$\text{standard error} = \sqrt{\left(\frac{(\text{Observed} - \text{Computed})^2}{N}\right)},$$

where N is the number of observations.

Table 12.3. (*In crores of Rs.*)

Accounting head	Standard error
Expenditure	73·84
Income	145·10
Excess of Expenditure over Income	88·67

The standard error for the excess of expenditure over income has been calculated from the following formula:

Let σ_E and σ_Y be the standard error for the estimates of expenditure and income and σ_{ex} the standard error for excess, then σ_{ex} is given by the formula

$$\sigma_{ex} = \sqrt{(\sigma_{E+}^2 + \sigma_Y^2 - 2r \cdot \sigma_E \, \sigma_Y)},$$

where r is the correlation coefficient between income and expenditure. Assuming the deviations to be normally distributed, ± 2 standard error covers nearly 97 per cent of the deviations. We now obtain the most optimistic and the most pessimistic picture. If things go well then the excess of expenditure over income may be taken as -2 standard error giving us a deficit of Rs. 587 crores, assuming foreign aid is not subject to any error. The corresponding picture if things go wrong, is given by adding 2 standard error to the expected deficit bringing it up to a total of Rs. 941 crores.

The above projection, as already stated, assumes that the Government announces a financial plan and holds on to it, in spite of price increases, thus depreciating the actual growth in real terms.

Projections on the Basis of the Second Set of Assumptions

What will happen if the Government wants to keep to its physical plan by an upward revision of the financial targets in the case of a price-rise? This will mean that with a price-rise each year there will be an upgrading of the plan thus affecting the projection of the succeeding year. The following tables give the sequence on the assumption that a price rise in the first year forces the Government to upgrade the Plan in the second year and so on.

Thus $I_g(t+1)$ (Revised) $= I_g(t+1)$ (Original) $\times \dfrac{P_{t+1}}{P_t}$.

Then with the revised plans the consequent rise in expenditure, income and price, will be as follows:

Table 12.4. (*In crores of Rs.*)

| Year of Plan | Original Plan target (at 1960–1 price) | Revised plan target (at 1960–1 price) | Revised | | |
			Expenditure (at 1960–1 price)	Income (at 1960–1 price)	Excess of expenditure over income (at 1960–1 price)
1	1032·00	1032·00	1828·88	1398·73	430·15
2	1441·50	1520·79	2227·84	1577·65	650·20
3	1632·75	1801·58	2474·96	1751·71	723·25
4	1647·75	1864·42	2570·82	1872·31	698·51
5	1746·75	2024·13	2747·09	1931·65	815·43
Total	7500·75	8242·92	11849·59	8532·05	3317·54

Assuming foreign aid to be Rs. 2200 crores, deficit spending will be equal to Rs. 1117·54 crores at 1960–1 prices.

There will be some additional repercussions of the extra spending by the Government on price. This difference, which is small, may be seen from the following table:

Table 12.5. (*Base* 1952–3 = 100)

Year of Plan	Price indices with first set of assumption	Prices indices with second set of assumption
1	131·69	131·69
2	137·57	137·70
3	140·92	141·21
4	144·25	144·62
5	152·07	152·54

Thus the size of deficit spending will largely increase due to governmental upgrading of plan for the retention of the physical targets.

Projections on the Basis of the Third Set of Assumptions

We now come to the third variant. If the Government wants to keep deficit spending in the region of Rs. 550 crores, as announced in the Plan, what revision would be necessary on the basis of our model?

From the set of equations of our model, it is obvious that an increase of Rs. 100 crores in I_g leads to an increase of about Rs. 70 crores in E and an increase of about Rs. 22 crores in Y. Then for a reduction of the deficit by about 214 crores we have to reduce I_g by about 452 crores. Working on this we can obtain the following value of I_g and the corresponding series for targets of the plan, expenditure, income and excess of expenditure over income.

Table 12.6. (*In crores of Rs. at* 1960–1 *price*)

Year of Plan	Original Plan target	Plan target revised to maintain a deficit of Rs. 550 crores	Revised		
			Expenditure	Income	Excess of expenditure over income
1.	1032·00	940·99	1765·40	1378·69	386·71
2.	1441·50	1351·58	2109·76	1540·37	569·39
3.	1632·75	1542·53	2294·17	1694·62	599·55
4.	1647·75	1557·50	2356·67	1804·71	551·96
5.	1746·75	1656·10	2491·17	1850·58	640·59
Total	7500·75	7048·70	11017·17	8268·97	2748·20

Deficit spending at 1960–1 prices = 2748·20 − 2200 = 548·20 crores.

This is approximately the deficit spending anticipated by the planning authority. Thus to reduce the deficit to this level the original I_g is to be cut by Rs. 90 crores (approximately) each year, assuming a uniform reduction over the years.

This cut in I_g by about Rs. 90 crores every year will reduce the price indices projected for the third Plan period under the first set of assumptions by 0·15 every year.

In both these cases, however, once the investment I_g is allowed to be influenced by the price emerging in the model the exogenous nature of this variable would be affected. But we may look at it in this way. The model is supposed to run in discrete periods. At the beginning of each of these periods, starting from the first, I_g is revised, but during each time period, once decided, I_g is treated during the period as exogenous. Thus the revision of I_g is equivalent to a discontinuity of the model, with a fresh assignment of exogenous values. If the interaction between P and I_g is assumed to be working within the sample, then I_g ceases to be exogenous. We assume that interaction between P and I_g occurs at fixed breaks in the time period only.

CHAPTER 13

A GROWTH MODEL OF THE CALCUTTA METROPOLITAN REGION[1]

13.1

The object of this paper is to present the construction of a growth model for the Calcutta Metropolitan Region. The Calcutta Metropolitan Region is defined by a much bigger area than Calcutta City proper. It 'covers approximately 400 square miles in and around Calcutta. It encompasses two corporations, thirty-three municipalities and thirty-seven urban units covering the continuous area on both banks of the River Hooghly known as the conurbation'.[2] It includes such rural areas as fall within this boundary. The primacy of this metropolitan region in East India as a whole is unquestioned. The volume of employment it offers, the size of its output, the large volume of foreign trade, the density of its population, all these place it in a position of unique importance in India. With the growth of the steel and engineering industrial complex in the eastern belt, its position as the only available port for the region has become still more important.

The pre-eminence of this metropolitan region is due to a fairly long period of growth. It is not our purpose to go into the historical aspects of this growth but to try and locate the major demographic movements over the last few decades, the basic inter-relationship between the demographic and economic variables and to use this knowledge to construct suitable models for the approximate determination of future migration tendencies from adjacent rural areas into the Calcutta Metropolitan Region.

In § 13.2 a brief review is made of the main demographic components of the growth of the population of the region.

In § 13.3 some of the important characteristics of the migrant population, revealed by an occupational study, are discussed.

In § 13.4 we discuss information on the nature of empirical interdependence obtained in a study of migration and the corresponding natural population and similar inter-relationship between migration and employment.

In § 13.5 an outline of a model for the projection of migration figures on the basis of an assumed growth of industrial employment is given. An

---

[1] This is the original version of the paper presented to the World Population Congress in Belgrade in 1965.
[2] First Report 1962, Calcutta Metropolitan Planning Organization.

alternative model, where a complete system is presented, giving the growth of the migrant population, in an inter-dependent system with other variables like natural population, employment, etc. is also presented.

13.2

Table 13.1 gives the total population figures, and figures for natural population and migrant population, according to the Census from 1911–61 for Calcutta, Calcutta Metropolitan Region and urban India with the respective index of growth since 1911.

Table 13.1

Year of Census	Total population			Index of growth		
	Urban India	Calcutta Metropolitan Region	Calcutta	Urban India	Calcutta Metropolitan Region	Calcutta
1911	27592914	18044346	998012	100·00	100·00	100·00
1921	29821285	1927081	1031697	108·08	106·80	103·38
1931	35029084	2192678	1140862	126·95	121·52	114·31
1941	45594994	3715883	2108891	165·24	205·94	211·31
1951	61867109	4893982	2548677	224·21	271·23	255·38
1961	78835939	6596888	2927289	285·71	365·61	293·31

It can be seen that while growth in urban India during 1911–61 multiplied by around 2·8, growth in CMPO region has been over 3·6 times and for Calcutta City around 3 times. Table 13.2 gives the share of immigrants and natural population in the growth of population of the Calcutta Metropolitan Region.

Table 13.2

Year	Population of Calcutta Metropolitan Region		Percentage share in increase	
	Natural	Migrant	Natural	Migrant
1911	981191	823155	—	—
1921	1042257	884824	49·75	50·25
1931	1296050	896628	95·56	4·44
1941	2305908	1409975	55·14	44·86
1951	2145209	2748773	14·00 (50·00)*	86·00 (50·00)*
1961	3107767	3489121	56·62	43·48

Of the two sources, (e.g. natural increase and immigration) immigration has been quite as important as the natural increase, the population has nearly doubled, the increase being shown equally between the two sources.

The natural increase of the population is due to a net increase of births over deaths. Generally it may be assumed that in the short range the secular trends in birth and death rates are not significantly affected by economic movements.

The natural increase, therefore, can be computed from given figures of birth and death rates, more or less independently, at least in the short run, of economic forces. However the other component of growth, immigration, is assumed to be related to economic and other influences.

To analyse the nature of immigration and its determinants it is necessary to study the broad economic characteristics of the migrant population. These are given below, for different census years, for available regions which are comparable.

Table 13.3. Percentage composition

Occupation	Calcutta with suburbs (1931)	Calcutta Industrial Area (1951)	Calcutta Metropolitan Region (1961)
Industry	19·47	37·99	37·86
Transport	8·95	12·26	10·01
Trade	15·86	21·79	21·70
Public Administration	8·70	8·02	9·14
Profession and Service	4·61	2·19	5·22

It will be seen from the figures that industry, trade, transport, public service and the professions, between them, absorb most of the immigrants into the city and metropolis. By and large, therefore, the growth of the area through immigration is to be looked for mainly in the growth of industries, trade, communications, services and professions.

13.3

For our study occupations filled mainly by immigrants can be listed under two broad heads: industrial and non-industrial.

Industrial and non-industrial employment in the city and the Metropolis during 1911–61 is given in Table 13.4. The employment figures for the Calcutta Metropolitan Area include some non-agricultural employment in the rural areas of the CMPO which could not be isolated

Table 13.4. Calcutta Metropolitan Region

Occupation	Urban with non-agricultural employment					Only Urban	
	1921	1931	1941	1951	1961	1951	1961
Industry	438872 (36·04)	457473 (33·42)	615800 (35·46)	789527 (32·50)	894922 (34·32)	666395 (34·85)	876289 (34·46)
Non-industry	778877 (63·96)	911210 (66·58)	1121000 (64·54)	1639866 (67·50)	1712431 (65·68)	1245755 (65·15)	1666422 (65·54)
Total	1217749 (100·00)	1368683 (100·00)	1736800 (100·00)	2429393 (100·00)	2607353 (100·00)	1912150 (100·00)	2542711 (100·00)

from the urban figures for the years up to 1941. From 1951 the urban figures are given separately as they could be isolated.

The predominant role played by non-industrial employment over industrial employment and the rising trend in non-industrial employment over time in the city and in the Metropolitan area are immediately obvious.

A big Metropolitan area caters economically to a very large region and its growth can be traced ultimately to the growth of the entire market it serves. One way of studying the determinants of growth is to analyse these markets separately as stimulants to growth. Therefore a grouping was made of the registered industrial establishments in the CMPO area taking into account whether they catered for a national market, a regional market, or a local market. Table 13.5 divides employment into groups serving a national market, a regional market or a local market. Generally in making this division we tried to demarcate an industry as national, regional or local by commonly known facts—whether the product is consumed only locally, or whether it is an industry of a basic type catering to the Indian economy as a whole. Table 13.6 gives the percentage growth rate of different industrial sectors during 1950–9.

This shows that national market industries have increased quite fast. An almost similar increase has been registered by the regional market industries. Local market industries have not increased as fast. They have actually declined in many cases. In the Metropolitan area the main

Table 13.5

Total employment in the CMPO area (National market)

Industry	1921	1931	1941	1951	1961	% Growth during 1951–61
Jute Mills	272780	249492	302457	302620	224212	74·1
Basic Metal Industry	25557	14469	44500	125325	172303	137·5
Transport Equipment	159	—	6900	36366	51016	140·3
Paper and Printing	6706	471	—	36942	48379	130·9
Chemical and Products	14993	16931	16800	23108	39862	172·5
Petroleum and Coal	37	—	—	10607	20500	193·5
Public, Legal, Business, Services	85536	136351	455300	139984	213599	152·6
Transport and Communication	37197	31515	73200	79867	105838	132·5
Total	442965	449229	899157	754819	875709	116·0

Employment in the CMPO area (Regional market)

Industry	1921	1931	1941	1951	1961	% Growth during 1951–61
Cotton Textiles	17796	21878	60187	55153	975448	176·9
Textiles: Others	3417	6149	6456	55783	77743	139·4
Food, Drink, Tobacco	31356	42282	66200	93903	115728	123·2
Hides and Skins	2292	13164	26800	35550	34636	97·4
Transport	81325	73825	108500	201004	155237	77·2
Total	136186	151620	268143	441393	480892	108·9

Employment of the CMPO area (Local)

Industry	1921	1931	1941	1951	1961	% Growth during 1951–61
Trade	161584	194784	261200	587844	565937	96·3
House Services	124064	396166	184500	188430	180230	95·6
Construction and Maintenance	58305	36517	38300	62737	84364	134·5
Bricks and Tiles	(20588)	(14069)	n.a.	n.a.	n.a.	—
Cement, Potteries	12055	29662	38300	n.a.	n.a.	—
Clothing, Jewellery, Laundry	27350	41519	n.a.	n.a.	n.a.	—
Personal Services except Household Services	251454	56121	n.a.	380000	407226	113·1
Electric and Gas	2626	3053	11500	14170	12995	91·7
Glass and Glassware	1160	4334	35700	n.a.	n.a.	—
Total	638598	762156	569500	1233181	1250752	101·4

Notes

1. Basic Metal products include Manufacture of Machinery and Manufacture of metal product.
2. Transport: Transport by air and Transport by rails.
3. Petroleum and Coal includes Rubber.
4. In case of 1941 Public and Legal and Business means Public and all the Services except Household services.
5. Construction and Maintenance including Bricks and Tiles in all years.

Table 13.6. All-India registered factory employment

	Employment		% Growth
Industry	1950	1959	1950–9
Clothing, jewellery	6985	18394	263·34
Metal products	53495	115105	215·17
Cement, lime, etc.	21014	43548	207·23
Chemical and products	63670	126711	199·01
Gins, presses	83701	160972	192·32
Transport and equipment	152515	290992	190·80
Manufacture of machinery	120440	220720	183·26
Electricity	21989	37970	172·68
Basic metal industry	93738	151958	162·11
Glass and glassware	25878	39764	153·66
Rubber, rubber products	20829	31955	153·42
Paper and printing	89289	133717	149·76
Bricks and tiles	89877	132992	147·97
Hides, skins	18027	26269	145·72
Food, drink, tobacco	433290	619312	142·93
Petroleum, coal	12790	16653	130.20
Cotton mills	622339	787514	126·54
Textiles: others	87946	105692	120·18
Shipbuilding, repairing	28779	30965	107·60
Jute mills	303364	280394	92·43

impetus to industrial growth is coming from the all India market rather than from the local market.

It will also be seen that most of the manufacturing establishments cater to a national market rather than to a regional or local market.

Non-industrial employment, however, is more indirectly determined. There is a small component in non-industrial employment that is stimulated directly by national demand but a large part of non-industrial employment is generated indirectly. It can be said that basic industrial activities and their ancillaries, like transport, communications, etc., form the core of economic activity in the metropolis. This core depends on factors of national importance and the movement of these factors is determined as a part of the national economy itself. Given this the secondary groups of industries are generated as a kind of multiplier activity centering around the core. In the next section, we will propose a model of growth on this hypothesis. That is, we will employ All-India growth trends in national market industries to determine the growth trend of industry, while, for other non-industrial activities, the trends of industrial growth within the Metropolitan Region itself are taken as the determining variable.

13.4

The classification of industries into national, regional, or local importance is the starting point in the present model. We take the national market industries as the basic group which generate activity throughout the economy. They are the autonomous injections in Keynesian terminology. Since they have a nationally determined market their progress primarily depends on the national economy itself. We can assume that the trend of the national growth of these industries will give us an indicator of their overall future growth.

But, while All-India growth may be high, or low, the share of the Metropolis may move differently. So the second step is to determine the time-trend in the share of the Metropolis. These two, combined together, give us the pattern of growth of these industries in the Metropolitan Region.

The model for the national market group of industries can be formulated thus

$$E_{\text{CMPO}} = (E_{\text{India}}) \times \frac{(E_{\text{CMPO}})}{(E_{\text{India}})}.$$

To obtain this trend equations were fitted to the industrial growth of India by the least square method. Similar trend equations were fitted to the shares for the Metropolitan area, also by least squares. The two equations were used to obtain projections beyond 1961. The projected Indian growth and the share of the Metropolis were multiplied to obtain employment figures in the CMPO. Normally this procedure can lead to some bias. In this case, however, both being considered only as functions of time, they can be shown to lead formally to the same procedure as obtaining a trend directly for employment in the Metropolitan Region. This was not done as it was thought that the logic of our process of analysis is better revealed by showing it in two stages.

In the present method an added advantage was that we could follow the two stages of the analysis independently and change any equations we did not think reliable.

Table 13.7 column 2 gives the percentage growth for India as a whole for the national market industry during 1950–9, the figures referring to employment in registered factories only.

In general the figures show a steeply rising trend over the last ten years in most industries. It is likely that all these industries will have a similarly rising trend in the future. On this assumption exponential or modified exponential growth curves were fitted to the data. The equations obtained are also shown in Table 13.7.

Table 13.7

Name of the Industry	% Growth during 1950–9	Equation of All-India growth
Jute mills	92·43	$\log E = \log 103·4 - 0·0137t$
Manufacture of machinery	183·26	$\log E = \log 77 + 0·0459t$
Cotton mills	126·54	$\log E = \log 124·3 - (0·4848)^t \log 0·4580$
Basic metal industries	162·11	$\log E = \log 83·56 + 0·0337t$
Transport and transport equipment	190·80	$\log E = \log 84·92 + 0·0353t$
Manufacture of metal products	215·17	$\log E = \log 99·97 + 0·0454t$
		$(\log E = \log 142·90 + 0·0370t)$
Paper and printing	149·76	$\log E = \log 134·2 + 0·0205t$
Rubber and rubber products	153·42	$\log E = \log 145·6 + 0·0238t$
Chemical and chemical products	199·01	$\log E = \log 83·99 + 0·0332t$
Food, drink and tobacco	142·93	$\log E = \log 99·47 + 0·0300t$
Shipbuilding and repairing	107·60	$\log E = \log 80·79 + 0·0287t$
Textiles: others	120·18	$\log E = \log 239·3 - (0·4468) t$
Glass and glassware	153·66	$\log E = \log 93·65 + 0·0334t$
Bricks and tiles etc.	147·97	$\log E = \log 92·34 + 0·0400t$
Electricity, gas, steam, cement	172·68	$\log E = \log 87·40 + 0·0295t$
Lime and potteries	207·23	$\log E = \log 170·1 + 0·0205t$
Petroleum and coal	130·20	$\log E = \log 93·61 + 0·0279t$
Clothing, jewellery works, etc.	262·34	$\log E = \log 120·0 + 0·0439t$
Processes connected with hides and skins	145·72	$\log E = \log 110·9 + 0·0153t$
Gins and presses	192·32	$\log E = \log 202·5 - (0·4340)^t \log 1383$

A study of the growth curves reveals the nature of Indian industrialization during the last decade. Most of the basic, heavy and light industries, which are essential to rapid industrialization, have been growing at a rate of over 3 per cent per annum in India as a whole. These include, manufacture of machinery, basic metals, transport and equipment, metal-products, chemicals and products. The old industries of India like jute, cotton, textile etc. have not been growing, but declining slowly.

Power industries and cement were growing at just under 3 per cent per annum and so is petroleum.

The future of the various manufacturing industries assuming similar growth for next ten to twenty years may be predicated easily from these equations. The basic industries, on this assumption, will continue to grow fast. It is possible that power, petroleum, etc. will catch them up.

Traditional industries will decline or grow only very slowly. Some of the consumer's industries like food, drink, clothing, etc. would grow with increased urbanization as is shown by the fast growth over the last ten years.

Projections were made of All-India growth of the industries over the next two decades. Table 13.8 gives these figures for 1961, 1971 and 1981.

Table 13.8. *Estimates of All-India employment of selected industries from equation*

Names of industries	1961	1971	1981
Jute mills	226928	—	—
Manufacture of machinery	266895	767805	2212483
Cotton mills	141624	800468	800468
Basic metal industries	170228	369796	803335
Transport	343464	774471	1746297
Metal products	135972	386513	1100051
Paper and printing	211079	338494	382262
Rubber products	37257	64428	111453
Chemical	149017	319727	687591
Food, drink and tobacco	826732	1649671	3293022
Shipbuilding and repairing	41414	80225	155357
Textiles	137918	137918	137918
Glass and glassware	47175	101789	219664
Bricks and tiles	171298	430263	1080511
Electricity, gas, steam	43406	85647	168941
Cement, potteries, etc.	47823	76648	122891
Petroleum and coal	19720	37528	713022
Clothing and jewellery, etc.	23057	63291	192436
Hides and skins	27473	39046	82691
Gins and presses	159872	159822	159871

We now come to the second stage of the model. This is to determine the trend of the share of the Metropolis in All-India growth.

Table 13.9 gives the percentage increase in employment in each industry for India as a whole, with the share of the Metropolis in 1950 and 1959 and the difference in the share during 1950–9 and the equations fitted to the trend of the share.

It may be seen that in most of the industries the Metropolis has a falling share over the years.

Because this area is substantially industrialized it is not growing at the same fast pace as the industries in other parts of India.

There are a few industries which are favourably placed with an almost constant share. These include machine fabrication, paper and printing, food, drink and tobacco, textile and glassware, bricks and tiles, clothing and jewellery. All of these industries except the first two, have a high final demand content for consumers and therefore are almost functions of the rate of growth of the population. As such, in this Metropolitan area with its very large internal market, they are growing fast and keeping pace with the population.

In other industries, however, it is not to be supposed that there is an actual decline, except in a few cases. In most of them there is only a lower

Table 13.9

Industry	% Increase during 1950–9	Share of CMPO in India in percentage 1950	1959	Difference	Equations fitted
Clothing, jewellery	163·34	22·13	10·83	−11·30	$\log R = \log 37{\cdot}04 - 0{\cdot}0268\,t$
Metal products	115·17	37·83	27·07	−10·76	Share Constant: 5·20%
					(Average of last 5 years)
Cement, lime, etc.	107·23	14·87	11·66	−3·21	$\log R = \log 22{\cdot}67 - (0{\cdot}4420)\,t$
Chemical and products	99·01	28·31	15·97	−12·34	$\log R = \log 22{\cdot}67 - (0{\cdot}4420)^t \log 0{\cdot}5882$
Gins and presses	92·32	55·90	0·84	−55·06	$\log R = \log 21{\cdot}58 - (0{\cdot}0844)^t \log 211{\cdot}7$
Transport and equipment	90·80	16·09	11·16	−4·93	$\log R = \log 16{\cdot}69 - 0{\cdot}0167\,t$
Manufacture of machinery	83·26	30·37	24·77	−5·60	$\log R = \log 42{\cdot}71 - 0{\cdot}0258\,t$
Electricity	72·68	25·11	14·13	−10·98	Share constant 19·24
					(Average of last 5 years)
Basic metal industries	62·11	16·31	21·58	5·27	$\log R = \log 84{\cdot}47 - 0{\cdot}0134\,t$
Glass and glassware	53·66	22·82	21·28	−1·54	$\log R = \log 30{\cdot}96 - 0{\cdot}0235\,t$
Rubber products	53·42	80·10	66·81	−13·29	Share Constant 2·93
					(Average of last 5 years)
Paper and printing	49·76	23·08	19·31	−3·77	$\log R = \log 59{\cdot}05 - 0{\cdot}0267\,t$
Bricks and tiles	47·97	3·41	5·31	−1·90	Share Constant: 6·64
					(Average of last 5 years)
Hides and skins	45·72	n.a.	5·65	n.a.	Share Constant: 5·88
					(Average of last 5 years)
Food, drink and tobacco	42·93	3·89	2·91	−0·98	$\log R = \log 27{\cdot}90 - 0{\cdot}0299\,t$
Petroleum, coal	30·20	55·82	17·69	−38·13	$\log R = \log 8{\cdot}87 + 0{\cdot}0179\,t$
Cotton mills	26·54	4·49	5·45	0·70	$\log R = \log 54{\cdot}55 - 0{\cdot}0397\,t$
Textiles: others	20·18	7·78	6·93	−0·85	Share Constant: 13·60
					(Average of last 5 years)
Shipbuilding, repairing	7·60	38·77	42·79	4·02	$\log R = \log 2{\cdot}813 + 0{\cdot}0337\,t$
Jute mills	−7·57	92·98	68·79	−24·19	$\log R = \log 8{\cdot}56 - 0{\cdot}0998\,t$

Table 13.10. Estimated share of the Calcutta Metropolitan Area in percent of All-India employment

Industries	1961	1971	1981
Jute mills	91·42	*	*
Manufacture of machinery	19·98	10·78	5·82
Cotton mills	5·20	5·20	5·20
Basic metal industries	21·58	22·67	22·67
Transport	10·52	7·16	4·86
Metal products	23·58	13·02	7·19
Paper and printing	19·24	19·24	19·24
Rubber products	60·08	44·19	31·47
Chemical	14·52	8·45	4·92
Food, drink and tobacco	2·93	2·93	2·93
Shipbuilding	33·95	18·37	9·93
Textiles: others	6·64	6·64	6·64
Glass and glassware	21·72	21·72	21·72
Bricks and tiles	5·88	5·88	5·88
Electricity, gas, steam	12·22	6·14	3·08
Cement, limes and potteries	12·33	18·62	25·65
Petroleum and coal	15·17	6·08	2·44
Clothing, jewellery, etc.	13·60	13·60	13·60
Process of hides and skins	6·11	13·28	28·85
Gins and presses	0·43	0·03	—

* Not fitted.

rate of growth in the Metropolitan area, showing that, in many fields, the Metropolitan area has ceased to offer as large a growth prospect as other comparatively virgin regions.

On the basis of the fitted equations (Table 13.9) the projections (Table 13.10) were made for the share of the Metropolis in the growth of employment by selected industrial groups for 1961, 1971 and 1981.

Combining these two sets of projections, according to our model, we get the following projection for industrial employment in the Metropolitan area as far as registered factories are concerned for the years 1961, 1971 and 1981.

Table 13.11. *Estimated employment of selected industries in the Metropolitan Area*

Industry	1961	1971	1981
Jute mills	204235	153736	116552
Manufacture of machinery	53326	79240	128767
Cotton mills	41624	41624	41624
Basic metal industry	36735	73855	182116
Transport and transport equipment	36132	53104	85219
Manufacture of metal products	32062	48118	79094
Paper and printing	40612	62120	73547
Rubber products	22384	27771	35074
Chemical products	21637	26446	33829
Food, drink and tobacco	24223	45113	96486
Shipbuilding and repairing	14060	14668	15427
Textiles: others	9158	9158	9158
Glass and glassware	10246	20477	47711
Bricks and tiles	10072	23074	63534
Electricity, gas, steam	5304	5257	5203
Cement, lime and potteries	5897	13063	31522
Petroleum and coal	2992	2342	17398
Clothing, jewellery, etc.	3133	7779	26171
Hides and skins	1679	4629	23856
Gins and presses	687	80	—

We have so far considered only registered factory employment, which includes only employment in units of ten or more workers with power or twenty or more workers without power. To estimate total employment, both registered and unregistered, the registered employment in census years was compared with the total employment as recorded in the census. A curve was fitted to the registered employment and total industrial employment over census years, on the assumption that a similar relation will prevail over non-census years.

The following equation was fitted:

$$\log E_I = \log E_R + 0{\cdot}0335t.$$

The equation shows a progresssive rise in the rate of smaller un-registered units compared to the larger units over time. Table 13.12, below, gives the projection of total industrial employment on that basis from registered employment.

Table 13.12

| Year | Employment in 1000 | |
	Registered	Total
1960	568	829
1961	576	847
1962	585	868
1963	596	890
1964	608	916
1965	624	943
1966	637	973
1967	653	1005
1968	671	1041
1969	690	1080
1970	712	1122
1971	733	1199
1981	1112	1908

We now come to the non-industrial sectors. It is assumed that the non-industrial sectors are primarily dependent on the injections from the industrial sectors. That is, the industrial sectors generate demands which create corresponding demands in the non-industrial sectors. Some studies made on the relative growth of the immigrant population and employment in the non-industrial sector suggest that in a big metropolitan area employment in the non-industrial sectors is strongly influenced by immigrants coming in expection of work, while the local population goes into more well defined occupations. Petty trades, unskilled labour and similar low paid entry trades more naturally accommodate unskilled migrants. On these considerations the following model was fitted to the data

$$E_{ni} = \alpha + \beta E_i + \gamma . \Delta M,$$

where E_i and E_{ni} indicate industrial and non-industrial employment respectively and

ΔM = incremental migration during the year.

The equation was fitted on the census data for E_i, E_{ni} and ΔM for the census years 1921, 1931, 1941, 1951 and 1961.

To fit this equation only census data were available. Therefore the incremental migration ΔM was defined as increment between two consecutive census years, i.e. as $M_t - M_{t-10}$.

The coefficients of the fitted equation are given below:

$$E_{ni} = 79.30 + 1.70 E_i + 0.16 \Delta M.$$

An average rate of migration was calculated from the data for 1951 and 1961. This was assumed to be unchanged during 1971 and 1981 for calculating M for these periods.

The equation for predicting ΔM was as follows:

$$M_{1961} = M_{1951}(1+i)^{10}, \quad M_{1951} = (27487730), \quad i = 0.024.$$

Working on that basis we obtained the corresponding figures for E_{NI} from E_I and ΔM for 1961, 1971 and 1981 as below.

Table 13.13

Year	ΔM	Industrial employment	Non-industrial employment
1961	81776	861000	1476863
1971	103664	1199000	2054966
1981	1180937	1908000	3432629

13.5

It was seen in the previous section that non-industrial employment is significantly affected by immigration itself. We now go into the other side of the interaction, e.g. the impact of employment and population on immigration. In considering the flow of immigrants the East Pakistan immigrants were treated separately as they were immigrating for political reasons. Any attempt to fit a simple model on this flow is bound to be futile. This flow is considered exogenously determined and we concentrate mainly on the immigrant flow from provinces west of West Bengal.

The most logical way to start enquiring into this factor is to look into the nature of the growth of employment opportunities. The data, however, on direct expansion of full-time employment proper is very defective. While direct full-time employment has not grown very fast a very large growth has taken place in comparatively ill-defined casual or semi-casual employment of a tertiary type usual in a big city. It is not possible to get an adequate measure of this from any direct employment data. Therefore an activity index of a restrictive type was built up including in it series of production, export, import and several other indices together with suitable weights. A model was fitted to the data as follows:

$$_mP(t) = 869.75 + 0.669\,_nP(t) + 0.009\,\frac{X(t)}{X(0)} - 0.675\,_mP(t-1),$$

$X(0) = $ total output of base year,

where $X(t)/X(0)$ is an activity index of the area, other variables being defined as before.

Generally the fit was found to be good. The completed model was formulated as follows:

$$_nP(t) = {}_nP(t-1) + b.\,[_nP(t-1) + {}_mP(t-1)] - d.\,[_nP(t-1)],$$

$$_mP(t) = 0.669\,_nP(t) + 0.009\,\frac{X(t)}{X(0)} - 0.675\,_mP(t-1) + 869.75,$$

$$P(t) = {}_nP(t) + {}_mP(t).$$

The present formulation is a little more meaningful as it now brings into play the circular relation between the migrant population and economic activity.

Various alternative models were tried out for the purpose of estimating migrant flow. The initial experiment was conducted by considering the natural population itself as one of the variables while introducing some economic variables for the purpose of bringing in direct economic prospects. This was done as the data on economic activity was thought rather inadequate for building a good series.

In all these models, however, population seemed to swamp all other effects. The coefficient relating economic activity with migrant population seemed to be insignificantly small while the effect of population on the migrants was too large. This may again be due to the very casual way employment is defined in a census, so that it becomes partly synonymous with the labour force which is a direct function of the population. So that here again we get the same phenomena, i.e. the employment follows the population. This is an inverted Malthusian situation in the sense that the conclusions seem to emerge that population in the Metropolis is increasing willy nilly under its own momentum and employment is tagging along. People are not coming to the city lured by jobs but are being attracted into the city in search of a living because so many people living there creates a varied market.

The suitable approach in such a situation is to consider the flow of immigrants as being caused by two forces operating simultaneously. One of the forces is the positive one of actually existing jobs in the city. The other is the negative one of the growing lack of employment in the area from which they came. The 'pull' of economic activity in the Metropolis, as we saw, is not sufficiently strong. But we shall now show that if the 'push' from the origin of emigration is taken into account, together they become a much more potent factor in explaining the flow of immigrants.

Assuming that the bulk of the migrants from the West come from the agricultural labourer class of rural Bihar or Uttar Pradesh we prepared the following series showing the sown area per agricultural labourer in Bihar during the last several decades.

Table 13.14

Year	Net area sown per agricultural labourer (projected)
1931	6·99
1941	6·77
1951	6·67
1961	4·55

An equation was fitted to this index with time and the following projections were obtained for 1961, 1971 and 1981.

$$\log {}_B E(t) = \log 113 \cdot 9 - 0 \cdot 05 t.$$

Table 13.15

Year	Net area sown per agricultural labourer (projected)
1961	6·48
1971	5·70
1981	5·09

We assume that this projected index of sown area per agricultural labourer in Bihar may be used as an index of employment for the area.

This index gives us the relative employment prospects considering the forces of the 'push' factor, just as our former index gives the same from the demand side (the 'pull' factor).

Using these two indices we now fit an equation for the immigrant flow as follows:

$$_mP(t) = 1022880 + 1·33E(t) - 12100\,_BE(t),$$

where $_mP(t)$ = migration into the CMPO area in time t and $_BE(t)$ = employment indicator for neighbouring areas defined by the man–land ratio of Bihar in time t.

Putting the numerical values to the coefficients a complete formulation was as below:

$$E(t) = E_I(t) + E_{NI}(t), \tag{13·1}$$

$$E_{NI}(t) = 79·30 + 1·70E_I(t) + 0·16\Delta_{10}\,M(t), \tag{13·2}$$

$$M(t) = 1022880 + 1·33E(t) - 12100\,_BE(t). \tag{13·3}$$

The following table gives the computed values for 1961, 1971 and 1981 with the actual and observed values for 1961 for the same variables for employment in non-industrial enterprise, total employment and migration and $_BE(t)$ the index of employment at centres of emigration, which gives the 'push' factor.

Table 13.16

	Actual 1961	Computed		
		1961	1971	1981
E_{NI}	1712431	1474268	2225655	3744202
$_mP^{(t)}$	3489121	3427121	4901030	7924549
$E(t)$	2607353	2673268	3424655	5652202

Most models of growth start with employment possibilities and show how this job prospect attracts labour. In this sense, possibly, the growth in India (and in the whole of the underdeveloped and over-populated parts of the world) must follow a different pattern. Employment here is pushed up to meet a larger and still larger growth in numbers. If a planned increase in jobs takes place in urban areas it will lag behind the number wanting jobs. The creation of jobs temporarily may only result in a further acceleration of this influx into the urban area of people looking for jobs because of the comparative improvement in prospects between rural and urban employment. So long as we do not break even, i.e. create more jobs than are wanted, population pressures seem to lead economic development by the nose.

The model thus shows that we are still not masters of our economic destiny but are being led by situations created by the growth of the population in the surrounding region as a whole.

In building up a unified model these experiences are all combined together. It was seen that the non-industrial part of employment was influenced by the growth of migration. This was thought reasonable as the migrant population are often unskilled and come into the Metropolis looking for entry into any trade available. Hence non-industrial employment was made to depend on prospects for business in general as felt through the employment level and on the net increase in migration.

13.6

In this section a tentative formulation of a set of equations describing, in an interdependent system, the growth and interaction of population, employment and migration is described. Though there are many crudities in the model we venture to present it as we believe that, on the whole, the model gives us a structurally consistent set of figures. We give below the model with the parameters fitted by a straightforward least square process.

The following set of empirical values were obtained by a simple least square procedure.

1·1. $\quad _nP(t) = {}_nP(t-1) + b({}_nP(t-1) + {}_mP(t-1)) - d.{}_nP(t-1);$

1·2. $\quad _mP(t) = 1022\cdot88 + 1\cdot33E(t) - 12\cdot10\,{}_BE(t);$

1·3. $\quad E(t) = \dfrac{1}{\lambda(t)}.X(t);$

1·4. $\quad P(t) = {}_nP(t) + {}_mP(t);$

2·1. $\quad X(t) = X_1(t) + X_2(t);$

2·2. $\quad X_1(t) = 0\cdot2449X_1(t) + 0\cdot1006X_2(t) + F_{1h} + F_{1g} + E_{ext} - I_{ext} + K;$

2·3. $\quad X_2(t) = 0\cdot1134X_1(t) + 0\cdot0836X_2(t) + F_{2\Sigma};$

3·1. $\quad F_{1h} = 7000\cdot00 + 530\cdot89P(t) + 0\cdot002X(t)$ at base period (1950) price in 1000 Rupees;

3·2. $\quad F_{1g} = 467157\cdot00 - 0\cdot60P(t) + 84215\cdot00t$ at base period (1950) price in 1000 Rupees;

3·3. $\quad F_{2\Sigma} = 818154\cdot00 - 1\cdot30P + 66467\cdot00t$ at base period (1950) price in 1000 Rupees.

The following are the explanations of additional symbols used, other symbols have been explained previously.

X_1 = output of sector 1 (includes all primary and secondary productions);

X_2 = output of sector 2 (tertiary production);

a_{ij} = input coefficients relating input from sector i to output sector j;

F_{1h} = final demand of household or private account in sector 1;

F_{1g} = final demand on government account in sector 1;

$F_{2\Sigma}$ = final demand on government account and household account in sector 2;

E_{int} = flow to other regions in India for sector 1;

I_{int} = flow from other regions in India of products relating to sector 1;

E_{ext} = flow to other regions outside India for sector 1;

I_{ext} = import from other regions outside India in sector 1;

λ_t = average productivity of labour at time t;

$K = E_{int} - I_{int}$.

The model has three structural parts. The first part (1.1 to 1.3) is the demographic variables and their inter-relations with each other and with economic variables. The second part (2.1 to 2.3) is the input-output relations which is now introduced in only two sectors, but which is to be expanded subsequently. These give the interactions of the different sectors and their impact on output and, therefore, on employment. Finally, there are the equations giving the inter-relations between final demand population, and other variables (3.1 to 3.3). The equations are taken up one by one.

1.1 is an identity if birth and death rates are given.

1.2 is an equation determining the flow of immigrant population. The immigrant flow is governed by the activity index of the region from which migrants come and the index of activity of the Metropolis.

1.3 is an identity relation giving the total population as its two components, e.g. the natural and immigrant population. Emigration is ignored as small and insignificant.

As may be seen, the demographic equation depends partly on the immigrant population which in turn is determined, among others, by the volume of output or employment in the region. But it is also hypothesized that it is governed by the activity level of the region of the emigration which is exogenous.

2.1 is an identity relating total output with the output of the two sectors: secondary and tertiary. 2.2 and 2.3; these equations are the usual input-output equations of the open type which leaves the different components of the final demands exogenous. These equations will take the case of the inter-sectoral inter-actions and their impact on the level of output which eventually determines total output levels. In two sectors

Table 13.17. (*Unit* = 1000)

Symbol	Exp.	1955	1961	1971
$_mP$	Migrant	2765·29	3879·24 (3489·12)	4831·73
P	Population	5350·90	6987·01 (6596·89)	8403·18
E	Employment	2320·92 (2200·75)	2553·26 (2297·81)	3397·98
X	Total Output (Rs.)	3120714·20 (3090188·73)	3907804·20 (3647155·08)	6690405·19
X_1	Sector 1 Output (Rs.)	1666979·60	2096186·67	381441·31
X_2	Sector 2 Output (Rs.)	1453734·55	1940307·84	2875992·92
F_{1h}	Household F.D. (Rs.) sector 1	3032850·39 (2844368·34)	3641359·25	4511796·26
F_{1g}	Govt. F.D. Sector 1 (Rs.)	884795·86 (966100·00)	1389474·34	2234567·69
$F_{2\Sigma}$	Household and Govt. F.D. sector 2 (Rs.)	1143153·36 (1247900·00)	1540730·84	2214122·24
K		1404·15	1587·30	1953·60

it is almost trivial, but it has some use as the industrial and non-industrial groups are in these two sectors.

Equations 3·1 to 3·3 are demand equations which determine the level of final demand of the different final consumers. It is assumed that in sector 1, the level of household expenses towards consumption, or investments will be decided by population on the one hand and by the level of output on the other. The level of total output will be used in the place of income as a more easily measured variable, which will in any case also be highly correlated with employment and income. Government demand for goods, in sector 1, is assumed to be determined by the population and a time trend. It is also assumed that the total final demand in sector 2, will be governed partly by the level of the population of the region, partly by the level of total economic activity and partly by a secular trend. The level of export from Calcutta to other regions inside India as well as the level of import from these regions to Calcutta has been treated as exogenous. Foreign export and import are made entirely functions of time.

As will be seen the model has one coefficient λ-(productivity) which is exogenous and it is possible to make projections only for given values of productivity (λ = 1404·00, 1587·30, 1953·00 in 1955, 61 and 67.)

The model has a matrix of coefficients relating the exogenous variables where another exogenous value has to be assigned for K. K is the balance of inter-regional trade. There are two reasons for having this variable exogenous.

First, inter-regional trade data is hopelessly incomplete, especially with regard to industrial manufactures. Secondly, a growing import surplus is accumulating in sector 1 of the model, owing to the increasing use of Calcutta Port for the industrialization of the East Indian coal and iron belt. This import really is a re-export from Calcutta to other areas and should normally appear as re-export in our data but it does not. Gradually, therefore, K is increasing in a positive direction.

In the absence of any reliable data, therefore, we had no option but to work the model with various values of K and choose the K's that seemed reasonable. The observed and expected values for 1955, 1961 and 1971 are given above with assumed values of K, which stands for the balance of inter-regional trade.

The fit was very poor for 1951 owing to the fact that the estimate for government demand was too high compared with the actual value. This again was due to the fact that the post-independence stimulus to Government expenditure started a little later than 1951, making a sudden upward shift in the government demand function, which could not be approximated. The completely integrated approach, therefore, was upset because of the poor fit in one of the equations which could not properly be estimated due mainly to a sudden shift in decision for political reasons. Otherwise, the three sets of figures, relating to a period when no such change was evident between periods, are consistent and seem to go well with other forecasts.

CHAPTER 14

ON THE OVERALL STRATEGY OF
THE FOURTH FIVE-YEAR PLAN

The Five-Year Plans are put before the public as a set of attainable targets on the basis of the requirements of the country. For an outsider who has no part in the process through which such a set is arrived at it is extremely difficult to say anything very precise. One can, therefore, confine oneself to the broad strategies and assumptions behind the setting up of the targets and the relative importance placed on them.

To consider the fourth Plan strategy, one has to realize that, it starts with a very ominous background. Serious defence problems, an extremely desperate balance of payments position, a fast rising inflationary wave which is not under control and which is provoking serious internal discontent, these and a host of other very serious elements in the situation have taken up all the planners' room for manoeuvre. The days of playing with plans are over.

From a reading of the Plan it is difficult to get the impression that the planners do realize the gravity of the situation. One is forced to wonder how serious the planners are about the Plan. This impression is brought about by the very superficial analysis the planners make about crucial aspects of the economy and the equally casual happy-go-lucky remedies they suggest.

In two very important aspects planners should have gone into details before formulating the Plan. One of this aspect is the rising food prices and how this is to be controlled without stopping growth according to Plan and the other is the consequences to the economy of starting with a set of targets but not being able to achieve them. Both thus require serious study as they define the upper boundary of the growth targets.

The Plan has this to say about rising prices: 'These shortfalls in domestic production occurred at the same time as aggregate spending in the economy was rising in both the public and private sectors. In consequence, the third Plan period witnessed a steep increase in prices, especially prices of agricultural commodities.'

The following table gives the prices of rice and wheat the available supply including imports and the *per capita* income.

The figures make it obvious that prices have been rising steadily with a rise in per capita supply of both rice and wheat. The index for *per capita* supply of rice and wheat in 1964–5 was 124 and 200 compared with 1946–7, as base, while the price index was 129.

Year	Supply of *per capita* rice (md.) (R)	Wholesale price index of rice (base 1952–53 = 100) (P)	Supply of *per capita* wheat (md.) (W)	Wholesale price index of wheat (base 1952–53 = 100)	*Per capita* income at 1948–9 prices (Rs.) (Y)
1947	1·78	59	0·46	66	228
1948	1·75	83	0·54	121	233
1949	1·83	87	0·62	111	234
1950	1·82	91	0·60	94	234
1951	1·60	104	0·72	96	248
1952	1·62	100	0·32	98	250
1953	1·66	102	0·66	96	256
1954	2·04	86	0·58	79	266
1955	1·74	76	0·64	70	268
1956	1·77	93	0·64	86	268
1957	1·98	104	0·82	90	276
1958	1·69	108	0·70	96	267
1959	1·99	102	0·86	102	280
1960	2·01	109	0·91	91	279
1961	2·11	105	0·86	89	294
1962	2·07	109	0·90	92	293
1963	1·91	122	0·88	91	295
1964	2·12	139*	0·72	104	298
1965	2·21	151*	0·92	113	314

* Estimated.

A straightforward multiple regression was fitted to the data along with income as follows:

$$P = -64\cdot2 - 57\cdot3R - 22\cdot4W + 1\cdot07Y.$$

A simple calculation shows that a decrease of twenty-four points and ten points in price was actually achieved through an increased supply of rice and wheat but that a rise of seventy-two points was caused by rising income during this period.

Assuming that *per capita* income goes up on an average by 4 per cent, as envisaged in the Plan, the index for per capita income will go up to 250 (approximately). This will mean that there will be an addition of 53·5 units to the price, due to expansion of income. If we assume equal increments of supply of rice and wheat to neutralize the effect of this expanding income, the per capita rice and wheat supply must both increase in five years by approximately 0·33 mds. The *per capita* rise in supply during the last eighteen years has been 0·43 mds in rice and 0·46 mds in wheat including ever increasing imports. In other words, it would be necessary to raise the *per capita* rice supply (including imports) by about 16 per cent and the *per capita* wheat supply by 30 per cent in five years. Without imports these figures would easily go up to 25 per cent for rice and 50 per cent for wheat.

A detailed analysis thus shows that if planned expenditure goes up as visualized the expansion of agricultural output necessary to keep prices down (good weather or bad) would run into staggering figures.

Even with the most hopeful ideas on weather, attempts (i) to keep food prices stable, (ii) to reduce imports and (iii) to expand the economy as planned, are incompatible tasks unless much more serious institutional changes are made in the distributive system. To reconcile a slowly expanding food output with the two other objectives a very serious effort has to be made by the Government to become the dominant element in the buying and selling of food grains over the whole country.

The second aspect of the planning procedure worth detailed investigation is the cost of failing to achieve a Plan. This is necessary because the increasing risk of an unfulfilled Plan could provide an upper bound to various targets. To the public unfulfilled targets often mean only that some work could not be finished in time. Unfortunately, the situation is not so simple. There is a big cost to be paid for non-fulfilment of the Plan in terms of an inflationary pressure.

Physical and financial balances are counterparts of the blueprints of a planned economy. In a free enterprise economy the operation of market forces does equilibrate demand and supply for commodities and factors in physical terms and in money terms. In a planned economy, this is not done automatically but through the achievement of planned targets.

The imbalance between the financial and physical targets if any, comes in the shape of an inflationary pressure. This is because all such development is pushed through at high speed. As a result the physical plan often faces shortages and bottle-necks which were not anticipated in the beginning.

Since the financial plan precedes its actual physical execution it does not have the same rigid inhibitions and it often happens that during the period of operation the actual growth of the economy is smaller than the financial counterpart of the same period. This shows itself in an inflationary pressure, because of a more liberal flow of money than goods. It is, therefore, a very important task to the planning authority to devise a consistent and balanced financial counterpart to the physical plan. To be forewarned of the possible dangers of a rising discrepancy between these counterparts and to provide adequate safeguards against such possibilities is a sound line of defence.

A calculation can be made of the rate of price rise for each sector including interaction by assuming a simple input-output model.

The model described briefly elsewhere[1] estimates price rises in different sectors if a plan is started but expected output is not achieved. A three-sector economy for India was used for an exercise and it was found that the lower achievement of the third Plan with a spending as visualized in the Plan caused a price rise during the five years of 18·8 per cent for agriculture, 72 per cent for industry and 33 per cent for the tertiary sectors.

On the basis of these two points some broad conclusions regarding the strategy of the fourth Plan may be drawn. Progress in agriculture, even in

[1] For brief description see technical note at the end and also Inflation in a planned multi-sector growth process by A. Ghosh. *Arthaniti*, vol. III. no. II. (Paper 6 of this book.)

the most optimistic estimates will not be enough to keep prices down, given that a high rate of growth in economy is maintained. I unhesitatingly support the Commission in the stand that industrial expansion at a high rate is indispensable if we are ever to come out of our difficulties. But at the same time no false hopes should be put on an unwarranted growth of agricultural output. For reasons stated in earlier papers[1] I am convinced that under today's conditions with millions of scattered small poverty ridden peasant farms largely dependant on weather, even with a moderate availability of fertilizer, etc. agricultural progress will, at best, be slow.

Given that agricultural progress will be slow, the progress of the country as a whole will depend on the industrial progress that can be carried out with a comparatively backward agriculture. This means procurement and distribution: a painful but inevitable step to avert agricultural instability from seriously damaging the Plans. The entry of the public sector as a major competitor both in buying and selling in the grain trade is a *must* if plans are to be executed. Otherwise the future growth of the country will be conditioned by the monsoon and foreign aid and not by our plans.

With a backward and slowly moving agriculture and a very parasitical commercial grip on economic life the nationalization of the grain trade and the nationalization of banking is possibly the only way to save planned progress.

Technical Note

Let P denote the price vector, a the input-output coefficient matrix, C the vector of factor costs, X the vector of output, β and δ are the vectors of expected and actual growth rates of final demand, and F the final demand vector. We have according to the input-output model:

$$P = (1 - a')^{-1} C X^{-1} i,$$

where a' is transpose of coefficient matrix. The diagonal matrix $C X^{-1}$ is factor costs per unit of output. 'i' is the column vector $1, 1, \ldots, 1$ which transforms the diagonal matrix X into the vector X.

$$C = A_n X$$
$$= A_n (1 - a)^{-1} F,$$

where A_n is the diagonal elements of factor costs per unit of output. Therefore

$$P = (1 - a')^{-1} A_n i,$$

giving constant prices if output planned and achieved are according to plan.

Let actual output be given by

$$_a X(t) = (1 + \beta)^t X_0$$

---

[1] A. Ghosh, in Special No. *Yojana*. 1966.

and planned output by $\quad _pX(t) = (1+\delta)^t X_0,$

where X_0 is the base period output vector.

We write,

$$P(t) = (1-a')^{-1} A_n (1-a)^{-1} (1+\sigma)^t F(0) \left[(1+\beta)^t (1-a)^{-1} F(0)\right]^{-1}.$$

If $\delta > \beta$ $\qquad\qquad\qquad P(t) > P(0).$

INDEX

Contents

Introduction

A Trailer for the Docudrama of the Twenty-first Century

I n 2008, when the world realized the international economy had entered a sharp decline, I was sitting at a desk writing a book about why the international economy would boom. The decline that manifested itself in 2008 had the effect of focusing many people's minds. Those who lost jobs, or faced foreclosure, or saw their retirement savings damaged by swindlers masquerading as respectable bankers and Wall Street managers—their minds certainly were focused. My mind was focused on this question: Does it make sense to envision progress when the world seems to be sliding backward?

I came to the conclusion that this does make sense, and the result is the book you now hold. Before the downturn that became apparent in 2008, the larger global economic trend for three decades was rising prosperity for almost everyone, accelerating growth, higher living standards for average people, better education, increased ease of communication, low inflation, few shortages, and more personal freedom across most of the family of nations. History shows that when some crisis interrupts a larger trend, as soon as the crisis ends, the larger trend resumes. For example, global economic trends were mainly favorable before World War II; when the conflict ended, growth resumed, even in nations that were physically devastated by combat. All postwar recessions have ended in a resumption of previous trends. In places where natural disasters cause awful destruction, usually whatever larger trends were under way resume soon after the disaster stops; when the United States was hit by a manmade disaster in September 2001, the pattern of larger trends was not altered. Such precedents suggest that advancing global prosperity is likely to resume. If not this year, then soon, the global economy is likely to be fine. One purpose of a book is to step back from the drumbeat of headlines and consider larger trends. I write this preface knowing you may pick up *Sonic Boom* on a day when economic news is spooky. Notwithstanding, I believe a substantial rise in human prosperity is coming.

Here's the catch: just as favorable economic and social trends are likely to resume, many problems that have characterized recent decades are likely to get worse, too. Job instability, economic insecurity, a sense of turmoil, the unfocused fear that even when things seem good a hammer is about to fall—these also are part of the larger trend, and no rising tide will wash them away. For a writer sitting at a desk, the recession had a paradoxically useful impact, forcing me to spend just as much time contemplating the negative as the positive. The result is that the book you now hold, while envisioning the likelihood of a global boom, also warns that when it comes to anxiety, we ain't seen nothing yet.

What seemed scariest about the downturn that began in 2008 was not the dire unemployment rate, or specific data from bank lending departments or auto sales floors, but rather the fear that world economy was on the verge of unraveling. I don't think this will occur; I expect the reverse. But the fear may be here to stay. What happened in the economic downturn that began in 2008 was a trailer for the docudrama of the twenty-first century: a coming-attractions preview of the rest of your economic life. Don't worry about ordering tickets in advance, since you will be attending the show whether you wish to or not.

We're better off in a hectic, high-tech, interconnected world, for reasons *Sonic Boom* will spell out in detail. The coming global Sonic Boom may be the best economic news the world has ever received.

But being economically interconnected makes us feel vulnerable, because we can no longer control events—or at least, we can no longer believe events *can* be controlled. And that perception of loss of control is likely to accelerate. There will be tremendous pressure on government officials and policymakers to do something, anything, about the sense of accelerating change. Business leaders will be under tremendous pressure, too; soon, to the Fortune 500, Ralph Nader will seem like the good old days. New laws, policies and business plans might cushion the Sonic Boom, and this book will discuss them. But stop change? All the air, naval and ground forces in the world could not accomplish that. Get used to a ceaseless, low-grade sense of economic emergency, even if all goods and services are in ample supply, even if the local grocery store is fully stocked, busy and open twenty-four hours.

Why do I think a world boom is coming? Because though globalization may be driving you crazy, globalization is just getting started. The positive aspects—ease of communication, more freedom of speech, markets closely attuned to consumer demand, rising education levels in the developing world—are in their early stages. The world is going to become a *lot* more global. Though stress-inducing, this will be mainly good.

Because chip-based electronic devices are still relatively new and continue to rise in quality while declining in price, important technological improvements to the world economy are at hand. For example, fairly soon—meaning "really soon" at the current pace of change— most products will be manufactured using far less energy and producing less waste. That's the kind of advance for which we have all long hoped.

The conversion of the world to free economics remains in its early stages. You may not like free-market economics—let's hope someday there will be a saner, more compassionate system for organizing how we produce, work and spend—but it is inarguable that nearly all of the last century's improvements in standards of living for average people came from the free-market system. Just a few decades ago, most nations did not benefit from market economics. Most had controlled economies supervised by some form of dictatorship, or feudal economies—the feudal system, forgotten in the West, continues to be the primary tormentor of the world's poor—or economies that were free domestically but isolated behind import barriers. In the last generation, more and more of the world's economies have become reasonably free and begun to engage in reasonably open trade. Though the spreading of free economics is well-known, it's wrong to assume the impact has already occurred. Most of the impact lies in the future, because most of the world is just becoming accustomed to free markets, with their pluses and minuses. We should expect that in the near future, most of the world will attain the free-market advantages long enjoyed in the West, especially ample goods of rising quality and declining real-currency price.

Many of the benefits of the expansion of democracy remain in the future. A generation ago, according to United Nations figures, only one third of the world's nations held true multiparty elections; today 80 percent do, and the proportion continues to rise. Many nations have in recent years converted from despotism or autocracy to at least some halting form of democracy, while there is scant movement in the opposite direction. Dear Iran, North Korea and the Arab nations: become democracies. Do you really want to wake up some morning and find yourselves the world's sole holdouts against progress?

The concept of personal freedom, actively suppressed in much of the world through much of history, is only now spreading throughout most of the world. That people should make their own choices; that women should be as free as men; that individual decisions, not commands from palaces, should set the course of society—these are revolutionary concepts in many societies.

Until quite recently, only the Western nations benefited from technologically efficient agriculture and advanced manufacturing. Now most of the world is acquiring both, which means that soon billions of people will work with high productivity, rather than only those in affluent lands working productively.

One reason the United States and European Union have led the world in wealth and strength is that these are the first places where women achieved educational equality and personal freedom. Women could then contribute their ideas and effort to national success. As women achieve educational equality and personal freedom in developing nations, the supply of ideas and effort available to the world will roughly double!

And will an ever-more-interlinked globe reduce the odds of war? Military spending is among the least desirable uses of social resources. The best-case outcome for most defense spending is that it is totally wasted—that is, military force is never used. Worst-case outcomes go downhill from there. As most nations have begun spirited economic competition, they have reduced their competition in arms buildups. Stated in today's dollars, global military spending peaked in 1985 at $1.5 trillion, and by 2008 had fallen to $1.3 trillion.[1] Owing to world population growth through the period, military spending has declined from $312 per capita in 1985 (in today's dollars) to $194 per capita in 2008. Depressing numbers receive extensive coverage in the media; this splendidly positive number is unknown except to specialists.

Historically, the possession of military power has had a self-fulfilling aspect: nations with strong armies tend to use them. If the opposite is also true, then declining military spending ought to lead to reduced conflict. So far, that is the case. Wars in Iraq and a few other places are terrible exceptions to an overall trend of declining incidence and intensity of combat. As discussed in more detail later in the book, studies show that violent conflicts, both between and within states, rose steadily from 1955 to 1989, hit their post–World War II maximum in that year, declined steadily until 2003, the year of the U.S. invasion of Iraq, and since have risen slightly but remain below the level of the late 1970s. Owing mainly to this reduction in war, today a person's chance of dying by violence is the lowest it has been in human history. This is true broadly across the globe, except for a few places such as Sudan.

Perhaps twenty years is too little time from which to draw conclusions. But interconnected economics have arisen at the same moment that military spending has declined, and we should not be so cynical as to refuse to entertain the possibility that this means something good is happening. Hostile nationalism might reassert itself, but the globalized economy seems to make this less likely than in the past. In the late 1930s, Germany's export sector was just six percent of the country's GDP; the value of trade was not pressuring that country to avoid war. Today people worry about a revival of hostile nationalism in Russia, but that nation's export sector is 22 percent of GDP. Belligerence would be bad business for Moscow; the loss of export income would almost certainly outweigh anything Russia might gain through threats of fighting. China has an extremely large export sector, and China so far is a historical rarity, a great state *not* attempting to establish a dominant military.

Except, perhaps, for the hushed agrarian sunrises of a prehistory about which we may only speculate, the centuries have been marred by endless attempts at conquest by force. Today, in the early stages of globalization, there have been two decades without superpower confrontation, while most nations have shown more interest in acquiring market share than acquiring territory. Economists have long maintained that if only people and groups stopped fighting each other and cooperated, prosperity would rise for all. What a sly joke if free-market economists turn out to be history's peacemakers!

But bear in mind the seemingly iron law of human events: new problems always arise to replace old. Suppose the economic downturn ends and what comes next is a flowering of productive efficiency, higher material well-being and decreased military tension. The same forces that are likely to bring about these desirable ends will also have many unhappy consequences. Sudden economic tumult will become more frequent. Job anxiety will be endless; even if unemployment goes down, millions will fear it could return again quickly. The treadmill of work-and-spend will run ever faster, demanding we keep pace. Many jobs will become more physically convenient but will blur with home life, meaning there is never a time when you are not "at work." The velocity of change could become dizzying. Winner-take-all accumulation of wealth at the top, already the worst fault of capitalism and among the least attractive aspects of American society, may worsen in the West while infecting newly free nations. Every little thing that goes wrong anywhere in the world will scare us. And we will *know* every little thing that goes wrong anywhere in the world.

Through most of the past, even the recent past, most people on Earth had little to do with most other people on Earth. Knowledge of the world beyond the horizon was slight: during the height of ancient Egyptian civilization, during the pinnacle of the Roman Empire or the apex of dynastic China, most people on Earth were not in any way affected by these societies—indeed, they did not even know they existed. Through most of the past, most men and women interacted only with those in immediately adjacent communities, while international trade was rare and hardly a factor in the typical person's life. As recently as a century ago, most men and women were not touched by what happened on other continents: someone living in the American Midwest in the nineteenth century, for instance, might read a book about the places now called Malaysia or Pakistan, but events in those lands would never affect that person. Now, if something explodes in Pakistan or a new product from Malaysia challenges a Midwestern product, we have live television images within minutes. Increasingly we live not in isolation from the rest of the nation or world but in constant interaction, which means constant anxiety. This development appears irreversible, so don't waste valuable time complaining.

To date, commentary has tended to declare the evolving interconnected global economy either utterly marvelous or dreadfully awful. When some new force comes into play in society, there is a natural initial tendency to view the force as either all good or all bad. Our mental processing systems prefer such clear-line categorizations; after all, we've already got too much to think about. Eventually, though, people begin to sort out the constructive and destructive impacts of the new force. This book will offer such a second-phase, mixed-bag understanding of global trends—the global economy basically will be fine, while most things become better for most people, but the pressure of change will become close to unbearable.

The prospect of a world more prosperous, more free and less militaristic, yet ever more nervous, is the topic of *Sonic Boom*.

Gregg Easterbrook
Colorado Springs, Colorado
May 2009

One

SHENZHEN

The city did not exist thirty years ago, yet today has nearly 9 million residents, about the same population as the five boroughs of New York. Many of its residents were born into rural poverty—and today live a lifestyle approximately equivalent to that lived in Brooklyn. In mere decades the people of the city have transformed a rock-bound fishing village of tarpaper shacks into a leading urban center, if one whose existence is unknown to most of the world. Engineers flattened hills to make room for two dozen skyscrapers of forty-five stories or more—the tally will be larger by the time you encounter this paragraph—plus the world's ninth-tallest structure, a 1,260-foot-high office tower. The city contains numerous hospitals and power stations, plus hundreds of schools, almost all built during the lifetimes of those who use them. Crisscrossing the city are thousands of miles of roads and transit lines connecting tens of thousands of shops and cafés with more than a million dwellings, all structures that did not exist thirty years ago. Paris and London took many centuries to build; Manhattan's core was constructed in roughly one century; the glittering new cities of the American postwar imagination, Atlanta, Dallas, Denver,

Los Angeles, Miami, Phoenix and Seattle, each required roughly half a century to reach their current status of impressive-when-viewed-from-orbit. This new city has outflanked them all, becoming the fastest-built great metropolis in human history.[1] You're forgiven if you have never heard of Shenzhen.

What is really impressive about Shenzhen is not its boulevards and apartment towers but its harbor. A dense tangle of docks, warehouses, quays, slips and monstrous cranes, the Port of Shenzhen has gone in a single generation from nonexistent to the world's fourth-busiest harbor. Cargoes borne by oceangoing container ships are measured in the prosaically named Twenty-foot Equivalent Units, corresponding to metal boxes the size of the trailer on a semi truck; a TEU typically holds about ten tons of finished products. In 2007, some 21 million TEUs departed from Shenzhen to the markets of the world—more cargo than moved through Los Angeles and Long Beach harbors combined, and Los Angeles and Long Beach are America's two busiest ports. Twenty-one million TEUs in a year equates to a trailerload of goods departing Shenzhen harbor *every other second*. Rotterdam and Hamburg required centuries to reach central positions in global commerce; Shenzhen did this in less time than one person's life span. Export totals for 2008 and 2009 are expected to be down, but the basic accomplishment won't change—Shenzhen fashioned itself into a city of global importance in a remarkably brief period. Lines of enormous cargo vessels leave Shenzhen low in the water owing to the weight of the electronics, clothing, industrial equipment, toys, furniture and other manufactured goods they are bearing to the United States, the European Union, Latin America, the Middle East and other destinations. Batteries are a common cargo because BYD, the world's second-leading manufacturer of batteries, is based in Shenzhen. By the time you read this, BYD may be the world's number-one battery maker— and a decade from now may become the world's leader in manufacturing electric cars. BYD did not even exist until 1996.

Though the people of Shenzhen, China, do not hear it, the sound their city makes is a sonic boom. There have been booms before in various parts of the world: some brief, some long-lasting, some that were followed by busts, some that simply petered out. What is occur-